Praise for *Naturally Sweet & Gluten-Free*

"In this gorgeous book, Ricki Heller shows people with dietary concerns how they too can enjoy decadent desserts. It is solid proof that a seemingly restrictive style of eating can, in fact, be an absolute joy!"

Allyson Kramer, author of *Great Gluten-Free Vegan Eats* and *Great Gluten-Free Vegan Eats from Around the World*

"Ricki triumphs again with desserts that are free of gluten, dairy, egg, and refined sugar . . . [she] takes the treats we all love and works her magic . . . *Naturally Sweet & Gluten-Free* is a must in every kitchen!"

Iris Higgins, M.A., CH.t., author of *The Essential Gluten-Free Baking Guides* and host of thedailydietribe.com

"Ricki Heller's desserts are proof that food is activism! Her sweet treats will please every diner at your table."

JL Fields, coauthor of *Vegan for Her: The Woman's Guide to Being Healthy and Fit on a Plant-Based Diet*

"In every one of her creative recipes, Ricki proves that incredible taste and stellar nutrition can indeed coexist. With wisdom, enthusiasm, and a whole lot of heart, Ricki . . . offers [us] a heartfelt tribute to the soul-satisfying power of healthy cooking."

Hallie Klecker, author of *The Pure Kitchen* and *Super Healthy Cookies*

"This book is a triumphant, a gluten-free, sugar-free baker's bible, and a delightful blend of health and fun!"

Tess Masters, "The Blender Girl," host of healthyblenderrecipes.com

"What is life without dessert? Thanks to Ricki Heller's *Naturally Sweet & Gluten-Free,* anyone can enjoy decadent delights regardless of their food sensitivities or eating preferences. This book is thoughtful, well laid out, and highly informative."

Carol Kicinski, host of simplygluten-free.com

"*Naturally Sweet* is not only a visual delight, its recipes are amazing, too! I've come to rely on the fluffy pancakes and the oat muffins as staples, and plan to work my way through every healthy indulgence, one goodie at a time."

Alisa Fleming, author of *Go Dairy Free: The Guide and Cookbook* and senior editor of *Allergic Living* magazine

"What makes Ricki Heller's work so remarkable is her capacity to reinvent time-honored and traditional sweets with wholesome ingredients. Her recipes, which are crafted with meticulous attention to detail, will satisfy anyone — not only people who follow gluten-free or vegan diets."

Gena Hamshaw, C.C.N., host of www.choosingraw.com

"*Naturally Sweet & Gluten-Free* has recipes everyone will love, . . . but if you are allergy-sensitive this will soon become your go-to guide and dessert cookbook."

Christy Morgan, "The Blissful Chef," author of *Blissful Bites: Vegan Meals That Nourish Mind, Body, and Planet*

"Talk about tempting! Chocolate Pecan Pie and Butterscotch-Chocolate Chip Cookies? Yes please! . . . This book needs to be on your shelf!"

Kathy Patalsky, author of *365 Vegan Smoothies* and host of lunchboxbunch.com

Naturally Sweet & Gluten-Free

Allergy-Friendly Vegan Desserts

100 Recipes Without Gluten, Dairy, Eggs, or Refined Sugar

Ricki Heller

Photography by Celine Saki

Published by Sellers Publishing, Inc.

Book design by Rita Sowins, Sowins Design

Photography by Celine Saki
celinesaki.com

Sellers Publishing, Inc.
161 John Roberts Road, South Portland, Maine 04106
Visit our Web site: sellerspublishing.com
E-mail: rsp@rsvp.com

ISBN 13: 978-1-4162-0917-1

Library of Congress Control Number: 2013931255

10 9 8 7 6 5 4 3 2

Printed and bound in China

Notice

This publication contains the opinions and ideas of its author and is designed to provide useful advice in regard to the subject matter covered. The author and publisher are not engaged in rendering health or other professional services in this publication. This publication is not intended to provide a basis for action in particular circumstances without consideration by a competent professional. The author and publisher expressly disclaim any responsibility for any liability, loss, or risk, personal or otherwise, that is incurred as a consequence, directly or indirectly, of the use and application of any of the contents of this book.

Dedication

In memory of my mother, and
our shared time in the kitchen.

Contents

Easiest Almond Cookies, see page 112

Preface

Just before my fourth birthday party, I found myself sitting at my parents' kitchen table, excited to blow out the candles on an elaborately decorated birthday cake, its buttercream roses and chocolate swirls beckoning. I was surrounded by family and a pile of brightly wrapped presents waiting to be opened. Without warning, the entire scene disappeared; I awoke to find myself alone in my crib. At the sound of my piercing wails, my mother came running to see what was the matter. She soothed me, wiped away my tears, and patiently explained the concept of "dreaming," assuring me that the real party would occur later that day. I would, indeed, still enjoy all the things I'd been dreaming about.

When I look back on that morning, what I find most interesting about the experience is the source of my distress. My sorrow stemmed not from the disappearance of my family, the gifts, or even the entire party; no, what prompted me to cry inconsolably was the knowledge that I would lose out on eating that luscious chocolate cake.

My love of sweets, particularly those of the chocolate persuasion, has persisted unabated ever since that time. My mother was a traditional, naturally talented "from scratch" baker, and in one way or another, baking (and eating the spoils of my labor) has been a part of my life as long as I can remember. My dad, a dessert lover, was raised on a farm and couldn't tolerate "store bought" foods. As a result, our home was perpetually filled with the aroma of some newly baked treat: soft and chewy chocolate chip cookies; warm, aromatic apple crumble cake; light and airy summertime cheesecake topped with fresh berries. And, of course, everyone knew about my mother's incredible, legendary chiffon cake, over ten inches high and made with seven eggs!

Consequently, as a young child I became fascinated by what went on in the kitchen and baked my first batch of chocolate chip cookies, with my mom's help, at age six. I continued to bake — and eat — sweets regularly thereafter. It wasn't unusual for my sisters and me to consume dessert every night, several times on a weekend, and sometimes in place of the actual meal; we all loved desserts and easily preferred a cookie or piece of cake to just about any other foods. Ultimately, my love of sugary sweets was the catalyst to bringing about a massive change in my diet, and it prompted my devotion to a healthier lifestyle.

Many Diagnoses, One Turning Point

In my late twenties, I was first diagnosed with IBS (irritable bowel syndrome) and put on medication to control my symptoms (typically, the doctor never suggested any changes in my eating habits). Although the medication helped somewhat, my symptoms flared up intermittently, and I went on eating the way I always had. I just assumed this was how I'd live the rest of my life, never knowing when or why my symptoms would appear, and I tried, dejectedly, to accept my lot. During this time, I continued to consume my favorite foods — chocolate, cookies, and cakes — and even began a small catering company that provided desserts for birthday parties, weddings, and company meetings.

Several years later, after a particularly bad bout of ill health that kept me off work for almost a month, I finally found my way to a naturopathic doctor. She explained to me that my IBS was actually one symptom of a larger problem, systemic candida (or yeast) overgrowth. The candida causes the digestive problems of IBS as well as other symptoms, such as sugar cravings, foggy thinking, chronic sinus infections, and constant fatigue. By then, I was so desperate to feel better that I would have tried almost anything. I quickly agreed to the radical regimen she prescribed: an anticandida protocol that called for no gluten, no eggs, no dairy, no sweeteners of any kind — and that was just to start! What was there left to eat? I was devastated, to say the least, but still determined to make a go of it and rid myself of my debilitating IBS symptoms and the candida organism that caused them.

I clearly remember arriving home from my first shopping trip to the health-food store, bags of unfamiliar ingredients in hand, wondering if I'd ever get used to eating foreign foods like millet, tofu, or kale. Motivated by the powerful changes my naturopath had elicited, I took a leave of absence from my job to study natural nutrition and earn my RHN (Registered Holistic Nutritionist) designation. This led to the publication of my first book, *Sweet Freedom: Desserts You'll Love Without Wheat, Eggs, Dairy or Refined Sugar.* (The desserts in that book are great for anyone who can eat gluten and some higher-glycemic natural sweeteners like maple syrup or dates; turns out, that just wasn't me. While those are healthful sweeteners, over time they tend to trigger cravings and encourage my candida to flare up. I've found that I do much better without them.) Although I improved greatly on the diet and managed to follow it for almost a decade, I found myself slipping into old patterns each time I felt better. I would return to the naturopath, embark on the anticandida diet once again, and stay on it until I felt better. It took two major relapses for me to fully understand the pull that sugar has on me and the negative health consequences of straying from my whole-food diet.

When I was hit with my most recent bout of candida in December 2008, it finally became clear to me that I am simply not capable of eating refined sweeteners derived from sugar cane (e.g., "evaporated cane juice" or "cane sweetener") in moderation. Plain and simple, they are so addictive for me that even otherwise healthful natural sweeteners like maple syrup or dates could trigger my cravings. Similarly, after switching to a gluten-free diet as part of the anticandida regimen, I discovered that the bloating, abdominal pains, and other digestive distress I'd previously experienced had more or less disappeared. Today, I enjoy a whole-food diet filled with delicious foods and no absence of treats, but everything is made with sweeteners with a low glycemic index and without eggs, dairy, or gluten, and I know I will never consume refined sugar again.

How This Book Can Work for You

The recipes in this book are all free of gluten, eggs, and dairy; most are also soy free (or offer a soy-free option) and many are also nut free (or offer a nut-free option). On page 13, see the key to options that appear on each recipe. In addition, with the use of sweeteners such as coconut sugar, stevia, or, occasionally, agave nectar, every recipe has a reduced glycemic load. But even if you don't suffer from a major chronic condition like food allergies, diabetes, or candida, baking with natural, whole-food alternatives is a great way to transform your diet into something that's simply better for your body — and ultimately, your well-being in general — without sacrificing familiar taste or satisfaction. In other words, you won't be consuming processed, chemical-laden foods that may promote ill health in the long run.

The recipes in *Naturally Sweet & Gluten-Free* are made with products available in most health-food stores or the natural-foods section of your local supermarket. And while some of the ingredients, such as millet or coconut butter (made from pureed whole dried coconut "meat"), may be unfamiliar, you won't see any "out there" recipes in this book — no seaweed cookies, miso frosting, or maitake mushroom pudding. What you will find are many recipes for healthier versions of traditional favorites, such as Frosted Vanilla Cupcakes, Pumpkin Loaf, Chocolate Chip Cookies, or Chocolate Pecan Pie; a huge array of desserts made with creative combinations of ingredients (yep, some vegetables, too); as well as innovative and unusual uses of alternative ingredients to provide the greatest health benefits possible.

The process of baking without gluten, eggs, dairy, or refined sugar is a little different from that of conventional baking, so I've also included detailed instructions on how to best use whole-grain gluten-free flours, natural sweeteners, natural non-hydrogenated fats, and egg replacers in your existing recipes, as well as what to expect when cooking with whole-food ingredients.

With just a few easy adjustments to your familiar routines, you can create foolproof desserts every bit as delicious as the ones you're used to — but without the saturated fats, cholesterol, lactose, or refined sweeteners. As you'll quickly learn, a healthy lifestyle really can be sweet!

Making the Leap to Naturally Sweet & Gluten-Free Desserts

Nowadays, as more and more of us seek a healthier diet and lifestyle, finding a dessert that tastes great without contributing in some way to ill health can seem like an impossible task. After all, isn't a "healthy dessert" an oxymoron? Is there such a thing? With the rise in food allergies, type 2 diabetes, and other chronic illnesses, we've all become wary of dessert, especially when so many conventional baking ingredients can be hazardous to our health. We're taught that wheat contains gluten, butter is high in saturated fat, eggs are loaded with cholesterol, milk and cheese contain high amounts of lactose and casein, refined sugars and flours have been stripped of almost all their nutrients and can spike blood glucose levels . . . and the list goes on.

Perhaps even worse, what's often marketed as "healthy" isn't any better than white sugar– and white flour–laden confections. Low-fat options may be pumped with sugar to compensate for loss in flavor, and low-sugar confections often contain highly processed chemicals, fillers, or artificial sweeteners. Eating one of those so-called "healthy" sweet treats, in the end, may be even more harmful to our bodies than conventional desserts.

Delicious, appealing, and *truly* healthy treats seem to be the last unconquered frontier when it comes to today's health revolution. We're left wondering: Is it possible to enjoy authentic desserts without consuming any of these unhealthy foods?

With this book, I hope to prove that you can have your cake, and great health too! The desserts and other baked goods in *Naturally Sweet & Gluten-Free* were inspired by my own decision, after decades of baking and indulging in unhealthy sweets, to finally heed my body's wake-up call and radically alter my diet. Through years of recipe testing and selling the delicious results to health-food stores and farmers' markets, plus receiving feedback via thousands of comments on my blog, Diet, Dessert and Dogs, I've taken great care to ensure that every recipe you make from this book will taste just as good as a traditional dessert — and some, even better! Yet not one of them contains gluten, eggs, dairy, or refined sugars, and all have a lower glycemic index than "regular" desserts.

If you're accustomed to baking conventional desserts, you may notice that the ingredient lists for these recipes sometimes appear longer than those with which you may be familiar. Don't let this deter you! As I explain later in the book (see page 17), gluten-free all-purpose flour mixes work best when used with two or three other flours, and I've used sweeteners here, for the most part, in combination with stevia to lower the overall glycemic load of the recipes. These recipes still come together easily, and the ingredients have been carefully selected to ensure that the results will replicate — or even improve upon — the tastes and textures of "regular" baked goods.

So read on, bake some amazing sweet treats, and indulge freely, whatever your dietary restrictions.

Making the Leap

The transition from conventional baking to baking "free from" can be traumatic for some bakers. When I first switched to gluten-free flours, I assumed that they'd work in the same ways as the all-purpose wheat flour I knew and loved. While substituting for milk was easy, finding replacements for eggs and other forms of dairy and, eventually, for sugar, was more difficult, required extensive experimentation, and led to lots of botched results.

In this section, I'll share what I've learned from years of baking gluten-free, plus kitchen tips and techniques, and ingredient-substitution suggestions. You'll learn how easy it is to transform any recipe by replacing the ingredients that don't suit your diet (or may be absent that day from your cupboard!).

For general, but crucial, pointers about making naturally sweet and gluten-free desserts, read on. Additional helpful tips and suggestions can be found in the sections on ingredients, tips and techniques, and bakeware and tools, all of which are included so that you won't have to go through the same trial and error that I did!

Understanding the Recipes

All the recipes in *Naturally Sweet & Gluten-Free* are free from gluten, dairy, eggs, and refined sugar. In addition, many are also free from grain, soy, corn, and nuts. I have provided abbreviations to identify these additional allergy-free recipes, and, in some cases, a simple variation to the recipe. While I've done my best to ensure that each designation is correct, it is possible that in some rare instances, due to the large number of variables in each recipe, an incorrect abbreviation may have slipped through. As a result, I urge the reader to be vigilant in reviewing the recipe carefully where there may be a chance of including any known allergens.

Key to Abbreviations

Allergy-Free Option	Abbreviation
Grain-Free	GF
Soy Free	SF
Corn-Free	CF
Nut Free	NF

Baking Gluten-Free: Getting Started

Over the years, I've discovered a few key factors to successful gluten-free baking and conversion of conventional recipes. With this information, an adventurous spirit, and a bit of persistence, you can bake amazing gluten-free desserts without any of the usual flours, eggs, dairy, or refined sugars. Here are some points you'll need to remember for successful gluten-free baking.

- *Begin with a Mix.* Most experienced gluten-free bakers combine at least two or three different gluten-free flours in order to reproduce a texture that is reminiscent of wheat-based baking. As a rule, gluten-free flours don't work as well in isolation, something I learned the hard way. (Be sure you don't make the mistake I did when I began, and replace the wheat flour one-to-one by volume with rice flour. My banana bread came out much more like a banana brick!)

For this reason, when starting out, I always recommend a good all-purpose, gluten-free flour. All-purpose mixes can be used in place of wheat flour, using a one-to-one ratio; they make life much easier, since you won't have to purchase multiple bags of unfamiliar flours that you may never use again. An all-purpose mix also allows for guaranteed success in the beginning, which is great encouragement to keep at it! Once you learn about the different flours, their properties, and which you prefer, you may decide to veer from the all-purpose mix, but as a starting point, it's ideal.

I devised my own flour mix specifically to reproduce the same percentage of protein that exists in all-purpose wheat flour, while keeping starch to a minimum. In my experience, many commercial mixes lean a bit too heavily on starches since they are fine and white like wheat flour, which results in more conventional-looking baked goods. For me, it was most important that my mix could be used in quantities equal to what one would use for all-purpose wheat flour, and that it achieved similar results so substitutions could be easily made. I find that the starch-heavy mixes sometimes result in a slightly gummy texture, which I don't enjoy.

As you become more experienced and comfortable baking gluten-free, you will eventually learn which gluten-free flours appeal most to you. Some people love the neutral taste of rice flour, for instance; others prefer starches for their light texture; many include bean or legume flours for their protein; and so on. Like me, many gluten-free bakers ultimately decide to create their own all-purpose mix to have on hand whenever they need it, rather than having to purchase the prepackaged mixes.

Some of my favorite ingredients are unsweetened carob chips, raw unsweetened coconut, my all-purpose gluten-free flour mix, and coconut sugar.

I use my all-purpose mix in most of the recipes in this book (see page 22). I suggest mixing up a large batch to keep on hand, so you don't have to remeasure each time you wish to bake something. In most cases, you should be able to use any gluten-free all-purpose mix, as long as it can be substituted one-to-one for regular wheat-based all-purpose flour.

• *Give Your Baked Goods an Extra Lift.* Gluten-free flours don't rise as much as conventional wheat flour, so you'll need to add more than the usual amount of leaveners (such as baking powder or baking soda) to help the batter rise more effectively. Because I use neither eggs nor yeast, I rely on those two leaveners most often. Baking soda is naturally gluten-free, but be sure to check your baking powder, as some brands contain wheat. I also often add some apple cider vinegar or other acid (such as lemon juice) to the recipes, since it reacts with baking soda to create additional rise in baked goods.

• *Give Your Baked Goods an Added Binder.* Gluten-free baking requires an added binder to replace the gluten. According to the Celiac Sprue Association, the word "gluten" is a generic term that refers to any of the proteins found in many grains; it's used for the proteins in wheat, even though, technically, wheat contains more than one type of protein. It's the gluten or protein in wheat that provides the "glue" or binding qualities of the flour. Because gluten-free flours lack the same protein, any time you bake gluten-free you will need to provide an alternative means to bind your baked goods, or they won't hold together and will crumble like desert sand. The most common binders used are xanthan gum, guar gum, or whole psyllium husks. Each of these is discussed in "Binders" (see page 23).

• *Store Whole-Grain Gluten-Free Flours in the Refrigerator or Freezer.* Another reason I love gluten-free flours is because, in general, they are unrefined. A refined flour is one that has had both the germ and the bran removed from the grain, which extends the flour's shelf life and produces a more neutral flavor and lightly colored product. However, this process also removes most of the nutrients and healthy oils from the grain. Most wheat flour (even flour labeled "whole wheat") has been refined to some extent.

While some gluten-free flours (such as white rice flour) are also refined, almost all are not, so you benefit from the full nutritional value of the grain. Note, however, that whole-grain flours also tend to go rancid more quickly, since the natural oils have not been removed by the refining process. To keep them fresh as long as possible, store them in the freezer or refrigerator if not used within a couple of weeks.

• *Experiment!* One of the reasons I adore baking gluten-free — even more than I loved baking with wheat — is the incredible array of different flours, flavors, and textures available. The beauty of gluten-free flours is that there's a flour or flour combination to suit any recipe, occasion, or palate. Some flours, like millet or rice, or starches, such as arrowroot, tapioca flour, or potato flour, are delicate or mildly flavored and are therefore best for fancy cakes or pastries; others, like amaranth, quinoa, or buckwheat, offer a more robust flavor profile, working beautifully in rustic dishes like breads, biscuits, or muffins; still others, such as almond, coconut, or legume flours, work best with pizza or grain-free baking.

The more you play with the different flours, the more you'll learn about the individual properties of each, and before you know it, you'll be making adjustments to suit your own preferences. Soon you'll be so accustomed to the variety of gluten-free baking that you may find wheat-based goods to be bland and monotone!

At-a-Glance Pantry List

Here's a list of the ingredients I use most often in my kitchen, and the ones you'll find in the majority of recipes in this book. Check out the "Resource Guide" (see page 219) for some of my favorite brands.

- ❑ **Almond or soy milk** (plain or unsweetened)
- ❑ **Apple cider vinegar**
- ❑ **Arrowroot, tapioca, or potato starch**
- ❑ **Baking soda**
- ❑ **Carob chips** (unsweetened). It can be difficult to find unsweetened carob chips that are also free of dairy and gluten. If you can tolerate them, use dairy-free chocolate chips instead of carob chips.
- ❑ **Chia seeds or meal**
- ❑ **Cinnamon**
- ❑ **Coconut beverage**
- ❑ **Coconut butter**
- ❑ **Coconut flour**
- ❑ **Coconut milk** (canned) I use "full fat" coconut milk, as it mimics the richness of dairy cream best.
- ❑ **Coconut nectar**
- ❑ **Coconut oil** (preferably virgin organic)
- ❑ **Coconut sugar**
- ❑ **Coffee substitute** (for an instant-coffee substitute, I recommend Dandy Blend)
- ❑ **Fine sea salt**
- ❑ **Flax seeds or meal**
- ❑ **Garfava flour**
- ❑ **Gluten-free baking powder**
- ❑ **Millet flour**
- ❑ **Natural raw almonds**
- ❑ **Natural raw walnuts**
- ❑ **Natural smooth cashew butter**
- ❑ **Old-fashioned rolled oats** (closer to whole oats)
- ❑ **Organic sunflower oil**
- ❑ **Pure vanilla extract**
- ❑ **Psyllium** (whole husks)
- ❑ **Raw cacao** (the raw version of unsweetened cocoa is slightly less bitter than cocoa powder)
- ❑ **Stevia** (pure powder and/or liquid)
- ❑ **Sweet potatoes**
- ❑ **Tahini** (sesame seed paste)
- ❑ **Unsweetened cocoa powder**. There are two types of unsweetened cocoa powder: natural, which is non-alkalized; and Dutch-processed, which is alkalized. I prefer to use natural cocoa powder because it retains more of the natural antioxidants.
- ❑ **Xanthan gum** (use only Bob's Red Mill brand if you are concerned about a corn allergy)

Ingredients

When you first start baking with alternative ingredients, it can feel a little like a child's first visit to the county fair; there are so many options — and they're all unfamiliar! But with a little practice and a bit of experimentation, you'll quickly become familiar with the different flours, sweeteners, and other healthy replacements for conventional ingredients, and you'll be able to choose your favorite substitutions easily. In this section, I'll review the ingredients I use most often and explain how you can incorporate them into your own kitchen adventures for the greatest level of success.

Gluten-Free Flours

Most gluten-free flours fall into one of four main categories: grain and pseudo-grain, bean- and legume-based, starch; or nut- and seed-based. All-purpose mixes generally combine flours from at least two of the categories; many use three or more different flours. Again, once you begin to use the flours regularly, you'll discover your own perfect ratio and your preference for the heartier flours or those that are more delicate in flavor and texture.

Note: This list is not comprehensive; I include the flours I use most frequently in this book.

Grain & Pseudo-Grain Flours

Grain and pseudo-grain flours are made from gluten-free grains such as rice, amaranth, millet, quinoa, teff, corn, oats, buckwheat, and sorghum. Grain-based flours are similar to wheat flour in the way they're used and how they look and feel.

Some grain- or pseudo-grain-based flours can be ground at home with a high-powered blender, a coffee grinder, or a spice grinder. Home grinding comes in handy for some flours (such as millet or oat) that are not always widely available; it's also a more economical option if you have the time and inclination to grind your own, even for those flours that can be found easily in the grocery store. I've had good success grinding my own buckwheat, quinoa, millet, oat, and teff flours, though I wouldn't recommend attempting rice flour at home unless you have a grain mill (the hard grains may damage the blades in a regular grinder or blender).

- *Amaranth Flour.* Amaranth is a high-protein grain that can be used as a flour in conjunction with other flours. Because of its strong, distinctive aroma and taste, many people prefer to use amaranth in small quantities, combined with milder flours. I use amaranth rarely as a flour for this reason (though I do cook it in cereals). Amaranth flour can be ground at home (see page 35).

- *Buckwheat Flour.* Technically a seed, buckwheat contains no wheat (except in its unfortunate name!), so it's entirely and safely gluten-free. Buckwheat is a great flour to add to hearty breakfast dishes because of its lovely, nutty flavor and binding abilities. The dark color renders it most appropriate for muffins, bars, or other baked goods that are also darker in color. You'll find both raw buckwheat groats (a light greenish color) and toasted groats (also called kasha) — both can be ground at home (see page 35).

Gluten-free flour ingredients, clockwise: pumpkin seeds, whole millet grain, home-ground millet flour, home-ground oat flour, home-ground almond flour, natural raw almonds, raw walnuts, and whole oats in the center.

- *Millet Flour.* A mild, light grain that has been used for decades as the primary ingredient in bird feed, millet is my favorite flour to use as the main ingredient in my all-purpose flour. It has an extremely mild, neutral flavor that I feel works best for most baked goods and won't overpower delicate flavors such as lemon or vanilla. In fact, millet is the main ingredient in my dairy-free, nut-free, soy-free Pastry Cream or Custard (see page 167) which has won the hearts of hundreds of friends. It can be a little more difficult to find in stores, though it's easily found online. Millet flour can be ground at home (see page 35).
- *Whole Oat Flour.* Oat flour is made from whole-grain oats that are ground to a powder. Only recently have oats been deemed gluten-free, even though they never did contain gluten; most conventional oats, however, are cross-contaminated with wheat and can't be consumed by those on a gluten-free diet. In recent years, however, certain brands of oats have obtained gluten-free certification to ensure that they haven't been contaminated with gluten flours. Check labels carefully if purchasing oat flour. Oat flour can be ground at home, though note that only old-fashioned oats should be used in this case (see page 135).
- *Quinoa Flour.* Not actually a grain (quinoa is a seed), quinoa boasts a high protein content that is also present in the flour. It also provides a fairly distinctive, earthy, nutty flavor that is not enjoyed by everyone. For my purposes, quinoa flour works beautifully in rustic, more hearty recipes where it's tempered either by fruits or other prominent flavors, such as in the Low-Fat Cinnamon Walnut Loaf (see page 65). To prevent the quinoa from overpowering other flavors in a recipe, I always mix it with other flours, ensuring that the quinoa makes up no more than 25 percent of the total flour content in any recipe.

To mitigate the strong flavor, you could try this tip from Iris Higgins and Brittany Angell in their book *The Essential Gluten-Free Baking Guide, Part I*: Simply toast the flour on a parchment-lined, rimmed cookie sheet, spread about ¼-inch (.5-cm) thick, in a 215°F (100°C) oven for 2½ hours, stirring it once or twice during that time. Toasting removes the distinctive aroma and flavor, rendering the flour mild and ready to use in baking. Store in a covered container in the refrigerator for up to 3 months.

• *Rice Flour, White or Brown.* Probably the first widely used gluten-free flour, rice flour confers a slightly grainy, heavy texture to baked goods; however, the flavor is quite neutral, so it is preferred by some bakers. Many opt for superfine rice flour, a specially milled version that is much finer (available in most health-food stores and Asian groceries). I use rice flour in combination with other flours for recipes that are naturally hearty and grainy, such as shortbread or scones.

Unlike the white variety, which is refined, flour made from brown rice still contains the entire grain, so it boasts a much higher nutritional profile. For this reason, I rarely, if ever, use white rice flour (though you can substitute it in any of my recipes that call for brown rice flour). Because the natural oils are still part of the flour, brown rice flour is subject to rancidity if stored at room temperature. You should always store brown rice flour in the refrigerator, or, if you don't use it within a few weeks, the freezer. It's not advisable to grind your own rice flour at home unless you have a grain mill. Rice is extremely hard and could damage the blades in a regular grinder or blender.

• *Sweet Rice Flour.* This flour is derived from sweet rice (also called glutinous rice), a staple in both Japanese and Chinese cooking. I think of the name as a bit of a misnomer, however. Although it's a flour made from "sweet" rice, it is not sweet, it contains no gluten, and it looks and operates much more like a starch than a flour. I use sweet rice flour rarely, and usually in recipes that require a delicate crumb and fine texture, such as a white cake or cookie. As with regular rice flour, I wouldn't advise grinding your own sweet rice flour at home without a grain mill.

• *Sorghum Flour.* Best known in the American South where it's processed into a sweet syrup, sorghum is a versatile grain that also produces a fairly light-colored flour with a mild flavor. It's a great addition to cakes or pastries, and works much like millet in many recipes. Although I've never done it myself, I've read that you can grind sorghum at home.

• *Teff Flour.* The smallest known grain, this tiny, light-brown grain has a flavor slightly reminiscent of chocolate or carob. It also offers a relatively good amount of protein and fiber, and is used most commonly in the Ethiopian flatbread called injera. I love the subtle flavor of teff and often add it to recipes that are already dark in color, such as Ginger-Coconut Cookies (see page 115) or chocolate desserts. Teff can be ground at home (see page 35).

Bean- & Legume-Based Flours

These flours are usually higher in protein than other flours, as they are formulated from dried beans and legumes. Some examples include chickpea flour, lentil flour, pea flour, and garfava flour, which is made from garbanzo beans (also called chickpeas) and fava beans. As a rule, bean flours are rarely ground at home, as the process is fairly labor-intensive.

• *Carob Powder* (also called Carob Flour). Technically a legume, carob is an underrated ingredient that deserves its own hype apart from chocolate and not as a subpar chocolate substitute. I love the slightly sweet, slightly nutty flavor of carob, but I do know that not everyone feels the same way. I often use carob in recipes on its own; I also like to add a little carob powder to desserts made with unsweetened chocolate, as a way to mitigate the bitterness of the chocolate and add some additional sweetness without changing the overall flavor. Carob can be used in place of cocoa in recipes if you like, but note that it has a lower fat content, so you may need to add about a teaspoon (5 ml) more fat for each 3 to 4 tablespoons (45 to 60 ml) of carob used to compensate. Finally, while you can find raw carob powder in some specialty shops or online, most baked goods, including the recipes in this book, use the toasted variety (the basic carob found in most supermarkets is toasted).

• *Chickpea Flour.* Also called garbanzo bean flour, this is a high-protein flour made from dried chickpeas. I prefer chickpea flour in savory applications, but do occasionally use it in baked goods as well. If you're out of garfava flour for my all-purpose flour mix (see page 22), you can substitute chickpea flour instead.

• *Garfava.* Because of its mild flavor and naturally high starch content, garfava is a perfect flour to use in combination with other flours for your baking. I first learned about garfava when reading about New York's now-famous BabyCakes Bakery, which uses it in many recipes. While some people shy away from bean flours because of their taste, I love the fact that garfava adds a boost of protein without a heavy or prominently "beany" flavor. It's also high in fiber, which helps to lower the overall glycemic index of your baked goods.

Nut- & Seed-Based Flours

These are typically made from ground and/or powdered nuts or seeds. The most common is blanched almond flour, but you can also find flours from a variety of other nuts and seeds these days, such as hemp, sunflower, coconut, walnut, or pumpkin. Most of these can be ground into flour at home (see page 35).

Note: This list is not comprehensive; I include the flours I use most often in this book.

• *Almond Flour.* Almond flour is made from ground almonds; some brands use blanched and skinned almonds, while others use raw, natural (skin-on) almonds. Although it has become wildly popular among gluten-free bakers in recent years, you'll notice that I don't use almond flour in my recipes. Instead, I tend to include ground almonds as a regular component of any baked goods that do contain nuts. The primary reason is accessibility: I live in Canada, where the only really common brand of almond flour is Bob's Red Mill. The texture of this flour is very similar to ground almonds (in fact, I have noticed no difference between the two), so I find it more economical to grind my own. I have heard wonderful things about finely ground, blanched almond flour from Honeyville, but haven't had the opportunity to try it yet. Since most of my recipes rely on grain-based flours, this hasn't been a problem. Almond flour can be ground at home (see page 35).

Note: Home-ground almond flour will be slightly coarser than the really fine texture of packaged store-bought flour. This doesn't pose a problem for any of the recipes in this book, since they all use almond flour or meal made at home from whole almonds, but it's worth knowing if you wish to convert recipes from other sources.

• *Coconut Flour.* Coconut flour, a relative newcomer on the gluten-free stage, is made from the pulp left over after coconut oil is extracted from coconuts. It can be used to replace up to about 25 percent of the regular flour in a recipe without noticeable changes to texture. It's also a high-fiber flour (at 58 percent fiber, supposedly the highest percentage of any flour), and it absorbs liquid to a great extent, so it's useful if you're replacing a dry sweetener such as sugar with a liquid one such as agave or coconut nectar. Note, however, that the final results are often much more moist with coconut flour; if the batter is too thin, or the baked good is too thick (as in a cake), the flour may cause a sodden result after it's baked.

I rarely, if ever, use coconut flour as the only flour in a recipe. But for moist, dense baked goods like brownies or bars, it works beautifully to add an extra dimension of flavor and texture.

Starches

Starches are usually derived from grains or tubers. They appear white and very powdery, with an almost "squeaky" texture. Starches include arrowroot, tapioca starch, and potato starch. Sweet rice flour is sometimes included in this category because of its high starch content, even though it is technically a flour.

• *Arrowroot.* Best known as a major ingredient in the classic biscuits of the same name, arrowroot is a tuber from which starch is derived. It works much like tapioca starch in most baked goods, with an extremely neutral flavor. I use it in my all-purpose flour mix (see page 22). You can replace arrowroot with tapioca starch if you wish.

• *Tapioca Starch.* Derived from the cassava root, this starch is a great thickener and also lends body to baked goods, especially in vegan baking when eggs are absent. It can normally be used interchangeably with arrowroot in baked goods.

• *Potato Starch.* Sharing some characteristics of arrowroot and tapioca starch, potato starch is derived from potatoes. With a pure white color, its texture is slightly heavier than that of other starches. I love to use potato starch in grain-free cooking because of its neutral flavor; also, it won't become gummy when cooked, the way tapioca sometimes does.

All-Purpose Gluten-Free Flour Mix

Most of the recipes in this book call for "Ricki's All-Purpose Gluten-Free Flour Mix." I designed this mix based on my own preferences and a desire for a reliable all-purpose gluten-free flour. It can be used in place of all-purpose wheat flour in most recipes; use 1 cup (135 g) of this flour in place of 1 cup (140 g) of regular all-purpose flour. Then also add xanthan gum (or other binder) as the recipe directs.

You will also achieve good results with my recipes if you use packaged all-purpose mixes such as those from Bob's Red Mill or King Arthur Flour. Note, however, that you should use volume measures rather than weight when substituting one gluten-free flour mix for another. Because different flours have very different densities and weight per volume, 135 grams (the weight of 1 cup/240 ml of my all-purpose flour) may yield a different volume with heavier or lighter flours. For instance, 135 grams of brown rice flour is only slightly more than ¾ cup (180 ml). The same is true of all-purpose flours. If you substitute 1 cup (240 ml) for 1 cup (240 ml), however, the recipe should work. Because each all-purpose mix contains its own blend of gluten-free flours, some of which absorb more liquid than others, you may also need to adjust the liquid measurements if you use a different all-purpose flour.

Ricki's All-Purpose Gluten-Free Flour Mix

I created this mix after examining the protein (i.e., gluten) content of regular wheat-based all-purpose flour; I wanted a product that would approximate the same ratio of protein to starch as exists in the wheat-based product. This mix of grain, legume, and starches matches the values of wheat flour almost perfectly. I usually mix up a double batch of the flour at a time (I bake a lot!), then store it in a covered plastic food container for easy scooping.

2 cups (270 g) millet flour (see *Note* below)
⅔ cup (100 g) garfava bean flour
⅔ cup (90 g) arrowroot or tapioca starch
⅔ cup (120 g) potato starch (not flour)

Sift all ingredients into a large bowl, then stir with a whisk or spatula until very well combined and all flours are equally incorporated. Store in an airtight container in the refrigerator or freezer. Will keep, refrigerated, up to 6 weeks, or frozen up to 3 months.

Note: You can grind your own millet flour at home from the grain (see page 35).

Binders

Because they don't contain gluten, gluten-free flours require some other method to bind them together and perform the same function as the gluten. Most gluten-free baking includes some kind of alternative binder.

• *Psyllium Seed Husks.* Psyllium has been used as a natural thickener for some time by raw foodists and has recently been introduced as a binder in gluten-free baking. Psyllium absorbs liquids and softens to an almost gel-like texture that works well to replace gluten in baking without adding any noticeable texture (and it's also flavorless). I like psyllium for sturdier baked goods, such as cookies, muffins, or some pie crusts. Note that psyllium is available both as a powder and as whole husks (which look like a fine wheat bran); I use the whole husks in my recipes.

• *Xanthan Gum and Guar Gum.* Xanthan gum is usually made by fermenting corn to create a fine powder that becomes gluey when moistened; it replaces gluten in most gluten-free baked goods. It is possible to find corn-free xanthan gum — Bob's Red Mill is the brand I use and recommend, it is corn-free and gluten-free. In those recipes designated corn-free (CF), please ensure that you use only that brand, if ingesting corn is a health concern. Xanthan gum is expensive, but so little is called for in recipes that it will last a long time if tightly wrapped and kept in the freezer.

• *Sweet Potato Puree.* I use sweet potato puree frequently to add moistness, sweetness, and binding power to my baked goods. I love that sweet potatoes confer sweetness while remaining low on the glycemic index and full of fiber. I think sweet potato puree is a perfect means to add nutrition to your baked goods without sacrificing flavor or texture.

While you can find good canned sweet potato puree (be sure it's unsweetened, with sweet potato as the only ingredient), I prefer to make my own at home, both because it's so much more economical and because I find the flavor to be superior to the canned variety. Baking sweet potatoes helps to caramelize the natural sugars and bring out their uncommonly sweet flavor.

How to Make Your Own Sweet Potato and Pumpkin Puree

Bake a large (250 g) sweet potato with the skin on at 400°F (200°C) for about an hour, until very soft. Allow to cool and then peel off the skin. Cut the flesh into chunks and puree in a food processor until smooth. One large sweet potato (about 250 g) will yield about 1 cup (240 ml) puree. Store, covered, in the refrigerator for up to 5 days, or freeze up to 6 months.

For pumpkin puree, bake a small sugar or pie pumpkin (2 to 3 lbs. or 1 to 1.4 kg.) with the skin on at 400°F (200°C) for about an hour or until soft. Allow to cool, cut in half, then scoop out the seeds, and peel off the skin. Cut the flesh into chunks, then puree in a food processor until smooth. One small sugar pumpkin yields about 2 cups (480 ml) of puree. The puree can be stored, covered, in the refrigerator for up to 5 days or freeze for up to 6 months.

Sweeteners

It can be difficult to decide which sweeteners to use when terms like *natural*, *refined*, or *alternative* are often bandied about without much explanation. In much of North America, the term "natural" can legally appear on a product label even though the contents of the package may be far from what most of us would consider natural.

Categories of Sweeteners

For clarity, here are the terms I use and the definitions I attribute to sweeteners.

- *Natural.* To me, a natural sweetener is one that has been minimally processed, if at all, and is as close to the natural state of the plant from which it's derived as possible. Many natural sweeteners have been around for hundreds, if not thousands, of years, and could theoretically be made at home. A natural sweetener contains no chemical additives or fillers and doesn't require extensive filtering or bleaching to reach its usable form (as is the case with cane sugar, for instance).

Natural sweeteners provide better flavor and more nutrition than refined white sugar; in the latter, the vitamins and minerals are removed through processing. Because many natural sweeteners are available only as liquids, however, you may need to adjust both the levels of other liquids in a recipe and the dry ingredients. All the recipes in this book have been designed with these properties in mind, so they won't require any adjustments if followed as written.

- *Refined or Unrefined.* A refined sweetener is one that has been concentrated to extract its core part (sugar) by removing or separating out any other components or impurities. For instance, white sugar has been "purified" by removing any fiber, almost all of the nutrients, and all of the color. Given my definition of "natural," it makes sense that the sweeteners I prefer are either unrefined or as close to unrefined as possible.
- *Alternatives.* Alternative sweeteners are simply that: any sweetener than can be used as an alternative to sugar. However, just because a sweetener is alternative does not mean it's also natural. Alternatives to sugar abound in grocery stores these days, but few of them are whole-food products. For instance, aspartame and sucralose may be considered alternative (and both are low calorie and have a low glycemic index), but they are far from natural.

I'm aware that there are other sweeteners with a low glycemic index out there, many of which are recommended for those with diabetes or those on an anticandida diet, but I am not comfortable consuming sugar alcohols like xylitol or erythritol, which can cause digestive distress.

- *Conventional Sugar.* In this book, I use the term "sugar" to refer to refined (white) sugar made from either sugar cane or sugar beets. Although most natural sweeteners do contain naturally occurring sugars (these are the types of sugar listed on nutrition labels), they are usually unrefined, and they do provide nutritional value (unlike white sugar). In other words, my diet is sugar free, but it is not sweetener free.

If you are able to tolerate some sugar, you can always replace the sweeteners used in my recipes with some, or all, cane or beet sugar; note, however, that you'll need to adjust the other ingredients if you substitute sugar for a liquid sweetener (see the next section for specifics).

Specific Sweeteners

Having followed a strict anticandida diet for almost 13 years (primarily an organic diet without gluten, molds, animal products, or — most important — any refined sugars), I've found a variety of sugar-free options that really work for me. While the sweeteners I use in this book all have a lower glycemic index, I'm also including some of the other popular natural sweeteners that I think are healthful options if you're able to consume them. Here is a list of my favorites.

• *Agave Nectar.* In recent years, agave nectar (sometimes called agave syrup) has become the "go to" sweetener for vegans and those on lower glycemic diets. Made from sap extracted from the agave cactus, it's not as thick as coconut nectar and doesn't crystallize like honey. "Light" agave (versus the darker, "amber" variety) has a very mild, pleasant taste that won't dominate the other ingredients in your recipe. Although it's less refined, amber agave also has a stronger flavor that is not appealing to everyone. I use amber in chocolate desserts and combined with other robust flavors such as buckwheat, where it won't overpower the other ingredients.

There has been some controversy lately about the high levels of fructose in agave. However, agave nectar derived from traditional methods (that have existed in Mexico for centuries) is a natural sweetener that, in my view, is on par with other natural sweeteners like maple syrup. When included in special treats, agave is a useful low-glycemic sweetener that adds variety to your baking.

I use agave rarely, but find that it's indispensable in delicately flavored baked goods such as lemon or vanilla cake, or when you need a lightly colored product, such as pastry cream.

Substitution Tip: Agave can be swapped 1:1 in place of maple syrup. If using in place of coconut nectar or brown rice syrup, use about 25 percent less agave. For instance, if the recipe calls for one cup (240 ml) of coconut nectar, use only ¾ cup (180 ml) agave in its place. Finally, if replacing sugar with agave, reduce the amount by about 25 percent as well (that is, ¾ cup or 180 ml agave in place of 1 cup or 240 ml sugar; you'll need to increase the dry ingredients by about 25 percent as well in this case).

• *Blackstrap Molasses.* Molasses is the residual product after sugar cane has been processed into cane (granulated) sugar. While the light "Fancy" or "Barbados" varieties are formed early in the process and still retain a fairly high sugar content, blackstrap molasses contains very little sugar and actually retains all the nutrients that are removed from sugar during processing. The darker (or less sweet) the molasses, the more minerals it contains. Blackstrap molasses is the most nutritious form, with excellent levels of iron and calcium (in fact, it contains more calcium per volume than milk!) and good amounts of magnesium, potassium, and B vitamins.

Some people find the taste of blackstrap molasses too bitter (the unsulphured variety tastes best), so I always combine molasses with other sweeteners, and think of it as an addition rather than the main sweetener in any recipe.

• *Brown Rice Syrup.* After news stories surfaced in early 2012 about high levels of arsenic in brown rice syrup, many people who had been using this mildly flavored natural sweetener abandoned it. I would likely have continued to use brown rice syrup if I hadn't discovered coconut nectar as a suitable substitute. However, brown rice syrup is less expensive and provides a very similar flavor profile to coconut nectar, and so can be used in its place if you prefer; you may replace any coconut nectar in this book 1:1 with brown rice syrup.

• *Coconut Sugar.* A dry, granular sweetener with a flavor much like caramelized brown sugar, coconut sugar is made from the coconut palm flower. It is fairly low on the glycemic index, clocking in at 35. Its flavor is like a mild butterscotch or caramel, so it works beautifully in most sweet recipes.

Note: Because it doesn't dissolve as readily as cane sugar, I tend to add it to the wet ingredients in any recipe so that it will begin to dissolve before it's mixed into the batter.

Substitution Tip: While most cookbooks suggest that coconut sugar can be used 1:1 in place of white sugar, I have found that it is not quite as sweet as cane sugar, so I usually increase the amount by about 25 percent (or amp up the sweetness by supplementing coconut sugar with stevia). For each cup (240 ml) of refined sugar, I would use 1¼ to 1½ cups (205–250 g) coconut sugar, or ½ to ¾ cup (85–125 g) coconut sugar combined with 20 to 40 drops stevia liquid for a lower glycemic option.

• *Coconut Nectar.* A liquid sweetener sourced the same way as coconut sugar, coconut nectar is thick and sticky like honey or brown rice syrup. It has a low glycemic impact and can be used in place of other higher-glycemic liquid sweeteners, such as maple syrup or honey.

I would recommend combining coconut nectar with other sweeteners in baking, as it's not terribly sweet and you would require an enormous amount to achieve the desired sweetness. I tend to use it when a butterscotch or caramel flavor is desired, but in conjunction with at least one other sweetener.

Substitution Tip: Coconut nectar is expensive, and not everyone is a fan of its subtle caramel flavor. If you prefer, you may use brown rice syrup 1:1 instead of coconut nectar in my recipes (though note the concerns about brown rice syrup, above). You can also substitute agave nectar or maple syrup, but will need to reduce the liquid in the recipe by about 25 percent. In other words, if you use 1 cup (240 ml) agave nectar instead of 1 cup (240 ml) coconut nectar, reduce any other liquid in the original recipe by 25 percent.

• *Fruit Purees.* Two of the most common fruit purees are date and banana. In my early years baking with natural sweeteners, I relied heavily on both of these for added sweetness and body in my recipes. However, since both of these fruits are quite high on the glycemic index, I tend to avoid them today, and have substituted lower-glycemic pears and prunes, respectively. If you don't mind the high sugar content and prefer dates to prunes, feel free to substitute them in my recipes in equal measure. (You may need to decrease other sweeteners in the recipe somewhat if you use dates, however, as dates are sweeter than prunes.)

I find pear puree to be a wonderful addition, since it adds very little flavor to the final product; similarly, unsweetened applesauce works as well.

• *Lucuma Powder.* Lucuma powder is the dried and pulverized flesh of the lucuma fruit, native to South America. While I wouldn't use lucuma on its own as the sole sweetener in a recipe, it's a lovely addition to ramp up the sweetness and brings a slight caramel or butterscotch flavor to desserts.

• *Maple Syrup.* Maple syrup is a wonderful, delectable natural sweetener that provides a surprising number of nutrients. It's an excellent source of manganese (a cofactor in many enzymatic actions in the body) as well as zinc (a key antioxidant vital to immune functioning and prostate health). The darker the syrup, the more its sugar has been concentrated. I love its flavor and find it complements certain other ingredients (such as walnuts or apples) beautifully. Because it has almost the same glycemic index as white sugar, however, I tend not to use maple syrup in my recipes, but it remains a healthful, natural sweetner for those who can consume it.

Substitution Tip: You can replace agave nectar 1:1 with maple syrup. If you can tolerate the higher glycemic index of maple syrup, feel free to replace any coconut nectar in my recipes with maple syrup as well (though note that the flavor will change depending on the grade of maple syrup used). Since coconut nectar is so much thicker than maple syrup, when replacing with maple syrup, reduce the other liquid in your recipe by about 25 percent. In other words, for every 1 cup (240 ml) of coconut nectar, use ¾ cup (180 ml) maple syrup; or reduce other liquids by 25 percent.

• *Stevia.* The leaves of the Stevia rebaudiana (Bertoni) plant have been used as a sweetener for centuries in Latin America. The sweetener referred to simply as "stevia" is either a powder made from the dried leaves, or else a liquid suspension of the powder (in a glycerin or alcohol base). One of the major sweeteners in Japan, stevia is a natural sweetener that you could grow in your own backyard. Sold primarily as an herbal supplement in Canada, pure stevia is about 30 times sweeter than sugar, yet boasts a glycemic index of zero, so it doesn't affect blood-sugar levels. In the United States, stevia is available both in its pure form and in sugar substitutes that extract a single component of the plant and then combine it with fillers to create a new (and patentable) product. I don't consider those sweeteners equivalent to true stevia.

Most alternative-health professionals such as naturopaths or holistic nutritionists recommend pure stevia as a healthy alternative to sugar. Because the powder is so concentrated, anything under 1⁄16 of a teaspoon (.25 ml) becomes very difficult to measure accurately, and in those cases I use the liquid instead. If the stevia can be measured easily in either powder or liquid form, feel free to choose whichever form you prefer in a recipe. As a general rule, use twice as much liquid stevia as powder to achieve equal sweetness. For instance, ¼ teaspoon (1 ml) liquid is roughly equivalent to ⅛ teaspoon (.5 ml) powder.

While it adds a great deal of sweetness to foods, it cannot be substituted for sugar in baking without greatly altering a recipe's texture. I tend not to use stevia on its own, simply because of the change in volume and texture it would cause to the ingredients.

A second potential issue with stevia is that, when used in larger quantities, some people detect a slightly metallic or bitter aftertaste, particularly when used with unsweetened cocoa or chocolate. In those cases, I subscribe to the adage "less is more"; I prefer to use a little less stevia and aim for a bittersweet flavor (sort of like 70 percent chocolate bars). It's still sweet enough to really enjoy it, yet it doesn't possess a strange aftertaste.

I also buy the best-quality stevia possible, always seeking out 100 percent–pure stevia rather than any of the "baking blends" or one-for-one stevia mixes that are intended to replace sugar, since those invariably contain fillers (see "Resource Guide," page 219, for my recommendations).

• *Yacon Syrup.* Yacon is extracted from the roots of the yacon plant, found in the Andes mountains. A dark, sticky liquid, it's often compared to molasses, though its glycemic index is much lower (and its flavor not as sweet). I use yacon sparingly, and always in combination with another sweetener, as some find its tangy flavor a little too powerful.

Natural Egg Substitutes

There are numerous ways to replace eggs in baking. Because I'm inclined to use only natural, whole foods and ingredients, however, I'm not overly fond of the prepackaged or powdered replacers, such as Ener-G, which contains carbohydrate gum and chemical leaveners. Instead, I usually opt for one of the following ways to replace eggs.

• *Avocado.* Yes, avocado is technically a fruit, but since most people don't think of it that way, and since it has its own distinctly nonfruit-like characteristics, it has found its way here!

Avocado puree, made in a blender, can act as a wonderful egg substitute in certain dishes; avocado confers moistness, body, and healthy fat. Because avocados are already high in monounsaturated (heart-healthy) fats, they can be used to replace some of the other oils in your baking as well. I tend to use avocado where its flavor and color won't be detected, such as in Zucchini-Pineapple Mini Loaves or Muffins (see page 66).

Substitution Tip: About ¼ cup (60 ml) packed avocado puree replaces 1 large egg.

• *Ground Flax Seeds (or Meal).* Flax seeds are a high source of healthy omega-3 fats and add protein, fat, and fiber to your baked goods. When ground flax seeds are mixed with water, they develop a viscous, gel-like texture that resembles that of raw egg whites, enabling them to be used successfully as a replacement for the binding power of eggs in baking. However, since flax seeds don't contain the leavening power of eggs, you'll need to add more leaveners when using flax instead of eggs.

I tend to use ground flax more than any other egg substitute, as flax seeds are fairly easy to find (most bulk or health-food stores now carry them) and reasonably priced. You can certainly buy preground flax meal, but I find the cost isn't worth it; I purchase whole seeds (which can be stored at room temperature), grind them in a coffee grinder, spice grinder, or blender, and use as needed. As a general rule, the volume of flax seeds will double when ground; that is, 1 tablespoon (15 ml) whole flax will yield approximately 2 tablespoons (30 ml) finely ground flax.

Store ground flax seeds in a dark container in the refrigerator or freezer for no more than 6 weeks. (Their high omega-3 content makes them more perishable once ground.) If buying preground flax seeds, opt for the vacuum-packed bags, and then store opened bags in the freezer or refrigerator.

Note: Since my recipes have already been formulated to account for the moisture absorbed by the flax, there is no need to make any changes when you see flax in these recipes.

Seeds and seed-based egg replacers, clockwise from top right, hemp seeds, ground flax, grey chia seeds, psyllium husks, pumpkin seeds (pepitas), brown flax seeds.

For each egg you wish to replace, combine 1 tablespoon (15 ml) of ground flax seeds with 3 tablespoons (45 ml) of water in a small bowl; allow to sit at least 2 minutes, or until the texture becomes gel-like. Add to your batter as you would regular eggs.

Another version of flax "eggs" can be made by boiling the seeds in water. To make, boil ½ cup (50 g) of the whole seeds in 3 cups (720 ml) water until glue-like, then strain, reserving the gel-like liquid. One regular, large egg is equal to about ¼ cup (60 ml) of the gel. Because the fiber from the flax seeds is not included in these "eggs," I use them in lighter or more delicately flavored baking.

Substitution Tip: Flax "eggs" can replace up to 2 large eggs in baked goods without any noticeable change to the final product; any more than that, however, and the texture will be compromised. I do not recommend converting conventional recipes with more than 2 eggs in the original recipe.

• *Ground Chia Seeds (or Meal).* Chia is a more recent addition to the high-omega-3 group of foods. With an omega-3 content, protein content, and fiber content even higher than those of flax, chia has been touted as the next superfood. One of the great qualities of chia for my purposes, however, is that, once ground, it makes a wonderful egg substitute that can also absorb a fair amount of liquid in a recipe, which is useful for those recipes that are meant to remain quite moist, such as Carrot Snack Cake (see page 157) or Pear and Ginger Mini Loaves or Muffins (see page 53).

Although chia is more expensive than flax, I've become quite enamored of the tiny white or gray seeds. Once ground, they form a fine powder, which is less visible than flax in the final product. They also retain moisture differently from flax seeds, resulting in a more tender crumb for baked goods.

Although the white and gray seeds are both easily available in health-food stores and both work equally well in baked goods, I'd recommend the white ones for any light-colored treats, such as Sugar-Free Sugar Cookies (see page 116), to ensure a pleasing appearance of the final product. As with flax seeds, preground chia "meal" is also available in many health-food stores and can be used if you prefer not to grind your own. Once opened, chia meal should be stored in the refrigerator or freezer for up to 3 months.

For more delicate results, I use chia in some recipes, such as the Holiday Apple Cake (see page 150), but in almost all cases you can use flax as a substitute for chia in any recipe; use 1 tablespoon (15 ml) ground flax to replace every 1½ teaspoons (7.5 ml) of ground chia in my recipes. The resultant product will have a slightly denser texture, however.

Substitution Tip: For each large egg you wish to replace, combine 1½ teaspoons (7.5 ml) finely ground chia seeds with 3 tablespoons (45 ml) water and allow to sit for 2 to 5 minutes, until a gel-like texture is formed.

You can make your own chia meal by grinding the seeds in a coffee grinder, spice grinder, or blender until powdery; store as flax, above. One tablespoon (15 ml) of whole seeds will yield roughly 2 tablespoons (30 ml) of finely ground meal. As with flax, I do not suggest replacing more than 2 eggs from an original recipe with chia "eggs."

• *Fruit Purees.* Many bakers use fruit purees instead of eggs in their baking, as they add moistness and help the batter to bind together. As a general rule, about ¼ cup (60 ml) of any puree equals 1 large egg. I tend not to use fruit purees as the only egg substitute in my baking, as I find they alter the flavor of the product significantly (in general, you'll be able to taste if some banana or prunes have been added to your baked good, for instance). However, I do use purees where the flavor and texture will complement the original recipe, such as in banana bread, brownies, and so on.

• *Silken Tofu.* Silken tofu usually comes water packed in a plastic tub in the refrigerated section of your supermarket. This Chinese-style (with water) tofu is a great egg substitute, as is the soft silken Japanese-style tofu (packed in non-refrigerated, aseptically packaged cartons known as Tetra Pak boxes). Either form works well in most recipes, but when one or the other is essential to a particular recipe, I will specify that type. In the United States and Canada, the most popular Japanese-style brand, Mori-Nu, offers varying levels of firmness, though all are considered "silken" (from soft silken to extra-firm silken). I most often use the firm or extra-firm style.

A key quality of silken tofu is its resemblance in both appearance and texture to custard. As a result, when used in baking, this custard-like texture helps to bind and firm up the baked good in question. It's also moister than flax or chia, so is often used in cookies or squares that require moistness, such as brownies. And silken tofu makes a great "cheesecake" base.

I recommend using only organic brands of tofu, if at all possible, since some brands may contain genetically modified (GMO) soybeans, which are not always identified on the label. Organic products by law can't contain GMOs, so they are a safer bet.

Substitution Tip: For each large egg you wish to replace, use ¼ cup (60 ml) packed silken tofu of either type. Simply scoop the tofu from the package and into a ¼-cup (60-ml) measuring cup, pressing down and chopping it up with a spoon to eliminate any air pockets. Because it will hold its shape, silken tofu must be pureed in a food processor or blender before being added to any batter; my recipes include this step in the preparation of the wet ingredients.

While tofu has been proven a great source of protein and helpful in alleviating some cardiovascular problems as well as symptoms associated with menopause, some health-food advocates recommend avoiding tofu because it can cause digestive problems or issues for those with low thyroid function. Because I don't have these reactions to tofu, I feel comfortable using it in moderation. Of course, you should do what feels right to you. Any of the other egg substitutes listed here can be used to replace tofu "eggs" in my recipes.

Silken tofu is available in health-food stores, some bulk stores, and in the natural-foods section of some supermarkets (though many conventional brands in supermarkets aren't organic).

Better Fats & Oils

After learning in nutrition school about the various chemical structures of most cooking oils and how heat causes them to oxidize and produce free radicals, I began to narrow down my choices for fats that I'd comfortably use in baking. My list of preferred fats and oils for baked goods is probably shorter than the one you're used to, and certainly you're welcome to use almost any oil in my recipes, and the flavor and texture won't change dramatically. If your purpose is to prevent damage to the chemical structure and nutritional qualities of the oil, however, you might like to read on.

- *Coconut Oil.* For years, coconut oil received a bad rap because of its high saturated-fat content; it was also, in the past, often hydrogenated. Today, however, high-quality, unrefined (generally called "virgin"), and organic coconut oils are an ideal butter substitute for those who don't eat dairy. Like butter, coconut oil is solid at room temperature (it melts at 76°F/24.5°C). I use it chilled as a substitute for butter or lard in pastries, softened at room temperature in cookies and bars, and melted when a liquid oil is required. Depending on the brand you buy (see page 219 for my recommendations), it need not add a coconut flavor to your baked goods; refined coconut oil is tasteless and useful when you wish to avoid the mild hint of coconut from virgin oils.

The best characteristic of coconut oil, however, is that, as a naturally saturated fat, it is safe to use with relatively high heat. Undamaged by the heat of baking, coconut oil will preserve the integrity of baked goods where other fats might not. And unlike animal-based saturated fats, coconut oil has been shown in some studies to help improve cholesterol levels and heart health, rather than destroy them.

Substitution Tip: Use coconut oil in the same quantities as butter in a recipe. When substituting for butter, your coconut oil should be soft, but still solid. In recipes that require the oil to be melted first, I'll state that in the recipe.

• *Nut Oils.* Oils derived from nuts, such as macadamia, walnut, and almond (as well as other oils, such as avocado), have begun to appear on supermarket shelves in recent years and are useful additions to baked goods, providing subtle flavor and fragrance to your desserts. Because unrefined oils will confer the flavor of the nut or seed from which they are made, choose oils carefully to match the flavor profile of the baked good you're making. (For instance, walnut oil is lovely with any cinnamon-flavored treats, macadamia works well with vanilla, and so on.)

• *Olive Oil.* A source of healthy monounsaturated fat, olive oil would be my first choice of oil for baking, as it can withstand higher heats than most polyunsaturated oils. A good-quality, unrefined, and cold-pressed olive oil, however, will taste like its source — olives. So I confine my use of olive oil to those recipes where there is very little oil (about 2 tablespoons/30 ml) per recipe, or where the other flavors in the recipe are strong enough that the olive flavor won't be detected. If you like the flavor, feel free to use an equal amount of olive oil wherever sunflower oil is mentioned in my recipes.

• *Sunflower Oil.* Sunflower oil is the oil I use most often, and the main liquid oil mentioned in my recipes. It's a light-tasting oil that produces lovely results; however, as a polyunsaturated oil, it can be somewhat damaged by heat. Still, because some recipes absolutely require a liquid (rather than solid) fat, sunflower oil works best in those situations. If you can find high-oleic sunflower oil, buy that, as it can better withstand heat without damage to the chemical structure of the oil.

Why Not Canola?

Most people are surprised to discover that I don't use canola oil in my baking. Although it is a polyunsaturated oil, many brands of canola, if not organic, tend to contain GMO (genetically modified) ingredients, and some of the organic varieties may be cross-contaminated with GMO crops. They also have been highly processed to remove the strong flavor. Because of the tendency toward so much processing, I prefer not to use it in my cooking and baking.

Non-Dairy Milk Alternatives

Nowadays, there are so many varieties of alternative milk in stores that even if you don't drink them, you're probably aware of soy milk, almond milk, and perhaps rice milk. While all can be useful as an alternative in daily cooking, I've found that the properties of different milks create different results in baked goods.

Here are some of the more common milk substitutes I use, and a description of where they're most useful.

• *Almond Milk.* Made from boiled, crushed, and strained almonds, almond milk is a wonderful alternative for those avoiding soy (though it is a bit more expensive than soy milk). It can be used anywhere soy milk is used. As with soy milk, I tend to use unsweetened or "original" flavors. It can be used 1:1 in place of cow's milk or soy milk.

• *Coconut Milk and Coconut Beverage.* Full-fat or "lite" coconut milk is available in cans and is a great substitute for dairy cream, and it can be used to add richness to baked desserts (a mix of half coconut milk and half another alternative milk works beautifully in this way). In addition, coconut-based beverages in cartons have recently been introduced as another milk alternative, with a thinner consistency, lower fat content, and lower caloric values. Coconut milk beverage in a carton can be used much like any other milk substitute, but will bring a richer flavor to your final product.

• *Rice Milk.* While it's probably my favorite in terms of taste, rice milk is quite a bit thinner than soy or almond milk, and so isn't a perfect replacement for either of those in baked goods; the result is sometimes a bit too light or delicate, and may crumble easily. In other instances, it is actually a better alternative when a light and airy texture is preferred. If you do use rice milk instead of soy or almond in my recipes, be aware that your final product may lack the intended density. Rice milk is also naturally sweeter than other milks (even without added sugar), so it should be used in moderation by anyone avoiding increased blood-sugar levels.

• *Soy Milk.* Soy milk is probably the most well-known milk alternative, as well as the most popular. Despite some recent controversies about the problems with soy for children, those with low thyroid function (see "Silken Tofu," page 30), or people with cancer, I believe that, used in moderation, organic soy milk can be a great addition to baked goods and desserts. Because of its relatively high protein content, it seems to work in baking much like cow's milk does, and produces similar results.

In general, I use unsweetened, "plain" or "original" flavors for baking. You can use soy milk 1:1 instead of cow's milk.

Supporting Cast (Other Key Ingredients)

Below is a list of ingredients that I use often as add-ins or to boost the flavor or texture of baked goods. They are rarely the "star" of the recipe (that is, not one of the main ingredients) and can often be exchanged for something else (such as chocolate chips for carob chips), but they are all key ingredients nonetheless, and ones I use frequently.

• *Gluten-Free Rolled Oats.* You'll notice that I use oats in my recipes on occasion. Technically, oats are all gluten-free; but in the past, because of growing patterns and the fact that oats were often processed on the same equipment as wheat, most oats were off the table (and plate!) for those on gluten-free diets. I use Bob's Red Mill certified gluten-free oats, but there are other equally good products on the market today

Steel-cut oats (sometimes called "Scottish oats") are simply the whole oat groat that has been chopped into smaller pieces. These are hard, seed-like bits that take some time to cook (up to 45 minutes) and result in a chunky, nubby oatmeal that is, in my opinion, divine. For those with less time on their hands, rolled oats are a delicious alternative.

Most of my recipes call for "old-fashioned" oats (often referred to simply as "rolled oats"), which are the least processed type of rolled oat. In this case, the whole oat groats are steamed and rolled flat before being dried. This type of oat takes a little longer to cook than other rolled oats (about 20 minutes), but it also retains the most nutrients. "Quick cooking" oats look like regular rolled oats, but they have been rolled even thinner, so they cook up faster; however, the texture of quick oats isn't quite as pleasing as that of "old-fashioned" oats. Finally, "instant" oats are processed even more to require minimal or no cooking (sometimes just hot water will do the trick), but they are inferior both in nutritional value and taste.

• *Fresh Nuts and Seeds.* Fresh, organic nuts and seeds are wonderful sources of protein and healthy fats (both mono- and polyunsaturated). However, with this high fat content comes the same caveat as with cooking oils (see page 31): because toxins reside in fats, buy organic whenever possible. In addition, preroasted nuts and seeds are often cooked in unhealthy fats (and have lots of added salt), and their lack of freshness may be concealed under their toasty exterior.

If possible, I recommend buying raw, unsalted organic nuts and seeds and roasting them yourself. Also, buy whole nuts whenever possible; the smaller the pieces (for instance, prechopped nuts), the more surface area has been exposed to air, heat, or light, all of which damage the fragile fats that have been exposed.

To roast them, spread a single layer of nuts or seeds on a rimmed cookie sheet (or use a square or rectangular cake pan) and bake at 350°F (180°C) for 10 to 15 minutes, until just golden and fragrant. Cool and store, covered, in the refrigerator, for up to a month. Any raw nuts or seeds that won't be used within two to three weeks should be refrigerated as well, or frozen up to six months.

• *Instant-Coffee Substitute.* When I wish to produce a java-like taste in my baked goods, my first choice is Dandy Blend, a certified gluten-free coffee substitute with a very mild flavor, though any brand of coffee substitute will do in my recipes. You might have to adjust the amount with other stronger-flavored brands, however. Of course, you can always use instant-coffee granules where my recipes call for the caffeine-free substitutes. If converting to instant coffee, use about half as much coffee — that is, 1 teaspoon (5 ml) instant-coffee granules to replace 2 teaspoons (10 ml) instant-coffee substitute.

• *Nut and Seed Butters.* Toasted nuts and seeds make a perfect base for homemade nut or seed butters, which are much fresher and less expensive than the store-bought variety. Of course, I do keep jars of ready-made almond and cashew butters on hand for when I haven't the time or inclination to make my own — they work just fine in all the recipes! And while it's not technically a nut, coconut butter is also useful to have on hand, especially since it's stable at room temperature and will last for a year that way. Store-bought coconut butter can be pricey, so if you're able to make your own (see page 36), it's a great option.

Another reason I favor homemade nut butters over store bought is that I can control the amount of salt and the texture; the homemade variety is a bit thicker and spreads more easily than the jarred type (I find that prepared nut butters are sometimes a bit runny). In addition, I can blend a few different types of nuts in one nut butter according to my taste, rather than relying on just strictly almond or cashew butter. One of my favorite combinations consists of two parts almonds to one part each walnuts and pecans. For instructions on making homemade nut or seed butter, see pages 35–36.

• *Unsweetened Carob Chips.* As soon as a brand of dairy-free, gluten-free chocolate chips sweetened with stevia or coconut sugar hits the market, I aim to use it. Because I've yet to find a brand that is both gluten-free and dairy-free without containing sugar, I rely on unsweetened carob chips whenever a recipe would include whole (unmelted) chocolate chips, such as when sprinkled on Dalmatian Cheesecake Brownies (see page 143) or in Butterscotch-Chocolate Chip Cookies (see page 100). For me, they work beautifully in these situations.

Carob chips don't melt the same way chocolate chips do, however, so I wouldn't use them as a substitute in recipes that require melted chocolate.

Tips & Techniques

It's often said that baking is more of a science than cooking is. While that may be true, I've always found that becoming comfortable with your ingredients and equipment is just as important as following a recipe accurately. Here are some tips to simplify the process, while increasing your success and enjoyment in baking naturally sweet and gluten-free.

Grinding Your Own Flours

Many grains, nuts, or seeds can be ground into flour at home. To grind your own flour, take a small amount (about ¼ cup/30–45 g) at a time of raw nuts, such as almonds; seeds, such as pumpkin seeds; or small, dry grains (such as millet, whole oats, quinoa, buckwheat, or teff) and grind to a powder or very fine meal in a coffee grinder, spice grinder, or high-speed blender (such as Vitamix). Avoid grinding nuts too long, however, or you'll have nut butter! Transfer to a bowl and repeat until you have enough flour for your recipe. Then measure and use as you would prepackaged flour. Store, tightly covered, in the refrigerator.

Note: This method isn't suitable for all nuts and seeds. Those with a higher fat content, such as walnuts, will simply turn to nut butter fairly quickly. In addition, grinding larger grains or legumes could damage your grinder.

Here's a quick reference chart for those home-ground flours I make most often.

Quantity of Whole Grain, Legume, Seed, or Nut	Quantity of Flour	Texture of Flour
¼ cup (25 g) old-fashioned rolled oats	¼ cup whole oat flour	Very fine meal to powder
¼ cup (40 g) raw, blanched almonds or natural raw almonds	⅓ cup almond flour	Coarse meal to fine meal
¼ cup (35 g) raw seeds (sunflower, pumpkin, or hemp)	⅓ cup seed flour	Fine meal to very fine meal
¼ cup (45–50 g) small, round grains or pseudo-grains (quinoa, millet, buckwheat, teff, or amaranth)	6 Tbsp flour	Very fine meal to powder

Grinding Nut or Seed Butters

To make homemade nut or seed butters, simply toast natural (unroasted, unsalted) nuts or seeds of choice and let cool. Place in a powerful food processor and process until crumbly. Then keep processing until the mixture becomes finer and eventually forms a ball that rolls around the processor bowl; keep processing past this point, and the ball will eventually smooth out and become nut or seed butter. You'll need to stop periodically and scrape the sides of the processor; be patient — it can take up to 10 minutes — but the result is worth it. Occasionally, if your nuts or seeds are dry, you may need to add up to 1 tablespoon (15 ml) coconut or sunflower oil to help smooth out the final product. In general, I find that cashews, sunflower seeds, and pumpkin seeds tend to require added oil. Store your nut or seed butter in clean jars in the refrigerator for up to 1 month.

You can also make nut or seed butter in a high-speed blender, if you have one. Begin with a smaller quantity of raw nuts or seeds (about 1 cup/150 g) and, using the tamper to push the ingredient toward the blades, blend until liquefied. This should take only a minute or two.

While it's not technically a nut, dried coconut can be made into coconut butter easily and quickly in a high-speed blender as well. Start with 2 cups (135 g) of shredded, unsweetened coconut and use the tamper to blend. You'll need a little longer to achieve a fluid texture with coconut butter, up to 5 minutes, scraping the sides as necessary. Coconut butter will keep up to 6 months at room temperature; note that it will solidify at room temperature, and should be gently melted before use.

Here's a quick reference chart for the homemade nut and seed butters I make most often (other seeds, such as sesame, flax, or chia, are generally not suitable, as they won't liquefy in a food processor).

Quantity of Whole Seed or Nut	Quantity of Butter
1 cup (140 g) toasted almonds	½ cup (120 ml)
1 cup (150 g) toasted cashews or hazelnuts	½ cup (120 ml)
1 cup (115 g) toasted walnuts	½ cup (120 ml)
1 cup (120 g) toasted pecans	½ cup (120 ml)
1 cup (approximately 135g) of toasted pumpkin or sunflower seeds	½ cup (120 ml)
1 cup (120 g) toasted hemp seeds (or hemp hearts)	½ cup (120 ml)

Measuring Ingredients Correctly

My recipes are based on specific combinations of ingredients and will work best when the measurements are exactly the same as those in the recipes. It's worth noting how I measure my ingredients, as I've learned that not everyone automatically uses the same methods I do. To achieve the best results, I recommend following these guidelines.

- *Dry or Thick Ingredients.* For dry ingredients (such as flour) and thick, moist ingredients (such as nut butters), I use individual metal or plastic measuring cups in incremental amounts of ⅛ cup (equivalent to 2 tablespoons/30 ml), ¼ cup (equivalent to 4 tablespoons/60 ml), ½ cup (equivalent to 8 tablespoons/120 ml), and 1 cup (equivalent to 16 tablespoons/240 ml).

For dry ingredients, I scoop the ingredient (using the cup itself as a scoop), then level the top with the back of a knife. I don't pack down the dry contents further by shaking the cup. (When using metric measures, I simply weigh the dry ingredients.) I measure small amounts of dry ingredients — baking powder, salt, and so on — the same way, using a tablespoon or teaspoon and leveling the top.

I also always sift my dry ingredients *after* measuring them (to break up any small lumps or to reveal impurities like little pebbles or grain husks) by stirring the dry ingredients in a fine-mesh sieve. You can also use a sifter, of course.

For moist ingredients, I spoon the ingredients, such as nut butter, solid coconut oil, or silken tofu, into the cup and pack it in with the back of the spoon to eliminate air pockets; then I level the top, as above.

• *Liquid Ingredients.* For liquid ingredients, such as milk or oil, I pour the ingredient into a clear, spouted, glass or plastic measuring cup, stopping when the liquid reaches the desired amount when viewed at eye level.

I also always scrape out the cups as cleanly as possible with a rubber or silicone spatula (even the last drops of milk or oil from a glass measuring cup!).

Metric Conversions

When converting from American to metric measures, I've used the following methods:
Dry ingredients: measured by weight (grams), except for smaller amounts (less than 60 ml), which are measured by volume (milliliters).
Wet ingredients (including thick, moist ingredients, such as silken tofu and nut butters): measured by volume (milliliters).

Is It Done Yet?

The traditional toothpick-in-center test for baked goods won't always work for the recipes in this book. Batters based on whole grains are already fairly dark or golden, and darken even more when baked; the color is so close to that of a toothpick that I find I cannot always distinguish the batter from the wood. Instead, I use a small, very sharp steak knife and insert it in the center of the cake, muffin, or cupcake. If the knife comes out clean, it's ready. I find this method fairly easy — and it provides a good use for my otherwise unused steak knives! (Of course, a metal skewer will work well, too.)

Storing Your Naturally Sweet & Gluten-Free Baked Goods

Unlike conventional baked goods, my recipes don't contain preservatives or refined sugar (which acts as a natural preservative). In addition, moist sweeteners such as coconut nectar or agave nectar can begin to ferment if kept too long at room temperature.

Consequently, it's best to store your baked goods in the refrigerator in a closed container or tightly wrapped with plastic to prevent drying out. For items that are best eaten at room temperature, simply remove them from the fridge 20 to 30 minutes before serving. Most of the baked goods will keep for 4 to 5 days in the refrigerator, and can be frozen for longer periods (in the recipes, I indicate which items can be frozen).

Bakeware & Tools

As someone who was raised in a frugal home, I am not the type of cook who likes to possess every "next best thing" when it comes to appliances and kitchen gadgets; I believe that you can create fabulous food without having to use a lot of fancy tools and utensils. At the same time, though, I am willing to invest in those better-quality appliances and tools that I find necessary to streamline and perfect my recipes.

Here's a list of items that I think of as essential (or, at least, extremely useful) in my kitchen. Some of these, like my food processor, I use every single day. Others, like an offset spatula, may be employed less frequently but prove to be indispensable when I need them.

• *Food Processor*. I love my food processor! In fact, I hadn't realized how much I use it in these recipes until I started typing them out for the book. A good food processor is essential for some of the desserts (particularly the cheesecakes and those involving ground nuts), and I often use it as a single vessel in which to mix the entire batter for a recipe. My first food processor was a 9-cup (around 2.2 L) capacity, and I've since graduated to a full 14-cup (about 3.5 L capacity), which is great for making large-batch nut butters at home (see pages 35–36). However, most home cooks don't require the largest size as long as the bowl is big enough for a basic cookie dough or, say, for grinding the nuts for a recipe. I recommend owning one large processor (7 or 9 cups/1.6 L or 2.2 L) for major tasks and a mini processor for smaller jobs (see page 39).

Cleaning Tip: Here's a nifty trick for scraping out all the contents of the processor and cleaning off the blades in a snap. When working with thick or sticky batters (such as cakes, brownies, or nut butter), simply scrape out as much as you can into your mixing bowl or pan, but don't worry too much about the blades. Place the almost-clean bowl back on the base, leaving the blades inside. Cover once more and process for a few seconds; the centrifugal force of the spinning blades will throw any excess batter onto the walls of the processor bowl, leaving the blades virtually clean. Then open it up again, remove the blades, and scrape out the last bits of your batter from the processor bowl.

• *Powerful Blender*. Until I studied holistic nutrition and learned about "green smoothies" (smoothies with added leafy greens, such as baby spinach or kale), I had never heard of a "high-speed blender." These are large and ultra-powerful blenders that began in industrial kitchens and are now part of many health-conscious homes. I own a Vitamix (though I know many people who own a Blendtec for the same purpose). While a high-speed blender is an expensive kitchen appliance, and I wouldn't recommend one unless you are serious about blending green smoothies or other recipes that require it, it does come in handy for a few of my recipes, such as Best Bean Brownies (see page 139) or Mascarpone "Cheese" in the Rustic Glazed Peach and Mascarpone Tart (see page 179). However, all the recipes in this book can be made in a regular blender as well, by blending for a little longer and in smaller batches.

• *Coffee (or Spice) Grinder.* I use a coffee grinder to make flax or chia meal at home, to break up cacao nibs into smaller pieces, or to grind grains, nuts, or seeds into flours on occasion. We have two grinders in our house that we keep separate according to use: one for spices and one for all of my baking exploits. That way I never have to worry about the unwanted scent or flavor of curry powder making its way into my morning muffins!

• *Silicone Spatulas (but Not Muffin Cups).* Although I'm still wary of baking in silicone pans or muffin cups because of the extended time at high heat, I do use silicone spatulas for their versatility. Buy varying sizes so you'll have one to scrape out the mini processor or blender, a larger one for bowls and the full-size processor, and so on. Silicone spatulas are also great for stirring melted chocolate, since you don't have to worry about the heat. They're also flexible and can be cleaned easily in the dishwasher, unlike plastic or rubber spatulas.

A mini food processor, seen here with Chocolate "Buttercream" Frosting (see page 166), measuring cups, spoons, and scoops.

• *Mini Food Processor.* Along with my full-sized food processor, I also own a miniature one for smaller, quicker jobs, such as grinding nuts and seeds or mixing up small batches of frosting or nut butter. The mini processor is also perfect when I wish to bake up a half batch of cookies and don't want to dirty the larger one. This isn't an essential appliance, and I could definitely do without it, but it does make life a lot easier.

• *Offset Spatula.* While an offset spatula (a spatula with a long, thin metal blade that lies slightly below the handle) is something I don't use every week, it's indispensable when I do need it to spread batters smoothly and easily. It makes frosting a cake a breeze and is perfect for spreading a layer of filling or pastry cream over a crust. In a pinch, I also use my offset spatula to help ease a slice of brownie or cake out of a square pan.

• *Mini Whisk & Whisk.* I use my mini whisk to blend liquid ingredients in smaller bowls or glass measuring cups (ground flax tends to clump when it sits in a liquid; the whisk ensures that it's evenly dispersed before combining liquids with the dry ingredients). I use a large whisk to blend batters once they're combined in a larger bowl. I tend to keep two large whisks handy when I bake: one is to help stir the dry ingredients through a sieve to sift the flours, and one is to whisk the wet ingredients into the dry. Keeping one whisk entirely dry allows me to reuse it for sifting, without having to wash and dry each time, on those days when I'm baking two or three items one after the other (as when I bake up a selection of cookies for the holidays, for example).

• *Cookie Sheets.* I keep three flat and three rimmed cookie sheets in my kitchen. The flat ones are used primarily for cookies, while the rimmed sheets are ideal to toast nuts or seeds. I always line my sheets with parchment paper so that the baked good isn't placed directly against the metal, which could leach into the food.

• *Springform Pan.* A round pan with removable sides, a springform pan is generally considered a specialty item used for cheesecakes. However, an 8- or 9-inch (20- or 22.5-cm) springform pan can also double as a pie pan, round cake pan, or pan for Cinnamon Buns (see page 73), so I consider it a worthwhile investment.

• *Square Pans.* I'd recommend having two basic square cake pans of either 8 or 9 inches (20 or 22.5 cm). That way, you'll have them available for layer cakes if you wish, or for when you bake a double batch of, say, Ultra Fudgy Brownies (see page 134) or other bars. I recommend using glass pans if you can find them, as they are nontoxic and very durable. (Note that baked

Some of my most useful kitchen tools.

goods will brown more easily in glass than in aluminum or stainless steel, so the temperature when using glass should be reduced by 20–25°F/10–12°C from what is stated in the recipe). If using aluminum or other metal pans, I suggest lining them with parchment to prevent the batter from touching the metal directly.

- *Loaf Pans.* As with square pans, I own two standard (8-inch or 20-cm) loaf pans. They can be used for most regular loaf recipes, and if I encounter a recipe calling for a larger loaf pan, I simply divide the batter in half between the two smaller ones.
- *Wooden Spoons.* A good, sturdy wooden spoon or two is a useful utensil in any baker's kitchen. Wooden spoons are great for mixing batters, of course, but they're also useful to stir melted chocolate or puddings, as they can be used with nonstick surfaces when metal cannot be.
- *Muffin Pans.* My favorite muffin pans contain 12 muffin cups. If your recipe yields fewer than 12 muffins, you can simply leave the other wells empty. When I know my recipe will yield fewer than a dozen muffins, I begin pouring the batter in the cups around the edge of the pan (leaving the center empty), since the muffins will bake more evenly that way.
- *Sharp Knives.* A reliably sharp knife is a great tool for cutting firm or chewy bar cookies and dividing treats cleanly into squares. I use a 9-inch (22.5-cm) chef's knife for this purpose, but any sharp knife will do.
- *Measuring Cups.* For accurate measurements, I suggest owning both glass measuring cups (used for liquid measures) and graduated metal or plastic cups (for dry ingredients). The most common size for glass cups is a 2-cup (500-ml) capacity, which is sufficient to cover most recipes without having to measure twice. I also use my glass cup instead of a small bowl if the wet ingredients won't total more than 2 cups (480 ml), which saves me having to wash one more bowl! Dry cups are usually available in sets of graduated measures starting from ¼ cup (60 ml) up to 1 cup (240 ml). Years ago, I found a set of plastic cups that included a ⅛ cup (30 ml) measure, and it remains one of my most used measuring cups. Since ⅛ cup is equal to 2 tablespoons (30 ml), it's a handy way to measure that amount without dirtying a measuring spoon or having to measure twice.
- *Measuring Spoons.* As with measuring cups, I have two sets of graduated measuring spoons (from ⅛ teaspoon/.5 ml to 1 tablespoon/15 ml), so that I can reserve one for dry ingredients and one for wet while baking and save time not having to wash the spoons when I switch from wet to dry.
- *Scale.* Weighing dry ingredients is commonplace in Europe, the United Kingdom, and the antipodes, but we in North America are only now slowly coming to appreciate the ease and accuracy of weight rather than volume measures for flour, sugar, nuts, and seeds. And while my recipes have been tested extensively with volume measures by American and Canadian testers, I've been using weight measures myself for about ten years and love that I can be confident my flour and sugar are perfectly measured each time without having to dirty a measuring cup. Weighing ingredients also makes halving a recipe a breeze, since you don't have to estimate things like "half of ⅓ cup." These days, you can find a good kitchen scale for under $20.00. I think it's a great investment.

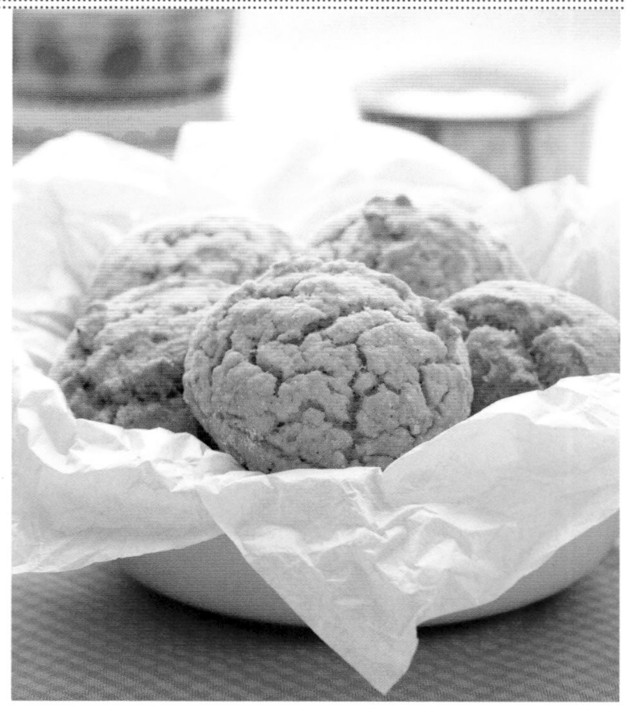

Chapter 1: *Breakfast Bakes*

(and toppings for pancakes & waffles)

Orange-Oat Muffins ✷ CF, can be SF or NF ✷

Makes 9

Although I no longer eat oranges very often, these remain one of my favorite muffins. They come together easily in the food processor, and in no time you've got some moist, hearty muffins for breakfast or snacks. If you are using a 12-cup muffin pan for this recipe, fill the cups around the edges (rather than the center) so the muffins will bake evenly.

- 1 medium seedless orange, washed, preferably organic (do not peel)
- 1 Tbsp (15 ml) finely ground flax seeds
- ⅓ cup (60 g) chopped prunes (dried plums) — they should be soft
- 3 Tbsp (45 ml) sunflower or other light-tasting oil, preferably organic
- ⅓ cup (55 g) coconut sugar
- 1 Tbsp (15 ml) yacon syrup or blackstrap molasses
- ¼ tsp (1 ml) pure stevia powder or ½ tsp (2.5 ml) pure plain, vanilla, or orange-flavored stevia liquid, or to taste
- 2 Tbsp (30 ml) whole psyllium husks
- ¾ cup (180 ml) plain or vanilla soy or almond milk
- 1 cup (135 g) Ricki's All-Purpose Gluten-Free Flour Mix (see page 22)
- 1 Tbsp (15 ml) baking powder
- 1 tsp (5 ml) baking soda
- ¼ tsp (1 ml) fine sea salt
- 1 cup (100 g) old-fashioned rolled oats (not instant or quick-cooking)

Preheat the oven to 375°F (190°C). Line 9 muffin cups with paper liners, or spray with nonstick spray.

Cut the orange into 8 sections. Trim the stem end to remove any hard bits, and remove any pith from the middle. Process in the bowl of a food processor until almost smooth. Add the flax seeds, prunes, oil, coconut sugar, yacon syrup, stevia, psyllium, and milk and process again until smooth (it's okay if you see tiny flecks of prune or orange still in the mixture, but none should be larger than sunflower seeds). Set aside while you measure the dry ingredients, or at least 2 minutes.

In a large bowl, sift the flour, baking powder, soda, and salt; add the oats and mix to combine.

Pour the wet mixture over the dry and stir just until combined (it's okay if a few dry spots remain here or there). Do not overmix! Using a large ice-cream scoop or ⅓ cup (80 ml) measuring cup, spoon the batter into the prepared muffin cups (they will be quite full).

Bake 15 to 20 minutes, rotating pan about halfway through. If you are using a 9-cup muffin pan, insert a tester (see page 37) in a center muffin; they are done when the tester comes out clean. Cool 5 minutes in the pan before removing to a rack to cool completely. These are even better the next day, as flavors develop. May be frozen.

Banana–Carob Chip Muffins * SF, CF, NF *

Makes 8

I rarely consume bananas anymore, but I do still love them. This recipe is a special treat for me, and my husband is grateful when I bake up a batch, since he's the one who gets to eat most of it! If you prefer chocolate chips and can tolerate them, feel free to substitute dairy-free chocolate chips for the carob. If you are using a 12-cup muffin pan for this recipe, fill the cups around the edges (rather than the center) so the muffins will bake evenly.

- 1 cup (265 g) banana puree (2 to 3 medium bananas)
- ⅓ cup (240 ml) light agave nectar
- Scant ¼ cup (60 ml) sunflower or other light-tasting oil, preferably organic
- 2 Tbsp (30 ml) finely ground flax seeds (from about 1 Tbsp or 15 ml whole seeds)
- 1 tsp (5 ml) pure vanilla extract
- ⅓ cup (65 g) unsweetened carob chips
- 1¾ cups (225 g) Ricki's All-Purpose Gluten-Free Flour Mix (see page 22)
- 1½ tsp (7.5 ml) baking powder
- ½ tsp (2.5 ml) baking soda
- 1¼ tsp (6 ml) xanthan gum (use only Bob's Red Mill brand if you are) concerned about a corn allergy)
- ⅛ tsp (.5 ml) fine sea salt

Preheat the oven to 350°F (180°C). Line 8 muffin cups with paper liners, or spray with nonstick spray.

In a medium bowl, whisk together the banana, agave nectar, oil, flax, and vanilla. Add the carob chips and stir to coat.

In a large bowl, sift the flour, baking powder, baking soda, xanthan gum, and salt. Add the wet ingredients to the dry and stir just to blend.

Using a ⅓-cup measuring cup or ice-cream scoop, scoop the batter and fill the muffin cups about ¾ full (these do not rise much during baking). Bake for 25 to 30 minutes. If you are using a 9-cup muffin pan, insert a tester (see page 37) in a center muffin; they are done when the tester comes out clean. Allow to cool completely before removing from the pan. See page 37, storing baked goods. May be frozen.

Gingered Apple Muffins * CF, can be SF or NF *

Makes 10

I'm not usually fond of baked apples, but diced in these muffins, they're perfect. Juicy chunks of apple and the tempting zing of fresh ginger abound in every bite. Be sure to cut the apples into small dice — the pieces should be the size of large blueberries or raspberries — so that they will soften completely while baking. Otherwise, your muffins will be filled with crunchy bits of apple!

- 2 small, crisp apples, such as Gala, Granny Smith, or Empire
- 2 tsp (10 ml) ground cinnamon
- 2 Tbsp (30 ml) finely ground flax seeds (from about 1 Tbsp or 15 ml whole seeds)
- ¼ cup (60 ml) coconut sugar
- 20 to 30 drops pure plain or vanilla stevia liquid, or to taste
- 1¼ cups (300 ml) unsweetened plain or vanilla almond or soy milk
- ¼ cup (60 ml) sunflower or other light-tasting oil, preferably organic
- 1 tsp (5 ml) apple cider vinegar
- 1 tsp (5 ml) pure vanilla extract
- 1 Tbsp (15 ml) grated fresh ginger
- 3 Tbsp (45 ml) whole psyllium husks
- 1⅓ cups (170 g) Ricki's All-Purpose Gluten-Free Flour Mix (see page 22)
- ⅓ cup (55 g) teff flour
- 1 Tbsp (15 ml) baking powder
- ¾ tsp (7.5 ml) baking soda
- ¼ tsp (1 ml) fine sea salt

Preheat the oven to 375°F (190°C). Line 10 muffin cups with paper liners, or spray with nonstick spray.

Wash, core, and dice the apples quite small (no need to peel), about ¼ inch (6 mm). You should have 2 to 2½ cups (275–300 g) of diced apple. In a small bowl, toss the apple with the cinnamon to coat. Set aside.

In the bowl of a food processor, blend the flax, coconut sugar, stevia, milk, oil, vinegar, vanilla, and ginger until the sugar has dissolved. Add the psyllium and pulse once or twice to incorporate.

In a large bowl, sift the all-purpose flour, teff flour, baking powder, baking soda, and salt. Pour the wet mixture over the dry ingredients and stir just to combine. Working quickly (the batter will thicken), gently fold in the apple mixture.

Using a large ice-cream scoop or ⅓-cup (80-ml) measuring cup, fill the muffin cups slightly overflowing (these won't rise much in the oven). Bake 20 to 25 minutes, until a tester inserted in a center muffin comes out clean. Cool 5 minutes in the pan before removing to a rack to cool completely. See page 37, storing baked goods. May be frozen.

Sweet Potato-Chocolate Chip Mini Muffins

✸ CF, can be SF or NF ✸

Makes 18 mini or 6 regular muffins

I love sweet potato on its own, and try to incorporate it in baked goods whenever I can. In this recipe, the sweet potato lends moistness and additional sweetness. If you are able to eat regular chocolate chips, go ahead and use them here. When I make these muffins for myself, I always use unsweetened carob chips, and they are equally wonderful. If you are using a 12-cup muffin pan for regular-sized muffins, fill the cups around the edges (rather than the center) so the muffins will bake evenly.

½ cup (40 g) coconut sugar
½ cup (120 ml) unsweetened plain or vanilla soy or almond milk
⅛ tsp (.5 ml) pure stevia powder or ¼ tsp (1 ml) pure plain or vanilla stevia liquid, or to taste
⅓ cup (80 ml) sunflower or other light-tasting oil, preferably organic
2 tsp (10 ml) finely ground flax seeds (from about 1 tsp or 5 ml whole seeds)
1 tsp (5 ml) pure vanilla extract
½ tsp (2.5 ml) apple cider vinegar
½ cup (120 ml) canned or homemade unsweetened sweet potato puree (see page 23)
2 Tbsp plus 2 tsp (40 ml) whole psyllium husks
1 cup (130 g) Ricki's All-Purpose Gluten-Free Flour Mix (see page 22)
2 tsp (10 ml) ground cinnamon
½ tsp (2.5 ml) ground ginger
¼ tsp (1 ml) ground cloves
Pinch ground nutmeg
½ tsp (2.5 ml) baking soda
½ tsp (2.5 ml) baking powder
¼ tsp (1 ml) fine sea salt
⅔ cup (135 g) unsweetened carob chips or dairy-free chocolate chips

Preheat the oven to 350°F (180°C). Spray 18 mini muffin cups or 6 regular muffin cups with nonstick spray, or line with miniature or regular paper liners.

In a medium bowl, mix together the coconut sugar and milk; stir until the sugar melts. Add the stevia, oil, flax, vanilla, vinegar, sweet potato, and psyllium; whisk until well combined. Set aside while you measure the dry ingredients, or at least 2 minutes.

In a large bowl, sift the flour, cinnamon, ginger, cloves, nutmeg, baking soda, baking powder, and salt. Pour the wet ingredients over the dry and stir to combine (do not overmix). Gently stir in the chocolate chips.

Using a small ice-cream scoop or tablespoon (15 ml), scoop the batter and fill the muffin cups about ¾ full.

Bake 15 to 20 minutes, or 25 to 30 for regular-sized muffins, rotating pan or cookie sheet about halfway through. If you are using a 9- or 12-cup muffin pan, insert a tester (see page 37) in a center muffin; they are done when the tester comes out clean. Allow to cool completely before removing from the pan. See page 37, storing baked goods. May be frozen.

Multi-Seed Muffins * CF, SF or NF *

Makes 12 to 14

I wanted to make a muffin that showcased all the healthy seeds that I love to eat, all in one place. These muffins were a favorite of mine when I sold them at an organic market in the Toronto area and were a huge hit with my recipe testers. The Chinese five spice powder provides just a hint of spice (without being too bold) in this moist and substantial muffin. If you would like the muffins to be entirely nut-free, use soy milk and substitute raisins or goji berries for the cashews.

3½ oz (110 g) prunes (dried plums), chopped (8–9 large or 13–16 small prunes)
⅓ cup (80 ml) boiling water
¼ cup (25 g) finely ground flax seeds (from about 2 Tbsp or 30 ml whole seeds)
⅓ cup (80 ml) sunflower or other light-tasting oil, preferably organic
¾ cup (55 g) coconut sugar
1 tsp (5 ml) pure vanilla extract
½ tsp (2.5 ml) apple cider vinegar
1½ cups (360 ml) plain or vanilla soy or almond milk
½ cup (75 g) coarsely chopped, natural raw cashews, lightly toasted
2 Tbsp (30 ml) poppy seeds
¼ cup (35 g) whole flax seeds
¼ cup (35 g) raw or toasted sesame seeds
¼ cup (35 g) raw or toasted pumpkin seeds
¼ cup (35 g) raw or toasted sunflower seeds
2 cups (265 g) Ricki's All-Purpose Gluten-Free Flour Mix (see page 22)
¾ cup (100 g) quinoa flour
1 Tbsp (15 ml) baking powder
1 tsp (5 ml) baking soda
¼ tsp (1 ml) fine sea salt
1¾ tsp (8.5 ml) xanthan gum (use only Bob's Red Mill brand if you are concerned about a corn allergy)
1½ tsp (7.5 ml) Chinese five spice powder, or 1 tsp (5 ml) ground cinnamon plus ¼ tsp (1 ml) ground cardamom

Preheat the oven to 350°F (180°C). Line 12 muffin cups with paper liners, or spray with nonstick spray.

Place the prunes in a small bowl and pour the boiling water over them. Allow to soak for 5 minutes, then transfer the mixture (both prunes and water) to the bowl of a food processor. Process until smooth.

To the processor, add the ground flax seeds, oil, coconut sugar, vanilla, and vinegar; process again until the mixture is very smooth and no large pieces of prunes are visible. Add the milk last and process just to combine. By hand, stir in the cashews, poppy seeds, whole flax seeds, sesame seeds, pumpkin seeds, and sunflower seeds until the seeds are covered with the mixture; do not process again. Set aside while you measure the dry ingredients.

In a large bowl, sift the all-purpose flour, quinoa flour, baking powder, baking soda, salt, xanthan gum, and Chinese five spice powder. Pour the wet mixture over the dry and stir just to blend; it's okay if a few small dry spots remain here and there.

Using a large ice-cream scoop or ⅓-cup (80-ml) measuring cup, scoop the batter and fill the muffin cups, dividing it evenly. The cups will be very full (if you prefer smaller muffins, you can make 14 muffins instead of 12).

Bake 30 to 35 minutes, rotating pan about halfway through. If you are using a 12-cup muffin pan, insert a tester (see p. 37) in a center muffin; they are done when the tester comes out clean. Cool 5 minutes in the pan before removing to a rack to cool completely. Serve with Quick Cranberry-Apple Compote (see page 88). See page 37, storing baked goods. May be frozen.

Tropical Lemon Coconut Muffins * SF, CF, NF *

Makes 6

The combination of coconut and zesty lemon in these muffins creates a spectacular breakfast treat. You won't taste the avocado in the final product, but it provides great binding power as well as the richness of monounsaturated fats, so you won't need extra oil. And don't worry — the Day-Glo green of the raw avocado softens when baked, so the final product is a deep, lemony yellow. If you are using a 9- or 12-cup muffin pan for this recipe, fill the cups around the edges (rather than the center) so the muffins will bake evenly.

- ½ cup (120 ml) packed pureed avocado flesh (about 1 large avocado)
- ⅓ cup (80 ml) agave nectar
- ½ tsp (2.5 ml) pure plain or vanilla stevia liquid or ¼ tsp (1 ml) pure stevia powder, or to taste
- 2 tsp (10 ml) finely grated lemon zest (about 1 large lemon), preferably organic
- ¼ cup (60 ml) fresh lemon juice (from 1 large lemon)
- 6 Tbsp (90 ml) water
- 3 Tbsp (45 ml) whole psyllium husks
- ¾ cup (100 g) Ricki's All-Purpose Gluten-Free Flour Mix (see page 22)
- ½ cup (60 g) whole oat flour (to make your own, see page 35)
- 1 tsp (5 ml) baking powder
- ¾ tsp (3.5 ml) baking soda
- ¼ tsp (1 ml) fine sea salt
- 1 cup (80 g) unsweetened coconut, medium shredded, (not fine)

Preheat the oven to 350°F (180°C). Line 6 muffin cups with paper liners, or spray with nonstick spray.

In a small bowl, combine the avocado puree, agave nectar, stevia, lemon zest, lemon juice, and water. Add the psyllium and whisk to remove any lumps.

In a medium bowl, sift the all-purpose flour, oat flour, baking powder, baking soda, and salt. Stir in the coconut.

Pour the wet mixture over the dry and stir quickly to blend. Do not overmix! It will begin to fizz and expand a bit; this is as it should be. Using a large ice-cream scoop or ⅓-cup (80-ml) measuring cup, fill the muffin cups very full (the muffins will not rise any more during baking).

Bake 20 to 25 minutes, rotating pan about halfway through. If you are using a 9- or 12-cup muffin pan, insert a tester (see p. 37) in a center muffin; they are done when the tester comes out clean. Cool 5 minutes in the pan before removing to a rack. Allow to cool completely before eating. May be frozen.

Pear and Ginger Mini Loaves or Muffins ✸ SF, CF ✸

Makes 8 mini loaves or 1 dozen muffins

Wonderfully moist and tempting, these loaves feature the winning combination of pear and ginger. Unlike most recipes for pear muffins, however, this one uses a pear puree, so you can taste the fruit in every mouthful.

- 1⅓ cups (320 ml) fresh or previously frozen pear puree (see *Note*)
- 2 tsp (10 ml) grated fresh ginger
- 2 Tbsp (15 ml) finely ground chia seeds or meal (from about 1 Tbsp or 15 ml whole seeds)
- ⅔ cup (110 g) coconut sugar
- ¼ tsp (1 ml) pure stevia powder, or ½ tsp (2.5 ml) pure plain or vanilla stevia liquid, or to taste
- ⅓ cup (80 ml) sunflower or other light-tasting oil, preferably organic
- 1 Tbsp (15 ml) balsamic vinegar or 1½ tsp (7.5 ml) apple cider vinegar
- 1 tsp (5 ml) pure vanilla extract
- ½ tsp (2.5 ml) pure lemon extract
- ⅔ cup (80 g) coarsely chopped walnuts
- 1⅓ cups (180g) Ricki's All-Purpose Gluten-Free Flour Mix (see page 22)
- ⅔ cup (85 g) whole oat flour (to make your own, see page 35)
- ¼ cup (20 g) whole psyllium husks
- 1½ tsp (7.5 ml) baking powder
- 1 tsp (5 ml) baking soda
- ¼ tsp (1 ml) fine sea salt
- 1 Tbsp (15 ml) ground cinnamon
- Scant ½ tsp (2 ml) ground cloves

Preheat the oven to 350°F (180°C). Line 8 mini loaf pans or 12 muffin cups with paper liners, or spray with nonstick spray. If using individual loaf pans, place them on a cookie sheet.

In a medium bowl, combine the pear puree, ginger, chia, coconut sugar, stevia, oil, vinegar, vanilla, and lemon extract; whisk to combine, then stir in the nuts to coat. Set aside while you measure the dry ingredients, or at least 2 minutes.

In a large bowl, sift the all-purpose flour, oat flour, psyllium, baking powder, baking soda, salt, cinnamon, and cloves. Stir briefly to combine. Pour the wet mixture over the dry and stir just to blend (it's okay if a few dry spots remain here and there).

Using a large ice-cream scoop or ⅓-cup (80-ml) measuring cup, pour the mixture into the pans and fill about ¾ full (these won't rise much while baking).

Bake for 30 to 35 minutes, rotating the cookie sheet or muffin pan about halfway through baking, until the loaves or muffins appear domed and dry on top, and a tester inserted in the center of one of the loaves or a center muffin comes out clean but moist.

Cool at least 5 minutes in the pans before removing to a rack to cool completely. Store, tightly covered or wrapped in plastic wrap, in the refrigerator, for up to 5 days. May be frozen.

Note: You can make the pear puree easily by coring 3 to 4 very ripe, medium pears and whirring them in a food processor (no need to peel).

Oatmeal Poppy Seed Scones * CF, SF or NF *

Makes 6 to 8

These are a perfect addition to your weekend breakfast or brunch. The dough comes together incredibly quickly, and the scones can go from idea to table for a freshly baked, warm, and inviting treat in under 30 minutes.

- 1¼ cups (165 g) Ricki's All-Purpose Gluten-Free Flour Mix (see page 22
- 1 Tbsp (30 ml) poppy seeds
- 2½ tsp (12. 5 ml) baking powder
- ¼ tsp (1 ml) baking soda
- ¼ tsp (1 ml) fine sea salt
- 1 tsp (5 ml) xanthan gum (use only Bob's Red Mill brand if you are concerned about a corn allergy)
- ⅔ cup (70 g) old-fashioned rolled oats (not instant or quick-cooking)
- ¾ tsp (3.5 ml) apple cider vinegar
- ⅔ cup (160 ml) unsweetened plain or vanilla soy or almond milk
- 1 tsp (5 ml) pure vanilla extract
- 10 to 15 drops pure plain or vanilla stevia liquid, to your taste
- 3 Tbsp (45 ml) coconut oil, chilled, preferably organic, plus 1 Tbsp (15 ml), melted, for brushing tops of scones

Preheat the oven to 425°F (220°C). Line a cookie sheet with parchment paper, or spray with nonstick spray.

In a medium bowl, sift together the flour, poppy seeds, baking powder, baking soda, salt, and xanthan gum; whisk to blend. Stir in the oats and set aside.

Pour the vinegar into a glass measuring cup. Add enough milk to make ⅔ cup (160 ml) total. Add the vanilla and stevia and stir to blend. Set aside.

Drop the solid coconut oil in chunks over the flour in the bowl. Using a pastry cutter or a wide-tined fork, cut the oil into the flour to create pea-sized bits (don't overmix the oil into the flour — it's okay if there is still a lot of flour that's not mixed with the oil). Pour the liquid over the dry ingredients and quickly toss with a fork until it comes together in a rather soft dough.

Using a large ice-cream scoop or ⅓-cup (80-ml) measuring cup, scoop the dough and place in mounds on the prepared cookie sheet. Using a floured palm or the back of a silicone spatula, gently flatten the top of each scone. Gently brush the tops of the scones with the remaining tablespoon of melted coconut oil.

Bake for 15 to 20 minutes, until lightly browned on top. Cool 5 minutes before removing to a cooling rack. Serve warm with Fresh Berry Topping (see page 89). See page 37, storing baked goods. May be frozen.

Cranberry-Ginger Muffins with Sunflower Butter

✷ CF, can be SF or NF ✷

Makes 1 dozen

This is a moist, substantial muffin with a burst of cranberry and a hint of ginger in each bite. I often pack one of these muffins for my husband to enjoy when he gets to the office in the morning; the sunflower butter provides additional protein so he won't be hungry until lunchtime. Be sure to choose prunes that are still soft and moist, rather than ones that have dried out, for best results.

3 oz (8.5 g) pitted unsweetened prunes (dried plums), 6 to7 large or 11 to 14 small prunes
⅓ cup (25 g) coconut sugar
1½ cups (360 ml) unsweetened plain or vanilla soy or almond milk
⅔ cup (160 ml) natural smooth sunflower butter, at room temperature
¼ cup (60 ml) sunflower or other light-tasting oil, preferably organic
2 Tbsp (30 ml) finely ground flax seeds (from about 1 Tbsp or 15 ml whole seeds)
¼ cup (20 g) whole psyllium husks
1 tsp (5 ml) pure vanilla extract
1 tsp (5 ml) apple cider vinegar
⅜ tsp (1.5 ml) pure stevia powder or ½–¾ tsp pure plain or vanilla stevia liquid, or to taste
⅓ cup (45 g) dried cranberries or goji berries
2 cups (265 g) Ricki's All-Purpose Gluten-Free Flour Mix (see page 22)
2 tsp (10 ml) baking powder
½ tsp (2.5 ml) baking soda
½ tsp (2.5 ml) fine sea salt
2 tsp (10 ml) ground ginger

Preheat the oven to 350°F (180°C). Line 12 muffin cups with paper liners, or spray with nonstick spray.

In the bowl of a food processor, blend the prunes, coconut sugar, and milk to a paste. Add the sunflower butter, oil, flax seeds, psyllium, vanilla, vinegar, and stevia and blend again until smooth. Stir in the cranberries by hand; do not process again. Set aside while you measure the dry ingredients.

In a large bowl, sift the flour, baking powder, baking soda, salt, and ginger. Pour the wet mixture over the dry and stir just to blend, taking care not to overmix (it's all right if a few small dry spots remain here and there).

Using a large ice-cream scoop or ⅓-cup (80-ml) measuring cup, scoop the batter into the muffin cups, filling them about ¾ full.

Bake 30 to 35 minutes, rotating pan about halfway through. If you are using a 9-cup muffin pan, insert a tester (see page 37) in a center muffin; they are done when the tester comes out clean. Cool 5 minutes in the pan before removing to a rack to cool completely. See page 37, storing baked goods. May be frozen.

Lemon Blueberry Scones ✷ CF, can be SF and NF ✷

Makes 8

These aren't as dense as true scones, but they make a lovely breakfast treat in any case. With a whisper of lemon and juicy blueberries, they are the perfect accompaniment for a cup of tea or coffee.

- 2 tsp (10 ml) apple cider vinegar
- About ⅔ cup (160 ml) unsweetened almond or soy milk or coconut beverage (the kind that comes in a carton), plus about 2 Tbsp (30 ml) extra milk for brushing tops, if desired
- ¼ cup (60 ml) coconut sugar
- 20 to 30 drops pure plain or vanilla stevia liquid, or to taste
- 2 Tbsp (30 ml) ground flax seeds (from about 1 Tbsp or 15 ml whole seeds)
- 3 Tbsp (45 ml) sunflower or other light-tasting oil, preferably organic
- 2 tsp (10 ml) pure vanilla extract
- 2 tsp finely grated lemon zest (about 1 large lemon), preferably organic
- 1¾ cups (230 g) Ricki's All-Purpose Gluten-Free Flour Mix (see page 22)
- 3 Tbsp (45 ml) whole psyllium husks
- 2 tsp (10 ml) baking powder
- ½ tsp (2.5 ml) baking soda
- ¾ tsp (7.5 ml) fine sea salt
- ½ cup (75 g) fresh or frozen blueberries (if using frozen, DO NOT thaw first)

Preheat the oven to 400°F (200°C). Line a large cookie sheet with parchment paper, or spray with nonstick spray.

Place the vinegar in a glass measuring cup and add enough milk to reach the ⅔-cup (160-ml) mark. In a small bowl, combine the vinegar-milk mixture, coconut sugar, stevia, flax seeds, oil, vanilla, and lemon zest.

In a large bowl, sift the flour, psyllium, baking powder, baking soda, and salt; whisk to combine. Pour the wet mixture over the dry and stir just to combine (do not overmix!), then gently fold in the blueberries. You should have a very thick batter, but one that is firm enough to hold its shape.

Using a large ice-cream scoop or ⅓-cup (80-ml) measuring cup, drop mounds of dough onto the cookie sheet about 2 inches (5 cm) apart. Do not flatten; they will spread slightly as they bake.

Bake for 6 minutes, then remove and quickly brush the tops with the remaining 2 tablespoons milk, if desired. Rotate the pan, then return to the oven and bake another 8 to 12 minutes, until the edges are golden and the tops are just beginning to brown.

Cool 5 minutes before removing to a rack and cooling completely. See page 37, storing your baked goods. May be frozen.

Pear and Pecan Scones ✱ SF, CF ✱

Serves 6

The pears in these scones add sweetness more than they do any pear flavor, while rice flour provides body and a dense, scone-like crumb (making them more like conventional scones than the Lemon Blueberry Scones on page 57). I love these for breakfast slathered with Quick Apple-Cranberry Compote (page 88).

- 1 cup (240 ml) pear puree (from 2 large, very ripe pears, about 8 oz or 230 g total)
- 2 Tbsp (30 ml) coconut nectar
- 20 to 30 drops pure plain or vanilla stevia liquid, or to taste
- 3 Tbsp (45 ml) sunflower or other light-tasting oil, preferably organic
- 1 Tbsp (15 ml) pure vanilla extract
- ½ tsp (2.5 ml) pure almond extract
- 1 tsp (5 ml) apple cider vinegar
- 1 Tbsp (15 ml) finely ground flax seeds (from about 1½ tsp or 7.5 ml whole seeds)
- 3 Tbsp (45 ml) whole psyllium husks
- ⅔ cup (75 g) coarsely chopped pecans, lightly toasted or raw
- 1¼ cups (160 g) Ricki's All-Purpose Gluten-Free Flour Mix (see page 22)
- ⅔ cup (100 g) brown rice flour
- ½ tsp (2.5 ml) Chinese five spice powder or ground cinnamon
- 2½ tsp (12.5 ml) baking powder
- ¼ tsp (1 ml) baking soda
- ¼ tsp (1 ml) fine sea salt

Preheat the oven to 375°F (190°C). Line the bottom of an 8-inch (20-cm) round pan or springform pan with parchment paper, or spray with nonstick spray.

In a food processor, process the pear puree, coconut nectar, stevia, oil, vanilla, almond extract, vinegar, flax, and psyllium until smooth. Add the pecans and stir them in by hand, but don't process again.

In a large bowl, sift the all-purpose flour, rice flour, Chinese five spice powder, baking powder, baking soda, and salt. Pour the liquid mixture over the dry ingredients and stir just to blend (do not overmix).

Turn the mixture into the prepared pan and spread evenly until smooth on top. If desired, sprinkle with a few extra pecans and press lightly. Score the top by cutting about ⅛-inch (2-mm) deep to demarcate 6 large scones.

Bake for 25 to 35 minutes, until browned on the edges and a tester inserted in the middle comes out clean. Cool 10 minutes, then cut into wedges and serve with Fresh Berry Topping (see page 89).

Grain-Free Coconut Flour Biscuits * GF, CF, can be SF or NF *

Makes 8 to 10 biscuits

This is an updated version of a coconut flour biscuit that saved me when I first started the anticandida diet. No, they don't taste like bread, but they are very "bready" in consistency and flavor, and offer a great way to avoid grains while still feeling as if you've gotten your morning carb fix.

- 2 tsp (10 ml) apple cider vinegar
- About ⅔ cup (160 ml) unsweetened soy or almond milk
- ½ cup (60 ml) cooked, pureed spaghetti squash or unsweetened applesauce
- 3 Tbsp (15 ml) natural smooth almond butter, sunflower seed butter (see *Note*), or tahini (sesame seed paste), at room temperature
- 1½ tsp (7.5 ml) pure vanilla extract
- 10 drops pure plain or vanilla stevia liquid
- 2 Tbsp (30 ml) finely ground flax seeds (from about 1 Tbsp or 15 ml whole seeds)
- 2 Tbsp (30 ml) whole psyllium husks
- 2 Tbsp (30 ml) coconut oil, melted (at low temperature), preferably organic, plus more for brushing tops of biscuits
- ½ cup (75 g) coconut flour
- 1 tsp (5 ml) baking powder
- ¾ tsp (3.5 ml) baking soda
- ¼ tsp (1 ml) fine sea salt

Preheat the oven to 400°F (200°C). Line a cookie sheet with parchment paper, or spray with nonstick spray.

Place the apple cider vinegar in the bottom of a glass measuring cup, and add milk to reach the ⅔-cup (160-ml) mark. Pour into a medium bowl and add the squash, almond butter, vanilla, stevia, flax, psyllium, and coconut oil; whisk well to combine.

Sift the coconut flour, baking powder, baking soda, and salt over the wet mixture in the bowl. Stir to blend well.

Using a large ice cream scoop or ⅓-cup measuring cup, scoop the batter and place mounds on the cookie sheet. Flatten each mound slightly with your palm or a silicone spatula.

Bake for 25 to 35 minutes, rotating the pan about halfway through, until very well browned on the bottom and beginning to brown on top. If desired, remove cookie sheet after about 15 minutes and gently brush the tops of the biscuits with more melted coconut oil (this will help them to brown further). Cool completely before serving. (These will be very moist in the middle while warm and may even appear underbaked; they will firm up as they cool, and are best the next day). See page 37, storing your baked goods. May be frozen.

Note: If you use sunflower seed butter, it alters the usual acid/alkaline balance of the batter, and the center of your biscuits will turn green. This doesn't affect quality or taste, but it does look rather off-putting (though your four-year-old might get a kick out of it).

Spiced Tea Bread ✱ SF, CF, NF ✱

Makes 1 loaf (about 8 to 12 slices)

I used to make a loaf similar to this one around Christmastime, as the mix of spices and dried fruit suggested holiday festivities to me. I became so enamored of it that I now make it year-round. A moist, fruity, and fragrant loaf, it's equally delicious slathered with almond butter for breakfast or served with a steaming cup of tea for dessert. Teas that are naturally dark in color, such as apple, berry, or spice, work best in this loaf; I'd avoid lighter teas such as chamomile, as results won't be nearly as good.

⅓ cup (80 ml) coconut oil, at room temperature, preferably organic

1¼ cups (360 ml) hot brewed tea, such as apple cinnamon or spiced herbal

⅔ cup (140 g) raisins, goji berries, dried cranberries, chopped prunes (dried plums), or dates

1½ Tbsp (22.5 ml) finely ground flax seeds (from about 2¼ tsp or 12 ml whole seeds)

⅓ cup (55 g) coconut sugar

¼ cup (60 ml) coconut nectar

1 Tbsp (15 ml) blackstrap molasses or yacon syrup

¼ tsp (1 ml) pure stevia powder or ½ tsp (2.5 ml) pure plain or vanilla stevia liquid, or to taste

1 tsp (5 ml) apple cider vinegar

1¾ cups (235 g) Ricki's All-Purpose Gluten-Free Flour Mix (see page 22)

¼ cup (20 g) whole psyllium husks

1½ tsp (7.5 ml) baking powder

¼ tsp (1 ml) baking soda

2 tsp (10 ml) ground cinnamon

½ tsp (2.5 ml) ground nutmeg

½ tsp (2.5 ml) ground allspice

¼ tsp (1 ml) ground cloves

¼ tsp (1 ml) fine sea salt

Preheat the oven to 350°F (180°C). Line an 8-inch (20-cm) loaf pan with parchment paper, or spray with nonstick spray. (You can also use 6 to 8 mini loaf pans; spray each with nonstick spray).

Place the coconut oil in a medium bowl; break into small pieces if it is solid. Pour the hot tea over the oil and stir until the oil is melted.

Add the raisins (or other fruit), flax, coconut sugar, coconut nectar, molasses, stevia, and vinegar and stir to mix well. Allow to cool to room temperature, stirring occasionally.

In a large bowl, sift the flour, psyllium, baking powder, baking soda, cinnamon, nutmeg, allspice, cloves, and salt. Whisk or stir briefly with a fork to distribute the spices.

Pour the wet mixture over the dry and stir just to blend (it's okay if a few dry spots remain here and there) — do not overmix! The mixture may begin to fizz and bubble slightly; this is fine. Pour the mixture into the loaf pan and smooth the top.

Place the pan on a cookie sheet (to catch any overflow, depending on the size of the pan) and bake for 50 to 60 minutes, rotating the pan about halfway through, until a tester inserted in the center comes out clean. Cool completely before removing from the pan and cutting into slices (the bread is fragile when warm, but will firm up as it cools). See page 37, storing your baked goods. May be frozen.

Sunshine Breakfast Loaf ⁕ SF, CF ⁕

Makes 1 loaf (about 8 to 10 slices)

The prunes in this delightful loaf add sweetness, and the hints of orange and cinnamon are a lovely combination. For best results, be sure to choose prunes that are still soft and moist, rather than ones that have dried out.

3¼ oz (90 g) prunes (dried plums) (about 7 to 8 large prunes or 12 to 15 small prunes)
¾ cup (180 ml) canned or homemade unsweetened pumpkin puree (see page 23)
½ cup (40 g) coconut sugar
⅛ tsp (.5 ml) pure stevia powder or 25 to 30 drops pure plain or vanilla stevia liquid, or to taste
2 tsp (10 ml) finely grated orange zest, preferably organic (about 1 medium orange)
1 cup (240 ml) pure unsweetened orange juice (from 3–4 medium oranges)
¼ cup (60 ml) sunflower or other light-tasting oil, preferably organic
2 tsp (10 ml) ground chia seeds (from about 1 tsp or 5 ml whole seeds)
1 tsp (5 ml) pure vanilla extract
1 tsp (5 ml) apple cider vinegar
5 Tbsp (25 g) whole psyllium husks
¼ cup (35 g) unsalted pumpkin seeds, raw or lightly toasted
½ cup (50 g) walnut pieces, raw or lightly toasted
1¼ cups (165 g) Ricki's All-Purpose Gluten-Free Flour Mix (see page 22)
½ cup (80 g) teff flour
2 tsp (10 ml) baking powder
1 tsp (5 ml) baking soda
½ tsp (2.5 ml) fine sea salt
1 Tbsp (15 ml) ground cinnamon

Preheat the oven to 350°F (180°C). Line a 4.5 x 8.5-inch (11 x 22-cm) loaf pan with parchment paper, or spray with nonstick spray.

In the bowl of a food processor, process the prunes until they are almost smooth. Add the pumpkin, coconut sugar, stevia, orange juice, oil, chia, vanilla, vinegar, and orange zest and blend again until smooth. Add the psyllium last and pulse just to blend. By hand, gently stir in the pumpkin seeds and walnut pieces; do not process again.

In a large bowl, sift the all-purpose flour, teff flour, baking powder, baking soda, salt, and cinnamon; whisk to combine. Pour the wet mixture over the dry and stir just until blended (do not overmix). The batter will be thick (more of a spoonable consistency than a pourable one).

Turn the batter into t he pan and smooth the top. Bake 50 to 60 minutes, rotating the pan about halfway through baking, until a tester inserted in the center comes out clean. Cool 10 minutes in the pan before removing to a cooling rack. See page 37, storing baked goods. May be frozen.

Low-Fat Cinnamon Walnut Loaf ✱ CF, can be SF ✱

Makes 1 loaf (about 8 to 10 slices)

Despite what looks like a long ingredient list, this is really an easy bread to make. Its light, moist crumb will remind you of muffins, but it's a bit more sturdy and a bit less sweet . . . perfect with nut butter for breakfast, or even as a means to sop up some hearty, savory soup. Don't worry if the finished product doesn't reach the top of the pan; this isn't a tall bread, but it's packed with flavor nonetheless!

- 1 Tbsp plus 2 tsp (25 ml) whole psyllium husks
- 1 tsp (5 ml) apple cider vinegar
- 1 Tbsp (15 ml) pure vanilla extract
- 2 Tbsp (30 ml) natural smooth almond butter or tahini (sesame seed paste), at room temperature
- Enough unsweetened plain or vanilla soy or almond milk to total 1½ cups (360 ml) (see instructions)
- ⅓ cup (55 g) teff flour
- ½ cup (55 g) amaranth or quinoa flour
- ¼ cup (40 g) potato starch
- 1½ tsp (7.5 ml) baking powder
- ¼ tsp (1 ml) baking soda
- ¼ tsp (1 ml) fine sea salt
- 1 Tbsp (15 ml) ground cinnamon
- ¼ tsp (1 ml) pure stevia powder or ½ tsp (2.5 ml) pure plain or vanilla stevia liquid, or to taste
- ⅓ cup (40 g) walnut pieces or chopped walnuts, lightly toasted

Preheat the oven to 350°F (180°C). Lightly grease an 8.5- or 9-inch (20-22.5 cm) loaf pan, or line with parchment paper.

Place the psyllium, vinegar, vanilla, and almond butter in a 2-cup (500-ml) glass measuring cup. Add enough milk to reach the 1½-cup (360-ml) mark. Using a small whisk or fork, whisk everything together until the almond butter is well dissolved in the liquid and no lumps remain. Set aside while you measure the dry ingredients.

In a large bowl, sift all remaining ingredients except for the walnuts. Whisk well to distribute all the ingredients evenly. Add the walnuts and stir to distribute.

Whisk the liquid again to ensure that it's smooth and everything is incorporated, then pour the wet mixture over the dry ingredients and stir just to combine (do not overmix!). Turn the batter into the prepared pan and smooth the top. It will only fill the pan about halfway; this is as it should be.

Bake for 65 to 75 minutes, rotating the pan about halfway through baking, until the bread is well browned on the bottom and sides, and the top springs back when touched lightly (there will be a fairly thick crust by this time, but it should still spring back). A knife inserted in the center should come out moist but clean.

Allow to cool for 10 minutes, then remove from the pan and set on a cooling rack; allow to cool completely before slicing. The bread is very moist on the first day and dries a bit by the second. Store, tightly wrapped, in the refrigerator for up to 3 days. May be frozen.

Zucchini-Pineapple Mini Loaves or Muffins

✱ SF, CF, can be NF ✱

Makes 8 mini loaves or 10 muffins

A healthy version of a heavier standard, this bread mixes up easily and is a great recipe for using up leftover zucchini, pineapple, and overripe avocado. I love the hint of ginger in these loaves, but if you're not a fan, feel free to leave it out. If you are using a 12-cup muffin pan for this recipe, fill the cups around the edges (rather than the center) so the muffins will bake evenly.

- 5 oz (150 g) finely grated zucchini, fresh or previously frozen (about 1¼ cups), skin on
- ¼ cup (60 ml) avocado puree (from about ½ small avocado)
- ½ cup (110 g) very well-drained crushed pineapple (drain first, reserving juice, then measure)
- ¼ cup (60 ml) juice from drained pineapple
- ¾ cup (55 g) coconut sugar
- ¼ tsp (1 ml) powdered pure stevia
- 2 Tbsp (30 ml) finely ground flax seeds (from about 1 Tbsp or 15 ml whole seeds)
- 3 Tbsp (45 ml) whole psyllium husks
- 2 Tbsp (30 ml) sunflower or other light-tasting oil, preferably organic
- 1 tsp (5 ml) apple cider vinegar
- 1 tsp (5 ml) pure vanilla extract
- Generous ¼ cup (40 g) sunflower seeds or chopped walnuts
- 1½ cups (195 g) Ricki's All-Purpose Gluten-Free Flour Mix (see page 22)
- 1 tsp (5 ml) baking powder
- 1 tsp (5 ml) baking soda
- ¼ tsp (1 ml) fine sea salt
- 1 Tbsp (15 ml) ground cinnamon
- ½ tsp (2.5 ml) ground ginger (optional)

Preheat the oven to 350°F (180°C). Line 8 mini loaf pans or 10 muffin cups with paper liners, or spray with nonstick spray. If using individual loaf pans, place them on a cookie sheet.

In a medium bowl, combine the zucchini, avocado, pineapple, pineapple juice, coconut sugar, stevia, flax, psyllium, oil, vinegar, vanilla, and sunflower seeds; stir to mix well. Set aside while you prepare the dry ingredients, or at least 2 minutes.

In a large bowl, sift the flour, baking powder, baking soda, salt, cinnamon, and ginger. Stir to distribute the leaveners and cinnamon throughout.

Pour the wet mixture over the dry and stir just to blend (don't worry if a few dry spots remain here and there). Using a large ice-cream scoop or ⅓-cup (80-ml) measuring cup, fill each pan or muffin cup about ¾ full.

Bake for 25 to 30 minutes for loaves or 20 to 25 minutes for muffins, rotating the pan about halfway through baking, until a tester inserted in a center loaf or a center muffin comes out clean. Cool about 10 minutes in the pans before removing to a cooling rack. Store in an airtight container in the refrigerator for up to 5 days (these taste even better the next day). May be frozen.

Sweet Potato Buns ✱ CF, can be SF and NF ✱

Makes 5 to 7

A light and tender roll that's perfect for breakfast or afternoon snacks, these are sweet enough to eat on their own, but also work well with the usual toppings.

- ½ cup (120 ml) canned or homemade unsweetened sweet potato puree (see page 23)
- ¼ cup (60 ml) unsweetened applesauce
- 2 Tbsp (30 ml) coconut sugar
- ⅓ cup (80 ml) unsweetened plain or vanilla almond, soy, or rice milk
- ¼ tsp (1 ml) apple cider vinegar
- ½ tsp (2.5 ml) pure vanilla extract
- 10 drops pure plain or vanilla stevia liquid
- 2 Tbsp (30 ml) sunflower or other light-tasting oil, preferably organic
- 1¼ cups (165 g) Ricki's All-Purpose Gluten-Free Flour Mix (see page 22)
- 1½ tsp (7.5 ml) baking powder
- ⅛ tsp (.5 ml) fine sea salt
- ⅛ tsp (.5 ml) nutmeg
- 1½ Tbsp (22.5 ml) whole psyllium husks

Preheat the oven to 375°F (190°C). Line a cookie sheet with parchment paper or spray with nonstick spray.

In a small bowl, whisk the sweet potato puree, applesauce, coconut sugar, milk, vinegar, vanilla, stevia, and oil until smooth. Set aside.

In a medium bowl, sift the flour, baking powder, salt, and nutmeg. Add the psyllium and whisk until everything is evenly distributed.

Pour the wet mixture over the dry and stir just to blend. It should be a soft dough, but still able to hold a shape. Using a large ice-cream scoop or ⅓-cup (80-ml) measuring cup, scoop the dough onto the cookie sheet and flatten slightly.

Bake for 25 to 30 minutes, rotating the sheet once about halfway through baking, until the bottoms are well browned and the tops are dry. Cool 5 minutes before moving to a cooling rack; cool completely before serving. These will be very moist when warm, and more breadlike once cooled. May be frozen.

Cinnamon Buns ✱ CF, can be SF or NF ✱

Makes 9

This is my lower-glycemic, yeast-free version of the classic recipe. The buns are slightly denser than yeast-based ones, but they bring back all the joy of eating a "real" cinnamon bun for me. While the recipe appears long, the only challenging part is rolling out the dough and carefully spreading the filling over it. The rest comes together very easily! Don't be alarmed by the three tablespoons of cinnamon in the filling. It's not overpowering in the final product, I promise!

FOR THE FILLING:

⅔ cup (50 g) coconut sugar
1 Tbsp (15 ml) tapioca starch
1 Tbsp (15 ml) Ricki's All-Purpose Gluten-Free Flour Mix (see page 22)
3 Tbsp (45 ml) ground cinnamon
3 Tbsp (45 ml) sunflower or other light-tasting oil, preferably organic
1 Tbsp (15 ml) water plus up to 2 tsp (10 ml) more, if necessary

FOR THE DOUGH:

2 cups (265 g) Ricki's All-Purpose Gluten-Free Flour Mix (see page 22) plus extra for the dough, if needed, and for dusting work surface
1 cup (145 g) sorghum flour
2 Tbsp (30 ml) baking powder
½ tsp (2.5 ml) fine sea salt
2½ tsp (12. 5 ml) xanthan gum (use only Bob's Red Mill brand if you are concerned about a corn allergy)
¼ cup (60 ml) coconut oil, chilled, preferably organic
1½ cups (360 ml) pure, unsweetened orange juice (from 5–6 medium oranges)
2 Tbsp (30 ml) coconut sugar

FOR THE GLAZE (optional):

⅔ cup (50 g) coconut sugar
¼ cup (40 g) potato starch
4 tsp (20 ml) pure vanilla extract
Up to 2 Tbsp (30 ml) unsweetened soy, rice, or almond milk

Preheat the oven to 350°F (180°C). Set an oven rack in the middle of the oven. Line a 9-inch (22.5-cm) springform pan with parchment paper, or spray with nonstick spray. (Alternately, you can use a large pie plate). Have ready a rectangular cutting board, plastic place mat, or piece of waxed paper that's about 13 x 10 inches (32 x 26 cm).

Make the filling: In a medium bowl, combine the coconut sugar, tapioca starch, flour, and cinnamon; mix well. Drizzle the oil over the top and stir to combine and coat as much of the filling as possible. Add 1 tablespoon (15 ml) of water and mix it in completely to create a thick but spreadable paste. IMPORTANT: It will seem FAR too thick at first, and you'll wonder if the sugar will absorb all the liquid. Before you add more water, let it stand for 5 to 10 minutes, then stir again. You do NOT want the filling to be pourable, but more the consistency of a thick nut butter, so that it won't ooze out of the roll too easily. If, after 10 minutes, the mixture is still too thick, add more liquid, ½ teaspoon (2.5 ml) at a time; be careful not to add too much liquid, or the filling will be too thin! Set aside.

Make the dough: In a large bowl, sift the all-purpose flour, sorghum flour, baking powder, salt, and xanthan gum; use a whisk or fork to mix together. Drop the cold coconut oil by teaspoons (5 ml) over the surface of the dry mixture. Using a pastry cutter or wide-tined fork, cut the mixture by pressing through the lumps of coconut oil and into the flour, just enough to create pea-sized pieces of oil (some bits may be smaller, but none should be larger). Toss the flour mixture with a fork to distribute the oil throughout. Resist the temptation to pinch this together with your fingers as you would a crumb topping; the oil should not be completely blended into the flour mixture, but just scattered throughout in little lumps, as with pie crust.

(continued on page 74)

Cinnamon Buns *continued* • CF, can be SF or NF •

In a glass measuring cup, whisk the juice with the coconut sugar until the sugar dissolves. Pour this wet mixture over the dry ingredients in the bowl and toss with a fork until it comes together in a ball. You should have a very soft and moist dough; this is as it should be. If it is too moist to hold together, add an extra 2 tablespoons (30 ml) all-purpose flour and mix together quickly.

Form and bake the buns: Flour the cutting board, place mat, or waxed paper with about ¼ cup (35 g) more all-purpose flour. Place the mound of dough on the board, pushing it into a ball with your hands, and dust the top of the ball with about 2 tablespoons (30 ml) more all-purpose flour. With a floured rolling pin, roll out the dough so it more or less covers the rectangle, starting in the middle and rolling toward the edges. (If you don't have a rolling pin, a clean, tall, empty glass or jar — or wine bottle — makes a good substitute).

Using an offset spatula or rubber spatula, gently spread the filling over the rectangle, taking care not to tear the dough. Come right to the edge on three sides, leaving a 1-inch (2.5-cm) border of dough on one of the longer sides. Begin to roll the dough, starting at the long side that has filling right up to the edge, and roll toward the long side with the 1-inch (2.5-cm) empty border. Once you get to the end, keep rolling so that the last long edge (the "seam") is underneath the roll. Cut the roll into 3 equal pieces (you can measure them, or just estimate — it doesn't need to be perfect). Then cut each piece into 3 more equal pieces, for 9 pieces total. Each piece will become 1 bun.

Place the pieces cut side up in the round pan with the seam facing the side of the pan. Start with 1 in the center and place 8 more around the outside of the pan (they won't be touching each other at this point).

Place the springform pan in the center rack of the oven. Bake for 25 to 30 minutes, rotating the pan about halfway through baking, until the rolls puff up a bit and the area around the filling is lightly browned. The tops of the buns should be dry and firm when done. Remove from the oven and cool for about 5 minutes before topping with the glaze, if using.

While the buns bake, prepare the glaze, if using: In a small bowl, combine the coconut sugar and potato starch. Add the vanilla and 1 tablespoon (15 to 30 ml) of the soy milk; mix well. Allow the mixture to sit for 5 minutes or so for the sugar to dissolve. If the glaze is still too thick at this point, add more milk, a teaspoon (5 ml) at a time, until the glaze is pourable but still thick; you want it to run off the tops of the rolls, but it should not be so thin that it pools at the bottom of the pans. (I always make it a bit thicker than I think it should be, and it works out perfectly that way.)

Drizzle the baked rolls evenly with the glaze. Allow to cool before cutting or pulling apart. Serve straight from the pan or remove to serving plates. May be frozen.

High-Protein Breakfast Waffles * CF, SF, NF *

Makes 12 to 16

Each one of these waffles contains 16 grams of protein — that's more than the protein in 2 eggs or a cup (240 ml) of yogurt, about the same as 2 cups (480 ml) of milk or ½ cup (120 ml) of cottage cheese, and about one-third of the average woman's daily needs. Each one also contains 4.5 grams of fiber, which is about 20 percent of your daily requirement. Slather one of these with a tablespoon of almond butter and grab it for a quick breakfast that will keep you charged until lunchtime.

- 1 cup (100 g) quinoa flour
- ½ cup (75 g) garfava flour
- ¼ cup (60 ml) arrowroot flour
- 2 Tbsp (30 ml) unflavored rice protein powder
- 1 Tbsp (15 ml) baking powder
- ½ tsp (2.5 ml) baking soda
- ¼ tsp (1 ml) fine sea salt
- ¾ tsp (7.5 ml) xanthan gum (use only Bob's Red Mill brand if you are concerned about a corn allergy)
- 2¼ cups (540 ml) unsweetened plain or vanilla almond or soy milk, or coconut beverage (the kind that comes in a carton)
- 1 tsp (5 ml) pure vanilla extract
- 6 to 8 drops pure plain or vanilla stevia liquid, or to taste
- 1 Tbsp plus 1 tsp (20 ml total) apple cider vinegar
- 3 Tbsp (45 ml) sunflower or other light-tasting oil, preferably organic

Set up a nonstick waffle iron and preheat according to manufacturer's directions.

In a medium bowl, sift the quinoa flour, garfava flour, arrowroot flour, protein powder, baking powder, baking soda, salt, and xanthan gum.

In a small bowl, whisk together the milk, vanilla, stevia, vinegar, and oil. Pour the wet ingredients over the dry and whisk to blend. Do not overmix.

Using a large ice-cream scoop or ⅓-cup (80-ml) measuring cup, pour batter over preheated waffle iron. Cook until the waffles are deep golden and crisp on the outside but still soft on the inside (5 to 7 minutes; time will vary depending on your waffle iron). Transfer to a platter and keep warm in a low (250°F/120°C) oven while you make the rest of the waffles. May be frozen.

Fluffy Fruited Pancakes * CF, can be NF and SF *

Makes 10 to 12

These light and foolproof pancakes are great when made with berries, apples, pears, or bananas. Unlike most dairy-free versions, they provide a good amount of protein on their own, due to the protein powder added to the batter. You can use leftovers for another day's breakfast or lunch: simply spread one pancake with your favorite nut butter and/or jam, then top with another pancake for a quick and delicious pancake "sandwich."

- 1¾ cups (420 ml) plain or vanilla soy, almond, or rice milk, plus up to ½ cup (120 ml) more, if needed
- 2 Tbsp (30 ml) finely ground flax seeds (from about 1 Tbsp or 15 ml whole seeds)
- 1 Tbsp (15 ml) apple cider vinegar
- 3 Tbsp (45 ml) sunflower or other light-tasting oil, preferably organic
- ¼ cup (20 g) whole psyllium husks
- 1¾ cups (235 g) Ricki's All-Purpose Gluten-Free Flour Mix (see page 22)
- 2 Tbsp (30 ml) unflavored rice or soy protein powder (substitute soy or chickpea flour, sifted)
- ⅛ tsp (.5 ml) pure stevia powder, ¼ tsp (1 ml) pure plain or vanilla stevia liquid, or 1 Tbsp (15 ml) coconut sugar or agave nectar
- 1 Tbsp (15 ml) baking powder
- ½ tsp (2.5 ml) baking soda
- ¼ tsp (1 ml) fine sea salt
- 1 cup (240 ml) fresh or frozen berries or chopped apple, pear, or banana (DO NOT thaw if using frozen fruit)

In a small bowl, combine the 1¾ cups (420 ml) milk, flax, vinegar, oil, and psyllium, stirring well.

In a large bowl, sift the flour, protein powder, stevia, baking powder, baking soda, and salt. Pour the wet ingredients over the dry and mix just to blend (there will still be a few lumps here and there; this is fine). Gently fold in the fruit.

Heat a nonstick frying pan over medium heat. Using a large ice-cream scoop or ⅓-cup (80-ml) measuring cup, pour the batter into the pan and spread slightly with the back of the scoop or measuring cup.

Cook each pancake about 3 to 4 minutes, until puffed and golden at the edges. Flip the cake and cook another 3 to 4 minutes on the other side. Serve immediately.

Refrigerate leftovers, tightly wrapped, for up to 3 days. May be frozen. (When reheating, place frozen pancakes directly in the toaster).

Note: If the batter thickens while you are cooking the pancakes, add a little more milk to the bowl to retain the consistency of the batter.

Rice and Spice Apple Pancakes * CF, can be SF and NF *

Makes 8 to 10 pancakes, 3½ inches (9 cm) in diameter

These pancakes offer a great means to use up leftover cooked rice or another grain. The combination of apple chunks with soft, chewy grains of rice and a touch of spice makes a perfect breakfast base. My preferred rice for these cakes is brown basmati, with its delicate flavor and firm texture.

1 cup (240 ml) leftover cooked rice (from about ⅓ cup or 80 ml dry rice)
1 cup (240 ml) unsweetened plain or vanilla almond, rice, or soy milk, plus more as needed
1 tsp (5 ml) apple cider vinegar
1 Tbsp (15 ml) finely ground flax seeds (from about 1½ tsp or 7.5 ml whole seeds)
2 Tbsp (30 ml) sunflower or other light-tasting oil, preferably organic
1 Tbsp (15 ml) coconut sugar
1 small or ½ medium apple, cored and cut in thin slices
1 cup (135 g) Ricki's All-Purpose Gluten-Free Flour Mix (see page 22)
2 Tbsp (30 ml) whole psyllium husks
2 tsp (10 ml) baking powder
¼ tsp (1 ml) baking soda
2 tsp (10 ml) ground cinnamon
½ tsp (2.5 ml) ground ginger
Pinch cloves
⅛ tsp (.5 ml) fine sea salt

In a medium bowl, combine the rice, milk, vinegar, flax, oil, coconut sugar, and apple. Set aside.

In a large bowl, sift the flour, psyllium, baking powder, baking soda, cinnamon, ginger, cloves, and salt. Pour the wet ingredients over the dry and stir just to combine (it's okay if there are a few small lumps here and there).

Heat a large nonstick frying pan over medium heat. Using a large ice-cream scoop or ⅓-cup (80-ml) measuring cup, pour the batter into the pan and spread it out with a spatula or the back of a ladle (the batter will be thick). Cook for about 4 minutes per side, until bubbles have popped on the surface of the pancakes and the edges are dry. Flip the pancakes and cook for 3 to 4 minutes more on the other side. Serve immediately. See page 37, storing your baked goods. May be frozen.

Plum Good Oaty Pancakes ✸ CF, SF or NF ✸

Makes 8 to 10 pancakes, 3½ inches (9 cm) diameter

While the plums in these pancakes provide a wonderful juiciness and tang, you could easily substitute sliced peaches or even apples. And they're a great way to consume your oatmeal and pancakes in one dish!

- ½ cup (50 g) old-fashioned rolled oats (not instant or quick-cooking)
- 1 Tbsp (15 ml) finely ground chia seeds (from about 1½ tsp or 7.5 ml whole seeds)
- 1½ cups (360 ml) plain or vanilla almond or soy milk
- 3 Tbsp (45 ml) coconut sugar
- 1 Tbsp (15 ml) sunflower or other light-tasting oil, preferably organic
- 2 tsp (10 ml) grated lemon zest, (about 1 medium lemon) preferably organic, or ½ tsp (2.5 ml) pure lemon extract
- 1 tsp (5 ml) apple cider vinegar
- 10 to 20 drops pure plain or vanilla stevia liquid, or to taste
- 3 to 4 small ripe red plums, pit removed and sliced into thin half-moons
- 1⅓ (180 g) Ricki's All-Purpose Gluten-Free Flour Mix (see page 22)
- ¾ tsp (3.5 ml) xanthan gum (use only Bob's Red Mill brand if you are concerned about a corn allergy)
- 2 tsp (10 ml) baking powder
- ¼ tsp (1 ml) baking soda
- ⅛ tsp (.5 ml) fine sea salt

In a medium bowl, combine the oats, chia, milk, coconut sugar, oil, lemon zest, vinegar, and stevia; whisk well to blend and to ensure there are no lumps of ground chia seeds visible. Stir in the plum slices. Set aside for 20 minutes.

Meanwhile, in a large bowl, sift the flour, xanthan gum, baking powder, baking soda, and salt.

Heat a large nonstick frying pan over medium heat. Stir the wet mixture to eliminate any lumps, then pour it over the dry ingredients and stir just to blend. The batter will be thick.

Using a large ice-cream scoop or ⅓-cup (80-ml) measuring cup, scoop the batter into the pan and spread to flatten it to about ½ inch (1 cm) thick. Allow to cook about 4 to 5 minutes, until the edges are dry and the top is beginning to dry. Flip and cook the other side for another 3 to 4 minutes, until golden. Repeat with the rest of the batter, keeping prepared pancakes warm until all pancakes are cooked; serve immediately with your choice of topping. See page 37, storing your baked goods. May be frozen.

Carob-Buckwheat Pancakes with Chopped Almonds and Chocolate or Carob Chips with Nut-Free Variation

✱ CF, can be SF and NF ✱

Makes 9 to 10 medium pancakes, about 3½ inches (9 cm) diameter

Although the ingredient list appears long, these pancakes actually come together very quickly. The only real "work" aside from measuring is to chop up the almonds if you toast them yourself, as ground almonds won't work here (though slivered almonds work well, too). If the batter seems too thin at first, don't worry; just cook the cakes thoroughly, and they'll rise high and won't remain wet in the middle.

1 cup plus 2 Tbsp (150 g) buckwheat flour
2 Tbsp (30 ml) coconut flour
3 Tbsp (45 ml) carob powder
1 tsp (5 ml) baking powder
½ tsp (1 ml) baking soda
⅛ tsp (.5 ml) fine sea salt
2 Tbsp (30 ml) finely ground flax seeds (from about 1 Tbsp or 15 ml whole seeds)
2 Tbsp plus 2 tsp (40 ml total) finely ground chia seeds (from about 1½ Tbsp or 20 ml whole seeds)
3 Tbsp (45 ml) finely chopped almonds or slivered almonds, lightly toasted
3 Tbsp (45 ml) unsweetened carob chips or dairy-free chocolate chips
2 tsp (10 ml) apple cider vinegar
About 1⅔ cups (400 ml) unsweetened plain or vanilla almond, soy, or coconut beverage (the kind that comes in a carton) to equal 1⅔ cups (400 ml) with the vinegar (see instructions)
2 Tbsp (30 ml) sunflower or other light-tasting oil, preferably organic
2 tsp (10 ml) pure vanilla extract
10 to 20 drops pure plain or vanilla stevia liquid, or to taste

In a medium bowl, sift the buckwheat flour, coconut flour, carob powder, baking powder, baking soda, and salt. Add the flax, chia, almonds, and carob chips and whisk to combine.

Place the vinegar in a glass 2-cup (500-ml) measuring cup and add enough milk to reach the 1⅔-cup (400-ml) mark. Add the oil, vanilla, and stevia to the cup and whisk briefly to combine. Begin to heat a nonstick frying pan over medium heat.

Pour the wet ingredients over the dry and mix just to blend; do not overmix.

Using a large ice-cream scoop or ⅓-cup (80-ml) measuring cup, scoop batter and pour it in the pan; spread out slightly if necessary to create a circle. Allow to cook until the pancakes are totally dry on the edges and begin to puff in the middle, 4 to 6 minutes. Flip and cook the other side another 3 to 4 minutes, until light golden. Keep pancakes warm as you continue to use all the batter in this manner. Serve with Walnut-Cacao Nib Butter (see page 90) and Quick Apple-Cranberry Compote (see page 88). See page 37, storing your baked goods; reheat to serve. May be frozen.

Variation:
Nut-Free Variation: To make the pancakes nut-free, use soy milk or coconut beverage, omit the chopped almonds, and increase the chips to ¼ cup (50 g).

Giant Baked Upside-Down Apple Pancake * CF, can be SF *

Serves 6 to 8

This is a perfect weekend breakfast or dish for a brunch crowd. Or, slice and wrap pieces of the pancake, then store them in the fridge for breakfast throughout the week. If your apples are very sweet, feel free to omit the coconut sugar in the apple layer if desired.

FOR THE APPLE LAYER:

1 large sweet apple, such as Gala or Delicious, peeled, cored, and cut in thin slices
1 Tbsp (15 ml) ground cinnamon
2 Tbsp (30 ml) coconut sugar

FOR THE PANCAKE BATTER:

⅓ cup (80 ml) natural smooth cashew butter, at room temperature
½ cup (120 ml) unsweetened applesauce
1 tsp (5 ml) pure vanilla extract
½ tsp (2.5 ml) pure almond extract (optional)
2 Tbsp (30 ml) agave nectar or 15 to 20 drops pure plain or vanilla stevia liquid
1 tsp (5 ml) finely ground chia seeds (from about ½ tsp or 2.5 ml whole seeds) or 1 Tbsp (15 ml) ground flax seeds (from about 1½ tsp or 7.5 ml whole seeds)
¾ cup (180 ml) plain or vanilla soy, almond, or rice milk
⅓ cup (50 g) brown rice flour
¼ cup (35 ml) coconut flour
¼ cup (25 ml) whole oat flour (to make your own, see page 35)
1 tsp (5 ml) ground cinnamon
2½ tsp (12.5 ml) baking powder
¼ tsp (1 ml) baking soda
⅛ tsp (.5 ml) fine sea salt

Preheat the oven to 350°F (180°C). Grease the bottom and sides of a large tart pan, springform pan, or pie plate. Then line with a circle of parchment paper and grease the top of the paper. (This is necessary to ensure that the fruit bottom unmolds properly; if you don't intend to flip the pancake over after it's baked and you plan to cut slices straight from the pan, you can omit the parchment paper).

Make the apple layer: In a small bowl, combine the apple, 1 tablespoon (15 ml) of cinnamon, and coconut sugar, if using. Toss with a spoon or your hands until all the slices are coated, taking care to separate any slices that stick together (discard any coating that's left at the bottom of the bowl). Place the slices in a single layer (or just slightly overlapping) over the bottom of the prepared pan in a decorative arrangement. Set aside.

Make the pancake batter: In a medium bowl, whisk together the cashew butter, applesauce, vanilla, almond extract, if using, agave nectar or stevia, and chia until combined. Slowly add the milk and whisk until well mixed.

In a large bowl, sift the flours, cinnamon, baking powder, baking soda, and salt. Whisk briefly to distribute the leaveners and cinnamon. Add the wet mixture to the dry and stir until well combined.

Assemble the pancake and bake: Carefully drop the batter by spoonfuls evenly over the surface of the apples, then spread gently to cover all the fruit, disturbing the slices as little as possible. Smooth the top as best as possible (it's okay if a few bits of apple stick out here and there).

(continued on page 84)

Giant Baked Upside-Down Apple Pancake *continued* ✷ CF, can be SF ✷

Bake for 35 to 45 minutes, rotating the pan about halfway through baking, until the top is golden, the edges are browned, and a tester inserted in the center comes out clean. Remove from the oven and allow to cool completely in the pan. Once cool, carefully run a knife along the outside edge of the pancake to loosen it. Place a serving plate over the pan and flip it over (the pancake should fall right out onto the plate). Gently peel off the parchment paper. The apples should be in the same position as they were when the pancake went into the oven; if they're not, carefully rearrange them on top of the pancake.

Serve with your choice of topping. I like mine with Caramel Ice Cream (see page 212.) See page 37, storing your baked goods. May be frozen.

Quick and Easy High-Protein Breakfast Pancakes for One * CF, can be NF and SF *

Serves 1

You can easily switch up the main grain or nut/seed butter in this versatile recipe. While my favorite combination is buckwheat and tahini, I've also enjoyed these with quinoa and amaranth, together with almond butter or sunflower seed butter. Keep in mind that your protein content will vary depending on which combination you choose. When looking for buckwheat groats, choose either raw or toasted (which are referred to as "kasha"); both work equally well.

- 2 Tbsp (30 ml) dry buckwheat groats (raw or toasted), amaranth, or quinoa
- 1 Tbsp (15 ml) unflavored rice protein powder
- 1 Tbsp (15 m) whole chia seeds
- 1 Tbsp (15 ml) ground flax seeds or meal (from about 1½ tsp or 7.5 ml whole seeds)
- 1 tsp (5 ml) ground cinnamon
- ½ tsp (2.5 ml) ground ginger (optional)
- ⅛ tsp (.5 ml) fine sea salt
- ¼ tsp (1 ml) baking powder
- 1 Tbsp (15 ml) tahini (sesame seed paste), natural smooth almond butter, or unsweetened sunflower butter, at room temperature
- 6 Tbsp (90 ml) unsweetened plain or vanilla coconut beverage (the kind that comes in a carton), or almond, soy, or flax milk
- 1 tsp (5 ml) pure vanilla extract
- 5 to 10 drops pure plain or vanilla stevia liquid, or to taste

Place the buckwheat groats, protein powder, chia, flax, cinnamon, ginger, salt, and baking powder in a coffee grinder and grind until powdered.

In a small bowl, whisk together the tahini, coconut beverage or milk, vanilla, and stevia. Add the dry ingredients to the bowl and stir until combined (it will be thick and sticky).

Heat a nonstick frying pan over medium heat. Divide the dough into two parts and spread out on the pan to create two pancakes that are about ¼ inch (.5 cm) thick. You will have to press down with the spatula, as the mixture won't spread on its own.

Cook about 5 minutes on one side, until the bottom is browned. Flip gently and continue to cook until the other side is also browned, another 4 to 5 minutes. Serve immediately. May be frozen.

"Notella" (Chocolate Hazelnut Butter)

✷ GF, SF, CF ✷

Makes about 1¼ cups (300 ml)

The trick to the extra-smooth texture here is starting with prepared hazelnut butter, which can be found in health-food stores. Or you can try making your own extra-smooth hazelnut butter (see pages 35–36). Either type will produce good results. If using store bought, be sure that the only ingredient is hazelnuts.

- 1 cup (240 ml) pure, natural hazelnut butter, very smooth, at room temperature
- ¼ cup (60 ml) coconut oil, melted (at low temperature), preferably organic
- 2 Tbsp plus 2 tsp (40 ml total) unsweetened cocoa powder, preferably non-alkalized
- 1 tsp (5 ml) pure vanilla extract
- ¼ tsp (1 ml) pure stevia powder or ½ tsp (2.5 ml) pure plain or vanilla stevia liquid, or to taste

Place all ingredients in the bowl of a food processor and process until well combined and very smooth (it will be almost liquid and very pourable), scraping down the sides a few times as you go. Pour the mixture into a clean jar and refrigerate at least 3 hours, until firm. Scoop and spread on whatever strikes your fancy. This nut butter would make a great truffle filling or tart filling as well. Store, covered, in the refrigerator, for up to 2 weeks.

Toppings: clockwise from top left: Fresh Berry Topping (see page 89), Strawberry Whipped Cream (see Variations, page 169), Chocolate Whipped Cream (see Variations, page 169), "Salted Caramel" Walnut Butter (see page 91), Lemon Whipped Cream (see Variations, page 169), Quick Cranberry-Apple Compote (see page 88), "Notella" (Chocolate Hazelnut Butter) (see this page).

Quick Cranberry-Apple Compote * GF, SF, CF, NF *

(see photograph on page 86)

Makes about 1½ cups (360 ml)

The brilliant hue of this tangy fruit spread creates great visual appeal as a topping for pancakes or a spread on muffins or scones. Or head over to the savory side of things and dollop it on burgers, tofu, or curries.

2 cups (210 g) fresh or frozen cranberries

1 large red apple, such as Spartan, McIntosh, Gala, or Delicious, cored, peeled or unpeeled

½ tsp (2. 5 ml) ground ginger

2 Tbsp (30 ml) water

¼ tsp (1 ml) pure stevia powder, ½ tsp (2.5 ml) pure plain or vanilla stevia liquid, or 2 Tbsp (30 ml) agave nectar, or to taste

Place the cranberries in a small, heavy-bottomed pot. Grate the apple into the pot and add the ginger and water; stir to combine. Turn heat to medium-low and cover the pot. Allow to cook, stirring frequently, for 15 to 20 minutes, until the apple is soft and most of the cranberries have popped. Stir well to combine the fruits. Add the stevia and stir well. Spoon into a clean jar and allow to cool. Store, covered, in the refrigerator, for up to 1 week.

Fresh Berry Topping ✱ GF, SF, CF, NF ✱

(see photograph on page 86)

Makes about 1½ cups (360 ml)

This fresh berry topping — almost like a light jam or pie filling — makes a great counterpoint to waffles, pancakes, or even ice cream. Try it over Fluffy Fruited Pancakes (page 76) for a real treat.

- 3 cups (475 g) fresh or frozen mixed berries, such as blueberries, raspberries, strawberries, or blackberries
- 1 Tbsp (15 ml) water
- 2 tsp finely grated lemon zest (about 1 large lemon), preferably organic
- Pinch fine sea salt
- 3 Tbsp (45 ml) coconut sugar
- ⅛ tsp (.5 ml) pure stevia powder or ¼ tsp (1 ml) pure plain or vanilla stevia liquid, or to taste

Place berries, water, lemon zest, salt, and coconut sugar in a medium pot and heat over medium heat until the berries begin to release their juices. Lower heat and simmer until berries are soft and the mixture has thickened somewhat, about 25 minutes. Add the stevia and adjust if necessary.

Remove from heat and cool completely. Store in an airtight container in the refrigerator for up to 10 days. May be frozen.

Walnut Cacao-Nib Butter * GF, SF, CF *

Makes about 1 cup (240 ml)

This is one of my very favorite nut butters. It can be drizzled on pancakes or ice cream, or spread on a muffin or scone. I love it melted over Carob-Buckwheat Pancakes with Chopped Almonds and Chocolate or Carob Chips (see page 81). Walnuts contain heart-healthy omega-3s, so you can even feel virtuous as you enjoy.

- 2 Tbsp (30 ml) cacao nibs, coarsely chopped unsweetened chocolate, or coarsely chopped chocolate chips
- 2 heaping cups (250 g) walnuts, lightly toasted
- ⅛ tsp (.5 ml) fine sea salt
- 10 to 15 drops pure plain or vanilla stevia liquid, or to taste

In the bowl of a food processor or coffee grinder, process the cacao nibs briefly to break up into crumbs. Don't overprocess, or you'll end up with cacao powder; you want a bit of texture. Remove the nibs to a bowl.

In the same processor bowl, whir the walnuts and salt until the mixture becomes almost perfectly smooth, 1 to 2 minutes. Stop the processor, add the stevia, and pulse a couple of times to blend. Add the cacao nibs back in and stir with a spoon to combine, but don't process again.

Turn the mixture into a clean jar. Store, covered, in the refrigerator, for up to 1 week.

Variation:
Almond Cacao-Nib: For an almond-based nut butter, replace the walnuts in the recipe with lightly toasted natural almonds. Note, however, that almonds take a bit longer to smooth out than walnuts (since they have a lower natural fat content), 5 to 10 minutes.

"Salted Caramel" Walnut Butter ✻ GF, SF, CF ✻

(see photograph on page 86)

Makes about 2 cups (480 ml)

The pairing of walnuts and coconut makes for a very indulgent-tasting spread that's firm when refrigerated and that softens as it stands at room temperature. The lucuma here provides the "caramel" flavor, making this a perfect topper for pancakes as well.

- 2 cups (340 g or 12 oz) walnut halves, lightly toasted
- 2 cups (130 g or 4.5 oz) unsweetened shredded coconut
- ¼ to ½ tsp (1 to 2.5 ml) fine sea salt, to your taste
- 2 Tbsp (30 ml) lucuma powder
- 1 tsp (5 ml) pure vanilla extract
- ¼ tsp (1 ml) pure stevia powder or ½ tsp (2.5 ml) pure plain or vanilla stevia liquid, or to taste

Place the walnuts in the jar of a high-speed blender, such as a Vitamix, and top with the coconut and salt. Blend, using the tamper as needed, until the mixture is liquefied (1 to 2 minutes). Add the lucuma powder, vanilla, and stevia and blend again. Pour into a clean jar or container and refrigerate until ready to use. Will keep, covered, in the refrigerator, for up to 3 weeks.

Chapter 2: *Cookies, Squares & Bars*

Chocolate-Flecked Pumpkin Seed Cookies * SF, CF, NF *

Makes 1 dozen

These rich-tasting, slightly chewy cookies come together quickly, for those times when you just need a snack pronto. Pumpkin seeds are a good source of zinc, they are involved in more body processes than any other mineral and they are important for healthy immune functioning.

- ⅓ cup (55 g) coconut sugar
- 20 to 30 drops pure plain or vanilla stevia liquid
- ¼ cup (60 ml) water
- 1 tsp (5 ml) pure vanilla extract
- ½ cup (120 ml) natural smooth pumpkin seed butter, at room temperature
- ¼ cup (25 g) finely ground flax seeds (from about 2 Tbsp whole seeds)
- ½ cup (75 g) brown rice flour
- ⅛ tsp (.5 ml) fine sea salt
- ¼ cup (50 g) unsweetened carob chips or dairy-free chocolate chips, coarsely chopped

Preheat the oven to 350°F (180°C). Line a cookie sheet with parchment paper, or spray with nonstick spray.

In a small bowl, whisk together the coconut sugar, stevia, water, and vanilla until the sugar dissolves.

Add the pumpkin seed butter, flax, flour, and salt and mix well to form a very thick and sticky dough. Stir in the chips.

Using a heaping teaspoon (5 ml), scoop the dough and roll it into small balls, placing them about one inch (2.5 cm) apart on the cookie sheet. Flatten slightly with your palm (or use a silicone spatula).

Bake for 10 to 12 minutes, rotating the sheet about halfway through, until the cookies are light golden brown (the dough will lighten as the cookies bake). Allow the cookies to cool completely before removing from the cookie sheet.

Store in an airtight container in the refrigerator for up to 5 days. See page 37, storing your baked goods. May be frozen.

Chocolate Mint Chocolate Chip Cookies

✱ SF, CF, NF ✱

Makes about 2 dozen

A popular vegan cookie company in Toronto sells a cookie similar to this, which I used to buy all the time. But at over $6.00 for a pack of 10 small cookies, I decided to develop my own version. When I switched to a gluten-free diet, I knew this recipe had to make the switch as well. These are soft, chewy cookies with a fudgy center, and a hit with everyone who's ever tried them.

- 3 oz (100 g) pitted prunes (dried plums), chopped (they should be soft)
- 2 Tbsp of prune soaking water (see instructions)
- ½ cup (85 g) coconut sugar
- ⅓ cup (80 ml) coconut nectar
- ⅛ tsp (.5 ml) pure stevia powder or ¼ tsp (1 ml) pure plain or vanilla stevia liquid, or to taste
- 20 to 25 fresh mint leaves, chopped, or ½ tsp (2.5 ml) pure mint extract
- 2 tsp (10 ml) pure vanilla extract
- 1 tsp (5 ml) apple cider vinegar
- ⅓ cup (80 ml) sunflower or other light-tasting oil, preferably organic
- 1½ cups (200 g) Ricki's All-Purpose Gluten-Free Flour Mix (see page 22)
- 1 tsp (5 ml) xanthan gum (use only Bob's Red Mill brand if you are concerned about a corn allergy)
- ¼ cup (35 g) unsweetened cocoa powder, preferably non-alkalized
- 1 tsp (5 ml) baking powder
- 1 tsp (5 ml) baking soda
- ¼ tsp (1 ml) fine sea salt
- ⅔ cup (135 g) unsweetened carob chips or dairy-free chocolate chips

Preheat the oven to 350°F (180°C). Line 2 cookie sheets with parchment paper, or spray with nonstick spray.

Place the prunes in a heatproof bowl and pour enough boiling water over them to cover (poke down any that float up, so that they are all submerged in water). Allow to stand for 5 minutes, then drain and reserve 2 tablespoons (30 ml) of the soaking water (you'll need it for the cookies).

Place the drained prunes, 2 tablespoons (30 ml) of the soaking water, coconut sugar, coconut nectar, stevia, fresh mint (or extract), vanilla, and vinegar in a food processor and process until you have a very smooth paste (be sure no large bits of prunes are visible). Add the oil and process again to blend. Set aside while you measure the dry ingredients.

In a large bowl, sift the flour, xanthan gum, cocoa, baking powder, baking soda, and salt; stir briefly to mix. Pour the wet ingredients over the dry and stir to combine. Add the chips last. You should have a soft and sticky dough.

Using a small ice-cream scoop or tablespoon (15 ml), drop mounds of dough about 2 inches (5 cm) apart on the cookie sheets. Wet your hands and use your palms (or use a silicone spatula) to flatten the cookies slightly.

Bake for 10 to 14 minutes, rotating the sheets about halfway through, until the cookies puff up and the tops begin to crack. They will still be quite soft. Allow to cool completely before removing from the cookie sheets (they will firm up as they cool). See page 37, storing your baked goods. May be frozen.

Carob Refrigerator Cookies ✵ SF, CF, NF ✵

Makes 12 to 16

Light and not too sweet, these cookies are perfect for an afternoon snack with tea or as the base for sandwich cookies. Made without the chips, they'd be great crumbled for a tart or pie crust.

- ¼ cup (40 g) coconut sugar
- 2 Tbsp (30 ml) water
- 1 tsp (5 ml) pure vanilla extract
- 20 to 25 drops pure plain or vanilla stevia liquid, or to taste
- ¼ cup (60 ml) coconut oil, melted (at low temperature), preferably organic
- 1 Tbsp (15 ml) finely ground flax seeds (from about 1½ tsp or 7.5 ml whole seeds)
- ⅔ cup (90 g) Ricki's All-Purpose Gluten-Free Flour Mix (see page 22)
- 3 Tbsp (45 ml) carob powder
- ½ tsp (2.5 ml) ground cinnamon
- ½ tsp (2.5 ml) baking powder
- ¼ tsp (1 ml) fine sea salt
- ½ tsp (2.5 ml) xanthan gum (use only Bob's Red Mill brand if you are concerned about a corn allergy)
- ⅓ cup (65 g) unsweetened carob chips (optional)

In a small bowl, whisk together the sugar, water, vanilla, and stevia until the sugar begins to dissolve. Add the oil and whisk vigorously to combine, or beat with electric beaters (it's okay if the mixture appears curdled). Mix in the flax.

In a medium bowl, sift the flour, carob powder, cinnamon, baking powder, salt, and xanthan gum. Add the wet mixture to the dry and stir to create a slightly sticky dough. Add the carob chips and gently stir to combine. Create a roll about 8 inches (20.5 cm) long, wrap tightly in plastic wrap, and refrigerate for at least 2 hours or up to overnight. (If you're in a rush, you can freeze the log for about 15 minutes, until firm, then proceed).

When you're ready to bake the cookies, preheat the oven to 375°F (190°C). Line a cookie sheet with parchment paper or spray with nonstick spray. Using a sharp knife, cut cookies about ½ inch (1.25 cm) thick and place them about an inch (2.5 cm) apart on the prepared cookie sheet. If the dough cracks or if the cookies are squished when cutting, press with your fingers to reshape them into circles.

Bake for 10 to 12 minutes, rotating the sheet about halfway through baking, until the cookies are slightly puffed and lightly browned on the bottom. Cool 5 minutes before removing from the cookie sheet. Store in an airtight container in the refrigerator for up to 5 days; serve at room temperature. May be frozen.

Grain-Free Cashew Carob Chip Cookies * GF, CF, can be SF *

Makes 8 to 10

A thin and chewy cookie with no grains, these firm up considerably as they cool. Since the chips aren't essential for the texture of the batter, feel free to use either carob or chocolate chips, or an equal amount of cacao nibs or raisins in their place.

- ¼ cup (60 ml) coconut nectar
- 2 Tbsp (30 ml) coconut sugar
- 20 to 30 drops pure plain or vanilla stevia liquid, or to taste
- 1 tsp (5 ml) pure vanilla extract
- 2 tsp (10 ml) rice, almond, or soy milk, or water
- ⅔ cup (160 ml) natural smooth cashew butter, at room temperature
- 1 Tbsp (15 ml) coconut oil, at room temperature, preferably organic
- 2 Tbsp (30 ml) finely ground flax seeds (from about 1 Tbsp or 15 ml whole seeds)
- ¼ cup (20 g) whole psyllium husks
- ⅛ to ¼ tsp (.5 to 1 ml) ground cardamom, or to taste
- ¼ tsp (1 ml) baking powder
- ¼ tsp (1 ml) fine sea salt (omit if cashew butter is salted)
- ⅓ cup (65 g) unsweetened carob chips or dairy-free chocolate chips

Preheat the oven to 350°F (180°C). Line a cookie sheet with parchment paper, or spray with nonstick spray.

In a medium bowl, mix the coconut nectar, coconut sugar, stevia, and vanilla to begin dissolving the coconut sugar. Add the milk or water, cashew butter, oil, flax, psyllium, cardamom, baking powder, and salt, if using, and stir until well combined. You should have a soft and sticky dough. Gently stir in the chips.

Using a small ice-cream scoop or tablespoon (15 ml), scoop batter onto the prepared cookie sheet about 2 inches (5 cm) apart. Do not flatten (they will spread as they bake).

Bake for 8 to 12 minutes, rotating the sheet about halfway through baking, until golden on the edges. Allow the cookies to cool completely before removing from the cookie sheet (they will firm up as they cool). See page 37, storing your baked goods. May be frozen.

Butterscotch-Chocolate Chip Cookies * SF, CF *

Makes 12 to 15

Just like the cookies grandma used to make . . . except with much healthier ingredients. In this recipe, the psyllium is essential to properly bind the cookies; I tried the recipe various ways with flax and/or chia, but the results were not nearly as good.

- ⅓ cup (80 ml) coconut sugar
- 1 Tbsp (15 ml) water
- 2 Tbsp (30 ml) coconut nectar
- 2 tsp (10 ml) pure vanilla extract
- 1 Tbsp (15 ml) nut oil, such as walnut, almond, or macadamia, or extra-virgin olive oil, preferably organic
- 5 to 10 drops pure plain or vanilla stevia liquid, or to taste
- 1 cup (110 g) old-fashioned rolled oats (not instant or quick-cooking)
- 1 cup (110 g) walnut pieces and halves, lightly toasted
- 1 Tbsp (15 ml) lucuma powder
- ¼ tsp (1 ml) baking soda
- ¼ tsp (1 ml) baking powder
- ¼ tsp (1 ml) fine sea salt
- 2 tsp (10 ml) whole psyllium husks
- ½ cup (100 g) dairy-free chocolate chips or unsweetened carob chips

Preheat the oven to 350°F (180°C). Line a cookie sheet with parchment paper, or spray with nonstick spray.

In a glass measuring cup or small bowl, mix together the coconut sugar, water, coconut nectar, vanilla, oil, and stevia; whisk to begin dissolving the coconut sugar. Set aside.

In the bowl of a food processor, process the oats until they resemble cornmeal. Add the walnuts, lucuma powder, baking soda, baking powder, salt, and psyllium and continue to process until the mixture is very fine and begins to stick together, moving in a solid "wall" around the edges of the processor. (The texture will be like a slightly moist sawdust at this point, and it should still fall apart in a powder when you separate it with your fingers, NOT like a regular dough that sticks together.)

Drizzle the wet mixture in a ring over the dry ingredients in the processor and process until it comes together in a dough. Lift the blade and scrape away any liquid that's hiding under there, then return the blade and process again briefly to incorporate. Remove the blade and stir in the chips by hand; do not process again.

Scoop the dough using a small ice-cream scoop or tablespoon (15 ml) and place in small mounds on the prepared cookie sheet. Use your wet palm or a silicone spatula to flatten the cookies to about ½ inch (1.25 cm) thick. Bake for 8 to 12 minutes, rotating the cookie sheet about halfway through baking, until the edges are golden. Allow to cool before removing from the cookie sheet. See page 37, storing your baked goods. May be frozen.

Chocolate Shortbread Cookies ✱ CF, SF, NF ✱

Makes 16 to 20

If you're a fan of shortbread, these buttery, sandy cookies will be sure to please. Not too sweet and very chocolatey, they also make the perfect tart crust for the Chocolate Satin Tart (see page 183).

- ⅓ cup (55 g) coconut sugar
- ¼ cup (60 ml) coconut nectar
- ¼ tsp (1 ml) pure stevia powder or ½ tsp (2.5 ml) pure plain or vanilla stevia liquid, or to taste
- 2 tsp (10 ml) water
- 1 tsp (5 ml) pure vanilla extract
- ⅓ cup (80 ml) coconut oil, at room temperature, preferably organic
- 1 cup (135 g) Ricki's All-Purpose Gluten-Free Flour Mix (see page 22)
- 2 Tbsp (30 ml) brown rice flour
- ¼ cup (35 g) unsweetened cocoa powder, preferably non-alkalized
- ¾ tsp (3.5 ml) xanthan gum (use only Bob's Red Mill brand if you are concerned about a corn allergy)
- ¼ tsp (1 ml) baking powder
- ⅛ tsp (.5 ml) fine sea salt

In the bowl of a food processor, combine the coconut sugar, coconut nectar, stevia, water, and vanilla until the sugar is dissolved. Add the coconut oil and process to blend. Add the all-purpose flour, brown rice flour, cocoa powder, xanthan gum, baking powder, and salt until evenly mixed and a soft dough is formed.

Form the dough into a roll 5inches (13 cm) long on a piece of plastic wrap, and roll it up like a sausage. Refrigerate until firm, at least 1 hour.

Preheat the oven to 350°F (180°C). Line a cookie sheet with parchment paper, or spray with nonstick spray.

Using a sharp knife, cut the roll into slices about ¼ inch (6 mm) thick and place about 1 inch (2.5 cm) apart on cookie sheet. Bake in the preheated oven 12 to 15 minutes, rotating the sheet about halfway through, until the cookies are browned on the edges. Allow to cool 5 minutes before removing to a rack to cool completely. See page 37, storing your baked goods. May be frozen.

Peanut-Free Peanut Butter Cookies * CF, can be NF *

Makes about 2 dozen

You'll be so delighted by the familiar taste, slightly grainy texture, and familiar crisscross pattern on this cookie that you may not believe it doesn't contain peanut butter! This is my version of the childhood classic, reimagined without peanuts, eggs, dairy, or refined sugar, yet every bit as appealing as the original. In fact, after you taste these irresistible confections, you may just find you have a new favorite "peanut butter" cookie.

¾ cup (180 ml) natural unsweetened sunflower seed butter, at room temperature

⅓ cup (80 ml) coconut nectar

⅓ cup (25 g) coconut sugar

20 to 25 drops pure plain or vanilla stevia liquid, or to taste

¼ cup (60 ml) unsweetened soy, almond, flax, or rice milk, or a little more, if absolutely necessary

¼ cup (60 ml) sunflower or other light-tasting oil, preferably organic

1 tsp (5 ml) pure vanilla extract

1 Tbsp (15 ml) ground chia seeds or meal (from about 1½ tsp or 7.5 ml whole seeds)

¼ cup (20 g) whole psyllium husks

2 cups (265 g) Ricki's All-Purpose Gluten-Free Flour Mix (see page 22)

1 tsp (5 ml) baking powder

½ tsp (2.5 ml) baking soda

½ to 1 tsp (2.5 to 5 ml) fine sea salt, or to taste (and depending on whether there's salt in your sunflower seed butter or not)

Preheat the oven to 375°F (190°C). Line 2 cookie sheets with parchment paper, or spray with nonstick spray.

In a medium bowl, stir together the sunflower seed butter, coconut nectar, coconut sugar, stevia, milk, oil, vanilla, chia, and psyllium until well blended. Set aside.

In a large bowl, sift the flour, baking powder, baking soda, and salt. Add the wet ingredients and stir until well combined (use your hands if necessary to blend into a fairly stiff dough).

Using a small ice-cream scoop or tablespoon (15 ml), scoop out small mounds of dough and roll them into balls. Place about 2 inches (5 cm) apart on the prepared cookie sheets. Using a fork, press down first in one direction, then in the opposite direction, to form a crisscross pattern and to flatten the cookies.

Bake for 12 to 17 minutes, rotating the cookie sheets once about halfway through baking, until the cookies are golden brown on the edges and just beginning to brown on top. Allow to cool completely before removing to a cooling rack. See page 37, storing your baked goods. May be frozen.

Hazelnut Mocha Cookies * SF, CF *

Makes about 2 dozen

I found an intriguing recipe for a similar cookie in a magazine, but the original was filled with butter, caffeine, and lots of sugar. I decided to re-create the effect with a healthier array of ingredients, and came up with this winning combination. This is a sophisticated little cookie, and it's one of my husband's favorites. (And don't be alarmed by the 4 Tbsp (60 ml) instant-coffee substitute in this recipe — it results in the perfect touch of mocha when baked into these cookies!)

½ cup (40 g) coconut sugar
2 Tbsp (30 ml) water
¼ cup (60 ml) coconut nectar
⅛ tsp (.5 ml) pure stevia powder or ¼ tsp (1 ml) pure plain or vanilla stevia liquid, or to taste
2 Tbsp (30 ml) finely ground flax seeds (from about 1 Tbsp or 15 ml whole seeds)
4 Tbsp (60 ml) instant-coffee substitute, such as Dandy Blend, or 2 tsp (10 ml) instant coffee (see page 34)
2 tsp (10 ml) pure vanilla extract
½ tsp (2.5 ml) apple cider vinegar
¼ cup (20 g) whole psyllium husks
½ cup (120 ml) coconut oil, melted (at low temperature), preferably organic
½ cup (75 g) coarsely chopped, skin-on hazelnuts, lightly toasted
1½ cups plus 2 Tbsp (210 g) Ricki's All-Purpose Gluten-Free Flour Mix (see page 22)
1½ tsp (7.5 ml) baking powder
½ tsp (2.5 ml) fine sea salt

Preheat the oven to 375°F (190°C). Line 2 cookie sheets with parchment paper, or spray with nonstick spray.

In a medium bowl, whisk together the coconut sugar, water, coconut nectar, and stevia until the sugar dissolves. Add the flax, instant-coffee substitute, vanilla, vinegar, and psyllium and stir until well combined, then whisk in the coconut oil. Stir in the hazelnuts to coat.

In the same bowl, sift in the flour, baking powder, and salt and stir to create a soft dough.

Using a small ice-cream scoop or tablespoon (15 ml), drop small mounds of dough 2 inches (5 cm) apart onto the prepared cookie sheets (no need to flatten these, as they spread quite a bit while baking).

Bake for 12 to 14 minutes, rotating the cookie sheets about halfway through baking, until the cookies are just turning golden on the edges and have puffed up a bit. Cool completely before removing from the cookie sheets (they will firm up as they cool). Store in an airtight container, see page 37, storing your baked goods. May be frozen.

From left: Hazelnut Mocha Cookies (*see this page*), Seed Jumble Cookies (see page 108), Chocolate-Almond Butter Fudgies (see page 109), Macadamia Sesame Cookies (see page 110).

Seed Jumble Cookies * SF, CF, NF *

(see photograph on page 106)

Makes about 20

Reminiscent of a granola bar, these cookies are chock-full of seeds and flavor. And they're incredibly easy to make!

- ⅓ cup (25 g) coconut sugar
- 2 Tbsp (30 ml) water
- ⅓ cup (80 ml) coconut nectar
- 20 drops pure plain or vanilla stevia liquid
- 2 tsp (10 ml) pure vanilla extract
- 2 Tbsp (30 ml) natural smooth sunflower butter, at room temperature
- ⅓ cup (80 ml) tahini (sesame seed paste)
- 1¼ cups (130 g) old-fashioned rolled oats (not instant or quick-cooking)
- ¼ cup (35 ml) Ricki's All-Purpose Gluten-Free Flour Mix (see page 22)
- ¼ cup (25 g) finely ground flax seeds (from about 2 Tbsp or 30 ml whole seeds)
- ½ cup (70 g) sunflower seeds, raw or lightly toasted
- ½ cup (75 g) pumpkin seeds, raw or lightly toasted
- ⅓ cup (50 g) sesame seeds, raw or lightly toasted
- ½ cup (100 g) dairy-free chocolate chips or unsweetened carob chips
- ⅓ cup (40 g) dried cranberries, goji berries, or raisins

Preheat the oven to 350°F (180°C). Line 2 cookie sheets with parchment paper, or spray with nonstick spray.

In a small bowl, whisk together the coconut sugar, water, coconut nectar, stevia, vanilla, sunflower butter, and tahini until smooth.

In a medium bowl, stir together the oats, flour, flax, sunflower seeds, pumpkin seeds, sesame seeds, chocolate chips, and dried cranberries. Pour the wet mixture over the dry ingredients and stir to combine well. The mixture will appear a bit crumbly and not very doughy; this is as it should be.

Using a small ice-cream scoop or tablespoon (15 ml), drop small mounds of the mixture about 2 inches (5 cm) apart on the prepared cookie sheets (you may need to press the edges a bit for it to hold together). Bake for 10 to 15 minutes, rotating the cookie sheets about halfway through baking, until golden. Allow to cool completely before removing from the cookie sheets (cookies will firm up as they cool). See page 37, storing your baked goods. May be frozen.

Note: You can use almost any combination of seeds to replace the sunflower, pumpkin, and sesame seeds, as long as they add up to the same volume (1⅓ cups or 320 ml). Use a variety of small and larger seeds for best results. I've used hemp or whole flax seeds instead of the sesame seeds with great results.

Chocolate-Almond Butter Fudgies * SF, CF *

(see photograph on page 106)

Makes about 30

These cookies are soft and almost cake-like, with a fudgy interior. You don't really taste the almond butter, but it adds a bit of crunch and a rich texture. If you can eat peanuts and prefer peanut butter here, feel free to use it instead.

- ½ cup (120 ml) natural crunchy almond butter, at room temperature
- ⅔ cup (50 g) coconut sugar
- ⅓ cup (80 ml) coconut nectar
- ¼ tsp (1 ml) pure stevia powder or ½ tsp (2.5 ml) pure plain or vanilla stevia liquid, or to taste
- ¼ cup (60 ml) sunflower or other light-tasting oil, preferably organic
- 1 Tbsp (15 ml) pure vanilla extract
- 1 tsp (5 ml) apple cider vinegar
- 1 Tbsp (15 ml) finely ground flax seeds (from about 1½ tsp or 7.5 ml whole seeds)
- ⅓ cup (80 ml) unsweetened applesauce
- ¼ cup (20 g) whole psyllium husks
- 1¼ cups (165 g) Ricki's All-Purpose Gluten-Free Flour Mix (see page 22)
- ¼ cup (40 g) teff flour
- ⅓ cup (35 g) unsweetened cocoa powder, preferably non-alkalized
- 1 tsp (5 ml) baking powder
- 1 tsp (5 ml) baking soda
- ½ tsp (2.5 ml) fine sea salt

Preheat the oven to 350°F (180°C). Line 2 cookie sheets with parchment paper, or spray with nonstick spray.

In a medium bowl or a food processor, cream together the almond butter, coconut sugar, coconut nectar, stevia, oil, vanilla, vinegar, flax, applesauce, and psyllium until smooth. Add the all-purpose flour, teff flour, cocoa, baking powder, baking soda, and salt and pulse a few times to incorporate, then process just until blended. You should have a very soft and slightly sticky dough, but one that will hold its shape.

Using a small ice-cream scoop or tablespoon (15 ml), drop small mounds of dough onto the prepared cookie sheets about 2 inches (5 cm) apart. Wet your palms (or use a silicone spatula) and flatten the cookies slightly, to about ¼ inch (6 mm) thick.

Bake for 10 to 13 minutes, rotating the cookie sheets about halfway through baking, until the cookies are puffed and cracked on top (they will still be quite soft). Cool completely before removing from the cookie sheets (they will firm up as they cool). See page 37, storing your baked goods. May be frozen.

Macadamia Sesame Cookies * SF, CF *

(see photograph on page 106)

Makes 10 to 12

Light and crisp, with an intense sesame flavor and buttery texture, these simple yet delicious cookies will become a favorite in no time. Sesame seeds are high in calcium, adding to the nutritional value of these chewy, crunchy bites.

- ¼ cup (60 ml) natural smooth macadamia butter, at room temperature
- 2 Tbsp (30 g) tahini (sesame seed paste)
- 2 Tbsp (30 ml) sunflower or other light-tasting oil, preferably organic
- ⅓ cup (25 g) coconut sugar
- 2 Tbsp rice milk, or water
- 20 to 30 drops pure plain or vanilla stevia liquid
- 1 tsp (10 ml) pure vanilla extract
- ¼ tsp (1 ml) apple cider vinegar
- ½ cup (60 g) whole oat flour (to make your own, see page 35)
- ¼ cup plus 2 Tbsp (55 g) sorghum flour
- 2 Tbsp (30 ml) whole psyllium husks
- ½ tsp (2.5 ml) baking powder
- ½ tsp (2.5 ml) baking soda
- ¼ tsp (1 ml) fine sea salt (omit if macadamia butter is salted)
- 2 Tbsp (30 ml) sesame seeds

Preheat the oven to 350°F (180°C). Line a cookie sheet with parchment paper, or spray with nonstick spray.

In a medium bowl, whisk together the macadamia butter, tahini, oil, coconut sugar, milk, stevia, vanilla, and vinegar. Set aside.

In a large bowl, sift the oat flour, sorghum flour, psyllium, baking powder, baking soda, and salt. Stir well to create a soft dough.

Use a heaping teaspoon (7 ml) to drop the dough about 1 inch (2.5 cm) apart onto the prepared cookie sheet. Wet your hands (or use a silicone spatula) and flatten the cookies until they are about ¼ inch (6 mm) thick. Sprinkle each cookie with some of the sesame seeds.

Bake for 10 to 14 minutes, rotating the cookie sheet about halfway through baking, until the cookies are just golden on the edges (they will still appear quite soft in the middle). Allow to cool completely on the cookie sheet before removing or eating. May be frozen.

Chocolate Whoopie Pies ✱ Can be CF, NF, or SF ✱

Makes 6 pies, about 3 inches (8 cm) in diameter

When I first developed this recipe, I put out a call on Twitter, asking folks about the texture of "authentic" whoopie pies, because I had never tasted one before. I was told they are halfway between a cake and a cookie; slightly denser than a cake but softer than a cookie — and that's just how these turn out. Even if they don't taste "authentic," I don't mind. They're delicious in their own right.

FOR THE PIES:

- ⅔ cup (160 ml) unsweetened plain or vanilla soy, almond, or rice milk or coconut beverage (the kind that comes in a carton)
- ⅓ cup (25 g) coconut sugar
- ⅛ tsp (.5 ml) pure stevia powder or ¼ tsp (1 ml) pure plain or vanilla stevia liquid, or to taste
- ½ tsp (2.5 ml) apple cider vinegar
- 2 tsp (10 ml) pure vanilla extract
- 2 Tbsp (30 ml) extra-virgin olive oil, preferably organic
- 2 Tbsp (30 ml) tahini (sesame seed paste)
- 2 Tbsp (30 ml) finely ground flax seeds (from about 1 Tbsp or 15 ml whole seeds)
- ¼ cup plus 2 Tbsp (60 g) teff flour
- ⅓ cup (50 g) millet flour
- ¼ cup (40 g) potato starch
- ¼ cup (60 ml) unsweetened cocoa powder, preferably non-alkalized
- 2 tsp (10 ml) baking powder
- ¼ tsp (1 ml) baking soda
- ½ tsp (2.5 ml) xanthan gum (use only Bob's Red Mill brand if you are concerned about a corn allergy)
- ⅛ tsp (.5 ml) fine sea salt

FOR THE FILLING:

- 1 batch Chocolate Buttercream Frosting (see page 166)

Preheat the oven to 350°F (180°C). Line a cookie sheet with parchment paper, or spray with nonstick spray.

Make the pies: In a medium bowl, whisk together the milk or coconut beverage, coconut sugar, stevia, vinegar, vanilla, oil, tahini, and flax until smooth. Set aside while you measure the dry ingredients, or at least 5 minutes.

In a small bowl, sift together the teff flour, millet flour, potato starch, cocoa powder, baking powder, baking soda, xanthan gum, and salt. Add the dry ingredients to the wet and stir until combined.

Using an ice-cream scoop or ⅓-cup (80-ml) measuring cup, scoop out the batter and place in mounds on the prepared cookie sheet. Wet your palms and flatten the mounds so that they are uniformly about ½ inch (1.25 cm) thick all over.

Bake for 10 minutes, then rotate the cookie sheet and bake another 5 to 7 minutes, until a tester inserted in the center comes out clean. Cool 5 minutes before removing to a rack to cool completely.

Assemble the pies: Once cooled, cut each pie in half horizontally (as if cutting a sandwich roll). Spread 1 to 2 tablespoons (15 to 30 ml) of frosting (or more, to taste) on the cut side of the bottom of each pie; replace the top of each pie over the frosting. Enjoy! See page 37, storing your baked goods. May be frozen, either as is or after they've been filled with frosting. Defrost, well wrapped, overnight in the refrigerator.

Easiest Almond Cookies * SF, CF *

Makes 15 to 20

I used to buy a similar cookie at the health-food store, but could never resign myself to the exorbitant price. I decided to devise my own version of the treats — and ended up preferring these, which are softer and chewier than the original.

- 2 cups (12 oz or 340 g) natural raw skin-on almonds, preferably organic
- ¼ cup (25 g) finely ground flax seeds (from about 2 Tbsp or 30 ml whole seeds)
- ½ tsp (2.5 ml) baking soda
- ¼ tsp (1 ml) fine sea salt
- ¼ cup (60 ml) agave nectar
- 2 Tbsp (30 ml) sunflower or other light-tasting oil, preferably organic
- 1 tsp (5 ml) pure vanilla extract
- 1 tsp (5 ml) pure almond extract
- 1 Tbsp (15 ml) water, if necessary

Preheat the oven to 350°F (180°C). Line 2 cookie sheets with parchment paper, or spray with nonstick spray.

In the bowl of a food processor, whir the almonds, flax, baking soda, and salt until you have a very fine meal (it should be the consistency of a coarse cornmeal or fine breadcrumbs, with no large pieces of almond visible). Watch that you don't blend so long as to obtain almond butter, however!

Add the agave nectar, oil, and extracts, and process again just until the mixture holds together and leaves the sides of the bowl. It should look like a moist dough. If the mixture is too dry, add the water and pulse quickly to blend.

Using a small ice-cream scoop or tablespoon (15 ml), scoop the dough and roll into balls; place them about 2 inches (5 cm) apart on the prepared cookie sheets. Wet your palms (or use a silicone spatula) and press down to flatten each ball to about ¼ inch (6 mm) thick.

Bake for 8 to 10 minutes, rotating the sheets about halfway through baking, until the edges are barely golden brown and the cookies are dry in the center (the tops will still be light). Allow to cool completely before removing from the cookie sheets; the cookies firm up as they cool. See page 37, storing your baked goods. May be frozen.

Ginger-Coconut Cookies ✷ CF, can be NF and SF ✷

Makes about 30

Redolent with ginger, these cookies are a chewy, spicy treat that's just decadent enough to bake as holiday gifts. But don't wait for the holidays — these are comforting all year-round.

- ½ cup (120 ml) coconut oil, at room temperature, preferably organic
- ⅔ cup (50 g) coconut sugar
- ¼ cup (60 ml) blackstrap molasses
- ½ tsp (2.5 ml) pure stevia powder or 1 tsp (5 ml) plain or vanilla stevia liquid, or to taste
- 2 Tbsp (30 ml) finely ground flax seeds (from about 1 Tbsp or 15 ml whole seeds)
- 2 Tbsp (30 ml) whole psyllium husks
- ¼ cup (60 ml) unsweetened plain or vanilla almond, soy, or rice milk
- 2 tsp (10 ml) grated fresh ginger
- 1 tsp (5 ml) pure vanilla extract
- 1½ cups (195 g) Ricki's All-Purpose Gluten-Free Flour Mix (see page 22)
- ½ cup (80 g) teff flour
- 1½ tsp (7.5 ml) baking powder
- ¼ tsp (1 ml) fine sea salt
- 1 tsp (5 ml) ground ginger
- ⅔ cup (55 g) unsweetened shredded coconut, medium shred (not fine)

Preheat the oven to 350°F (180°C). Line 2 cookie sheets with parchment paper, or spray with nonstick spray.

In the bowl of a food processor, whir together the coconut oil, coconut sugar, molasses, stevia, flax, psyllium, milk, fresh ginger, and vanilla until smooth. Set aside while you measure the dry ingredients, or at least 2 minutes.

In a large bowl, sift the all-purpose flour, teff flour, baking powder, salt, and ground ginger. Add the coconut and stir to combine.

Pour the wet mixture over the dry ingredients and blend well, until you have a fairly stiff dough. Using a small ice-cream scoop or tablespoon (15 ml), measure small mounds of dough and roll each into a ball. Place the balls of dough about 2 inches (5 cm) apart on the prepared cookie sheets and flatten slightly with the palm of your hand (or use a silicone spatula).

Bake for 10 to 13 minutes, rotating the sheets about halfway through baking, until the cookies are puffed, cracked slightly on top, and beginning to brown on the edges (they will still be soft to the touch). Allow to cool completely before removing from the cookie sheets (they will firm up as they cool). See page 37, storing your baked goods. May be frozen.

Sugar-Free Sugar Cookies * CF, NF or SF *

Makes 24 to 30

These simple, not-too-sweet cookies are the perfect base for cutouts or decorations. The dough remains soft and workable even when rolled and recut several times, but these will work well as drop cookies, too. They are great to make with kids — and don't worry if they snack on the raw dough, as it doesn't contain eggs!

6 Tbsp (90 ml) light agave nectar
1 Tbsp (15 ml) finely ground chia seeds (from about 1½ tsp or 7.5 ml whole seeds)
2 Tbsp (30 ml) plain or vanilla soy or almond milk
1 tsp (5 ml) pure vanilla extract
½ tsp (2.5 ml) pure lemon extract
2 cups (265 g) Ricki's All-Purpose Gluten-Free Flour Mix (see page 22)
1 tsp (5 ml) xanthan gum (use only Bob's Red Mill brand if you are concerned about a corn allergy)
1½ tsp (7.5 ml) baking powder
¼ tsp (1 ml) fine sea salt
½ cup (120 ml) coconut oil, at room temperature, preferably organic

Preheat the oven to 350°F (180°C). Line 2 cookie sheets with parchment paper, or spray with nonstick spray.

In a glass measuring cup or small bowl, whisk together the agave nectar, chia, milk, vanilla, and lemon extract. Set aside while you prepare the other ingredients, or at least 2 minutes.

In the bowl of a food processor, briefly process the flour, xanthan gum, baking powder, and salt. Drop the coconut oil in chunks over the flour mixture, then process again until incorporated. The mixture should appear crumbly, but hold together when squeezed in your hand. Pour the wet mixture in a ring over the dry and process until it comes together in a soft, sticky dough.

To make drop cookies, use the dough immediately. Drop from a small ice-cream scoop or tablespoon (15 ml) onto the prepared cookie sheets about 2 inches (5 cm) apart. Flatten slightly with your palm (or use a silicone spatula).

For rolled cookies, gather the dough together and form it into a disk. Wrap the disk in plastic wrap and refrigerate until firm, about 1 hour. Once firm, remove the dough and roll out on a piece of waxed paper to about ¼ inch (6 mm) thick. If it's very firm, it may begin to crack as you roll it, but if you persist, the dough will begin to warm and will roll beautifully. Cut into desired shapes and place 2 inches (5 cm) apart on the cookie sheets. Gather any remaining scraps of dough together and roll again; repeat until all the dough is used.

Bake for 10 to 13 minutes, rotating the sheets about halfway through baking, until the edges are golden. Cool completely before removing from the cookie sheets and decorating as desired. See page 37, storing your baked goods. May be frozen.

Coco-Nut Shortbread Buttons ✱ CF, SF ✱

Makes about 2 dozen

One of my favorite holiday cookies, these shortbread buttons are a breeze to make. Without any of the conventional ingredients, they offer a buttery shortbread texture and rich flavor nonetheless.

- ½ cup (85 g) lightly packed coconut sugar
- 2 Tbsp (30 ml) agave nectar
- 2 tsp (10 ml) pure vanilla extract
- ½ tsp (2.5 ml) coconut extract (optional)
- 2 Tbsp (30 ml) water
- 1 cup (110 g) lightly toasted walnuts
- Heaping ½ cup (40 g or 1.5 oz) unsweetened shredded coconut
- ⅔ cup (90 g) Ricki's All-Purpose Gluten-Free Flour Mix (see page 22)
- ½ cup (90 g) brown rice flour
- ½ cup (80 g) sweet rice flour
- 1 tsp (5 ml) xanthan gum (use only Bob's Red Mill brand if you are concerned about a corn allergy)
- ¼ tsp (1 ml) fine sea salt
- ⅓ cup (80 ml) coconut oil, melted (at low temperature), preferably organic

Preheat the oven to 350°F (180°C). Line 2 cookie sheets with parchment paper, or spray with nonstick spray.

In a medium bowl, combine the coconut sugar, agave nectar, vanilla, coconut extract, if using, and water and stir to begin dissolving the sugar. Set aside while you measure the dry ingredients.

In the bowl of a food processor, place the walnuts, coconut, all of the flours, xanthan gum, and salt. Process until the mixture has the consistency of a meal and there are no walnut crumbs larger than a grain of quinoa visible. Add the sugar-agave mixture and coconut oil and process until it comes together in a clumpy dough. This may take a while; at first, it will just look like dry crumbs. (Resist the urge to add more water until you have processed AT LEAST 3 minutes.) The dough should hold together when squeezed between your thumb and fingers.

Pack the dough into a small ice-cream scoop or tablespoon (15 ml) and place in mounds on the cookie sheets about 1½ inches (3.75 cm) apart. Press the tines of a fork into the top of each cookie to flatten it slightly and leave an indentation.

Bake the cookies in preheated oven for 20 to 22 minutes, rotating the cookie sheets about halfway through, until browned on edges and bottoms. Allow to cool before removing from the cookie sheets. See page 37, storing your baked goods. May be frozen.

Ginger Carrot Oatmeal Cookies ✸ CF, can be NF and SF ✸

Makes 16 to 20

A soft cookie with bright orange wisps of carrot throughout and a hint of ginger, this is a treat you can definitely feel good about eating. And who doesn't love vegetables in their baked goods?

- ¼ cup (35 g) lightly packed grated carrot (about ½ medium carrot)
- ⅓ cup (25 g) coconut sugar
- 1 Tbsp (15 ml) unsweetened plain or vanilla almond, soy, or rice milk
- 2 Tbsp (30 ml) coconut nectar
- 2 tsp (10 ml) pure vanilla extract
- 1 Tbsp (15 ml) nut oil or extra-virgin olive oil, preferably organic
- 5 to 10 drops pure plain or vanilla stevia liquid, or to taste
- 1 cup (100 g) plus ¼ cup (25 g) old-fashioned rolled oats (not instant or quick-cooking)
- ⅔ cup plus 1 Tbsp (110 g) hemp seeds
- 2 tsp (10 ml) ground cinnamon
- ¾ tsp (3.5 ml) ground ginger
- ¼ tsp (1 ml) baking powder
- ¼ tsp (1 ml) baking soda
- ¼ tsp (1 ml) fine sea salt
- 2 tsp (10 ml) whole psyllium husks
- ⅓ cup (45 g) raisins, goji berries, or chopped dates (optional)

Preheat the oven to 350°F (180°C). Line 2 cookie sheets with parchment paper, or spray with nonstick spray.

In a medium bowl, stir together the grated carrot, coconut sugar, milk, coconut nectar, vanilla, oil, and stevia until well blended. Set aside.

In the bowl of a food processor, process the 1 cup (110 g) oats until they resemble coarse cornmeal. Add the hemp seeds, cinnamon, ginger, baking powder, baking soda, salt, and psyllium and continue to process until it begins to stick together in a solid "wall" on the sides of the processor. At this point, it will resemble moist sawdust that will fall apart when you separate it with your fingers (it should not resemble a moist dough that sticks together).

Drizzle the wet mixture in a ring over the dry ingredients in the processor and process until it just comes together in a dough. Add the last ¼ cup (30 g) oats to the processor and pulse two to four times just to incorporate, but not enough to completely blend the carrots (the shreds should still be visible). If using the raisins or other fruit, stir them in by hand at this point, but don't process again.

Using a small ice-cream scoop or tablespoon (15 ml), scoop out the dough onto the prepared cookie sheet and flatten to about ½ inch (1.25 cm) thick. Bake for 10 to 14 minutes, rotating the cookie sheets about halfway through baking, until the edges are golden. Allow to cool completely before removing from the cookie sheets. See page 37, storing your baked goods. May be frozen.

Lemony Walnut-Cinnamon Cookies ✱ SF, CF ✱

Makes 15 to 20

This is a staple recipe in my gluten-free cooking classes. Quick and easy, the cookies have a light taste and chewy texture that brings to mind Greek cuisine, with their combination of lemon and cinnamon. And the walnuts provide some excellent omega-3 fats to the mix!

2 cups (230 g) raw walnut halves
¼ cup (25 g) finely ground flax seeds (from about 2 Tbsp or 30 ml whole seeds)
2 tsp finely grated lemon zest (about 1 large lemon), preferably organic
¼ cup (35 g) brown rice flour
1½ tsp (7.5 ml) ground cinnamon
½ tsp (2.5 ml) baking soda
¼ tsp (1 ml) fine sea salt
¼ cup (60 ml) agave nectar, light or dark

Preheat the oven to 350°F (180°C). Line 2 cookie sheets with parchment paper, or spray with nonstick spray.

In the bowl of a food processor, whir the walnuts, flax, lemon zest, flour, cinnamon, baking soda, and salt until you have a very fine meal (there should be no chunks of walnut visible). Take care not to overmix, however, or you'll end up with nut butter!

Add the agave nectar and process again until the mixture begins to leave the sides of the processor bowl. It should be a moist dough that holds together when squeezed between your fingers.

Using a small ice-cream scoop or tablespoon (15 ml), roll mounds of dough into balls and place about 2 inches (5 cm) apart on the cookie sheets. Wet your palms (or use a silicone spatula) and flatten each ball to about ¼ inch (6 mm) thick.

Bake for 8 to 10 minutes, rotating the sheets about halfway through baking, until the edges are golden and the cookies are dry on top. Allow to cool completely before removing from the cookie sheets (these will firm up as they cool). See page 37, storing your baked goods. May be frozen.

Twice-Spiced Ginger Cookies ⁕ CF, SF, NF ⁕

Makes 18 to 20

These crisp and not-too-sweet cookies are a classic "dunker": that is, they are perfect to dunk into a steaming cup of tea or frosty glass of milk. If you're a fan of ginger, you'll love them.

¼ cup (60 ml) coconut oil, at room temperature, preferably organic
¼ cup (40 g) coconut sugar
¼ cup (60 ml) coconut nectar
20 to 30 drops pure plain, vanilla, or orange-flavored stevia liquid, or to taste
1 Tbsp (15 ml) finely grated fresh ginger
½ tsp (2.5 ml) pure vanilla extract
½ tsp (2.5 ml) apple cider vinegar
1½ tsp (7.5 ml) finely ground flax seeds (from about ¾ tsp or 3.5 ml whole seeds)
1 cup (135 g) Ricki's All-Purpose Gluten-Free Flour Mix (see page 22)
⅓ cup (45 g) sorghum flour
¾ tsp (3.5 ml) xanthan gum (use only Bob's Red Mill brand if you are concerned about a corn allergy)
½ tsp (2.5 ml) baking powder
½ tsp (2.5 ml) baking soda
⅛ tsp (.5 ml) fine sea salt
1 tsp (5 ml) Chinese five spice powder (or cinnamon)
¾ tsp (3.5 ml) ground ginger
Extra coconut sugar for tops of cookies, if desired

Preheat the oven to 350°F (180°C). Line 2 cookie sheets with parchment paper, or spray with nonstick spray.

In the bowl of a food processor, blend the coconut oil, coconut sugar, coconut nectar, stevia, fresh ginger, vanilla, vinegar and flax until well combined and the sugar is dissolved.

Add the remaining ingredients and pulse once or twice to incorporate, then process until a soft dough is formed.

Using a small ice-cream scoop or tablespoon (15 ml), place mounds of dough about 2 inches (5 cm) apart on cookie sheets. Wet the bottom of a glass and dip it in coconut sugar, if using; use the bottom to flatten each cookie to about ⅛ inch (3 mm) thick, adding more sugar to the bottom of the glass as needed.

Bake in the preheated oven for 13 to 15 minutes, rotating the sheets about halfway through, until golden on the edges and dry on top. Cool 5 minutes on the cookie sheets before removing to racks to cool completely. See page 37, storing your baked goods. May be frozen.

Glazed Almond Bars * CF *

Makes 1 dozen

Almond lovers, rejoice! Although the "glaze" on these bars is a bit unconventional (made with silken tofu), I was pleasantly surprised when they were a hit with virtually everyone who tried them, including my picky sister. The squares offer a buttery, rich base with a subtle almond flavor, topped with chopped almonds and a sticky, gooey glaze. These are fancy enough to serve to guests, but you may find you bake up a batch just to have for yourself!

FOR THE GLAZE:

¼ cup (60 ml) packed silken tofu
2 Tbsp (30 ml) tapioca starch
⅓ cup (80 ml) light agave nectar
½ tsp (2.5 ml) pure almond extract
Pinch fine sea salt

FOR THE BASE:

⅔ cup (50 g) coconut sugar
¼ cup (60 ml) unsweetened almond, soy, or rice milk
2 tsp (10 ml) pure vanilla extract
2 tsp (10 ml) pure almond extract
2 cups (265 g) Ricki's All-Purpose Gluten-Free Flour Mix (see page 22)
2½ tsp (12.5 ml) baking powder
2 tsp (10 ml) xanthan gum (use only Bob's Red Mill brand if you are concerned about a corn allergy)
¼ tsp (1 ml) pure stevia powder
2 Tbsp (30 ml) finely ground flax seeds (from about 1 Tbsp or 15 ml whole seeds)
¼ tsp (1 ml) fine sea salt
½ cup (120 ml) coconut oil, at room temperature, preferably organic
⅔ coarsely chopped, natural raw almonds, preferably organic (or use slivered almonds, if you prefer)

Preheat the oven to 350°F (180°C). Line a 9-inch (22.5-cm) square pan with parchment paper, or spray with nonstick spray.

Make the glaze: In the bowl of a food processor, whir all ingredients until perfectly smooth and no traces of tofu are visible. Scrape into a small bowl and set aside.

Make the base: In a small bowl, whisk together the coconut sugar, milk, vanilla, and almond extracts until the sugar dissolves. Set aside.

In the processor bowl (no need to wash it), pulse together the flour, baking powder, xanthan gum, stevia, flax, and salt. Drop the coconut oil by large tablespoons over the top, and process until well incorporated (the mixture should still look fairly dry and powdery).

Pour the coconut sugar–milk mixture over the flour mixture and process to a soft, sticky dough.

Bake and glaze the bars: Scrape the cookie base into the pan and spread evenly, smoothing the top. Sprinkle the almonds over the top as evenly as possible; press slightly into the dough. Bake for 25 minutes, until the base begins to puff up and is light golden brown at the edges.

Remove from the oven, drizzle with the glaze (it's all right if there are still some bare spots here and there; it will spread as it continues to bake), then rotate the pan and return it to the oven to bake for another 10 to 15 minutes, until the edges are browned and the glaze is mostly set (it might jiggle a bit in the middle; this is fine).

Cool completely before cutting into squares. See page 37, storing your baked goods. May be frozen.

Date-Free Squares ✱ SF, CF, NF ✱

Makes 6 to 8

These are so reminiscent of date squares, you won't believe it. With beans in the filling and sunflower seeds in the topping, these bars are not only delicious, they provide a good hit of protein in each sweet bite.

FOR THE FILLING:

2 cups well-cooked, rinsed, and drained black beans (from about ¾ cup or 95g dried; or use one 15 oz/325 ml or 19 oz/540 ml can)

2 large ripe pears, washed and cored, peeled or unpeeled

2 Tbsp (15 ml) carob powder

⅓ cup (25 g) coconut sugar

Pinch fine sea salt

2 tsp (10 ml) finely grated lemon zest (about 1 large lemon), preferably organic

2 Tbsp (30 ml) fresh lemon juice

2 tsp (10 ml) pure vanilla extract

⅛ tsp (.5 ml) pure stevia powder or ¼ tsp (1 ml) pure plain or vanilla stevia liquid, or to taste

1 Tbsp (15 ml) finely ground flax seeds (from about 1½ tsp or 7.5 ml whole seeds)

FOR THE TOPPING:

⅓ cup (45 g) sunflower seeds, lightly toasted

¼ cup (20 g) coconut sugar

⅓ cup (45 g) millet flour

1½ cups (150 g) old-fashioned rolled oats (not instant of quick-cooking), divided

1 Tbsp (15 ml) ground cinnamon

Pinch fine sea salt

20 to 30 drops pure plain or vanilla stevia liquid

¼ cup (60 ml) sunflower or coconut oil, melted (at low temperature), preferably organic

Up to ¼ cup (60 ml) water, if needed

Preheat the oven to 350°F (180°C). Line an 8½-inch (21.5-cm) square pan with parchment paper, or spray with nonstick spray.

Make the filling: Combine the beans, pears, carob powder, coconut sugar, salt, lemon zest, and lemon juice in a food processor and process until very smooth and no pieces of bean are visible.

Transfer the mixture to a medium pot and heat over medium-low heat until it begins to heave and sputter (it will be trying to boil, but will be too thick to do so). If you have a splatter screen, now is a good time to place it over the pot. If not, keep the cover on but leave an edge uncovered to allow steam to escape. Reduce the heat so that the mixture is still cooking, but not quite as actively. Stir the mixture often (about once every minute or so) as it continues to heave and give off steam, scraping the bottom of the pot with a silicone spatula as you stir (it will scorch very easily — keep stirring!). After about 20 minutes, the mixture will begin to darken and thicken up considerably. When done, it should be thicker than applesauce, almost as thick as, say, a smooth almond butter (this could take up to 30 minutes total). Remove from the heat, stir in the vanilla, stevia, and flax, and set aside while you make the topping.

(continued on page 128)

Date-Free Squares *continued* ✸ SF, CF, NF ✸

Make the topping: In a food processor, process the sunflower seeds, coconut sugar, flour, 1 cup (100 g) of the oats, cinnamon, and salt until it resembles cornmeal. Add the stevia and oil and pulse until the topping comes together in clumps. It should be slightly moist and stick together when pinched between your fingers. If the mixture is too dry, add a tablespoon (15 ml) or so of water at a time until it comes together in moist clumps, adding no more than ¼ cup (60 ml) total. Add the final ½ cup (50 g) oats and stir them into the mixture by hand, but don't process again.

Press about half the topping into the prepared pan (you can measure, or just estimate). Spread the filling evenly over it, then crumble the rest of the topping over the top (it's okay if there are spots of filling uncovered here or there). Press gently into the filling. Bake for 30 to 35 minutes, rotating the pan about halfway through baking, until the edges are golden. Allow to cool before cutting into squares. See page 37, storing your baked goods. May be frozen.

Banana Oat Bars ✷ CF, can be NF or SF ✷

Makes 12 to 16

These bars are almost like a homemade granola bar — not too sweet and equally suitable for breakfast, a snack on the go, or dessert. Although I don't consume bananas very often because of their high sugar content, these bars are a good reason for making an exception, once in a while.

- ½ cup (40 g) coconut sugar
- 20 to 30 drops pure plain or vanilla stevia liquid, or to taste
- 1 Tbsp (15 ml) finely ground flax seeds (from about 1½ tsp or 7.5 ml whole seeds)
- ¼ cup (60 ml) unsweetened plain or vanilla soy or almond milk
- ¼ cup (60 ml) sunflower or other light-tasting oil, preferably organic
- 1 tsp (5 ml) pure vanilla extract
- 1 Tbsp (15 ml) natural smooth almond or sunflower butter, at room temperature
- 2 medium, very ripe bananas
- ⅓ cup (40 g) raisins or dried cranberries (optional)
- 1½ cups (160 g) old-fashioned rolled oats (not instant or quick-cooking)
- ½ cup (40 g) unsweetened shredded coconut
- ¼ cup (30 g) whole oat flour (to make your own, see page 35)
- ½ tsp (2.5 ml) baking powder
- ⅛ tsp (.5 ml) fine sea salt

Preheat the oven to 350°F (180°C). Line an 8-inch (20-cm) square pan with parchment paper, or spray with nonstick spray.

In a medium bowl, whisk together the coconut sugar, stevia, flax, milk, oil, vanilla, and almond butter until the sugar is dissolved, 1 to 2 minutes. (Alternately, grind the sugar to a powder in a coffee grinder before mixing. It will then dissolve very quickly.)

Cut the bananas into chunks and add to the bowl. Using a potato masher or large fork, mash the bananas into the mixture, leaving a few little chunks here and there (about the size of peas). Stir in the raisins, if using. Set aside.

In a large bowl, combine the oats, shredded coconut, flour, baking powder, and salt. Pour the wet mixture over the dry and stir well to combine. It may seem too wet for a bar dough; this is as it should be.

Scrape the mixture into the pan and smooth the top. Bake for 40 to 45 minutes, rotating the pan about halfway through baking, until the top is dry and a tester inserted in the center comes out clean. Cool completely before cutting into bars. See page 37, storing your baked goods. May be frozen.

Cinnamon Coffee Bars ✱ SF, CF ✱

Makes 1 dozen

These bars taste incredibly decadent — you may find it hard to believe they are made with only ¼ cup (60 ml) sunflower oil and no refined sugars. If you like the taste of cinnamon, you will adore these chewy, rich confections.

- 2 tsp (10 ml) instant-coffee substitute, such as Dandy Blend, or use 1 tsp (5 ml) instant coffee (see page 34)
- 4 tsp (20 ml) water
- 4 tsp (20 ml) pure vanilla extract
- ½ cup (40 g) coconut sugar
- ½ cup (120 ml) coconut nectar
- ¼ cup (60 ml) sunflower or other light-tasting oil, preferably organic
- 1 cup (135 g) Ricki's All-Purpose Gluten-Free Flour Mix (see page 22)
- ½ cup (75 g) sorghum flour
- 4 tsp (20 ml) ground cinnamon
- ½ tsp (2.5 ml) baking powder
- ¾ tsp (7.5 ml) xanthan gum (use only Bob's Red Mill brand if you are concerned about a corn allergy)
- ⅛ tsp (.5 ml) fine sea salt
- ¾ cup (85 g) pecan halves or pieces, lightly toasted

Preheat the oven to 350°F (180°C). Line a 9-inch (22.5-cm) square pan with parchment paper, or spray with nonstick spray.

In the bottom of a medium bowl, mix the coffee substitute, water, vanilla, coconut sugar, and coconut nectar until the sugar dissolves. Add the oil and blend well. Set aside.

In a large bowl, sift the all-purpose flour, sorghum flour, cinnamon, baking powder, xanthan gum, and salt. Pour the wet mixture over the dry and mix well to combine. Gently mix in the pecans. You will have a very thick and sticky batter.

Spread evenly in the pan and smooth the top. Bake for 20 to 25 minutes, rotating the pan about halfway through baking, until a tester inserted in the center comes out moist but clean (do not overbake!).

Allow bars to cool 5 minutes in the pan before removing to a rack (they will firm up considerably as they cool). See page 37, storing your baked goods. May be frozen.

Full of
of your

Apple Pumpkin Crumble Bars * CF, can be SF *

Makes 9 large bars

Dense, moist, and not too sweet, these bars may feel more like a breakfast food than dessert but are great either way. The filling here is almost like applesauce with a kick of pumpkin and is not meant to be gooey like pie filling. These bars are even better the second day, after the crust has a chance to absorb some of the moisture from the filling and softens up a bit.

FOR THE CRUMBLE:

- ⅓ cup (80 ml) coconut oil, melted (at low temperature), preferably organic
- 2 Tbsp (30 ml) coconut nectar
- ¼ tsp (1 ml) pure stevia powder or ½ tsp (2.5 ml) pure plain or vanilla stevia liquid, or to taste
- 1 Tbsp (15 ml) whole psyllium husks
- ½ cup (120 ml) plain or vanilla soy, almond, or rice milk, at room temperature
- 2 tsp (10 ml) finely grated lemon zest (about 1 large lemon), preferably organic
- ¾ cup (80 g) walnut pieces
- ½ cup (90 g) natural raw almonds with skins, preferably organic
- 1 cup (115 g) old-fashioned rolled oats (not instant or quick-cooking)
- ⅓ cup (45 g) coconut flour
- 2 Tbsp (30 ml) ground cinnamon
- 1½ tsp (7.5 ml) ground ginger
- ¼ tsp (1 ml) cardamom (optional)
- ⅛ tsp (.5 ml) fine sea salt

FOR THE FILLING:

- 3 medium sweet apples, such as Gala or Red Delicious, cored, and grated on large holes of a box grater or cut in chunks, peeled or unpeeled (see instructions)
- 1½ cups (360 ml) canned or homemade unsweetened pumpkin puree (see page 23)
- ¼ cup (40 g) coconut sugar
- 2 Tbsp (30 ml) whole psyllium husks
- 2 Tbsp (30 ml) freshly squeezed lemon juice
- 1 tsp (5 ml) pure vanilla extract
- ½ tsp (2.5 ml) drops pure plain or vanilla stevia liquid, or to taste

Make the crumble: Preheat the oven to 350°F (180°C). Line a 9-inch (22.5-cm) square pan with parchment paper, or spray with nonstick spray.

In the bottom of a large bowl, whisk together the melted coconut oil, coconut nectar, stevia, psyllium, milk, and lemon zest; set aside (don't worry if the mixture appears curdled at this point).

In the bowl of a food processor, blend together the remaining crumble ingredients until the mixture resembles a coarse meal (there should be no pieces of nuts visible). Add the dry ingredients to the wet mixture in the bowl and toss with a fork (as if making pie dough) until it comes together in a very moist yet crumbly dough (it might feel a bit too moist at this point, but should become more crumbly as it sits). Set aside while you prepare the filling.

Make the filling: If using grated apples, place all the filling ingredients in a bowl and mix together until well combined. Alternately, if using apple chunks, place the apples in the bowl of the food processor (you can just use the same processor bowl you used to blend the dry ingredients; no need to wash) and pulse to break up, then process until well chopped. Add remaining filling ingredients and process until smooth.

Remove about 1 cup (240 ml) of the crumble mixture, unpacked, and set aside. Press the remaining crumble into the bottom of the prepared pan. Top with the filling, spreading evenly. Sprinkle the remaining crumble mixture evenly over the filling (there will be spots of filling left uncovered) and press gently with the palms of your hands.

Bake in the preheated oven until the edges are browned and the top of the crumble begins to brown a bit, 40 to 50 minutes, rotating the pan about halfway through. (The filling won't bubble the way typical fruit-pie fillings do). Allow to cool to room temperature before cutting into squares; reheat to serve. See page 37, storing your baked goods. May be frozen.

Ultra Fudgy Brownies ✸ CF, can be SF or NF ✸

Makes 12 to 16

One of the gripes of vegan bakers is that it's difficult to achieve a brownie texture that is truly fudgy rather than cake-like. Well, here they are: the ultimate fudgy brownies! The addition of pureed avocado creates a little miracle of chemistry, combined with just ¼ cup (60 ml) oil. The result is one of the richest-tasting, fudgiest brownies I've ever had.

- ¼ cup (60 ml) packed avocado puree (see page 28) (from about 1 small, barely ripe avocado)
- ¾ cup (55 g) coconut sugar
- ⅓ cup (80 ml) coconut nectar
- ½ tsp (2.5 ml) pure stevia powder or 1 tsp (5 ml) pure plain or vanilla stevia liquid, or to taste
- 2 tsp (10 ml) pure vanilla extract
- ¼ cup (60 ml) sunflower or other light-tasting oil, preferably organic
- 1 Tbsp (15 ml) finely ground flax seeds (from about 1½ tsp or 7.5 ml whole seeds)
- ⅓ cup (80 ml) unsweetened plain or vanilla almond or soy milk
- 2 tsp (10 ml) instant coffee substitute, such as Dandy Blend, or 1 tsp (5 ml) instant coffee (see page 34)
- ¾ cup (100 g) Ricki's All-Purpose Gluten-Free Flour Mix (see page 22)
- ½ cup (50 g) whole oat flour (to make your own, see page 35)
- ¾ cup (80 g) cocoa powder, preferably non-alkalized
- 1 Tbsp (15 ml) whole psyllium husks
- ½ tsp (2.5 ml) baking powder
- ¼ tsp (1 ml) baking soda
- ¼ tsp (1 ml) fine sea salt
- ⅓ cup (65 g) unsweetened carob chips, dairy-free chocolate chips, or walnut pieces

Preheat the oven to 350°F (180°C). Line an 8-inch (20-cm) square pan with parchment paper, or spray with nonstick spray.

In the bowl of a food processor, combine the avocado, coconut sugar, coconut nectar, stevia, vanilla, oil, flax, milk, and coffee substitute until smooth. Add the all-purpose flour, oat flour, cocoa powder, psyllium, baking powder, baking soda, and salt and process until combined. Resist the urge to add more liquid; this batter is very thick! Stir in the chips, but do not process again.

Turn the batter into the pan and spread evenly (you may need to hold the parchment paper in place with your thumb as you do so, or the batter might pull the paper with it as you spread). Smooth the top.

Bake for 20 to 25 minutes, rotating the pan about halfway through baking, until a tester inserted in the center comes out moist but clean. Do not overbake (longer baking time will result in cake-like brownies).

Cool for at least 15 minutes, then refrigerate until completely chilled before slicing into squares. The brownies will firm up as they chill. (Alternately, you can freeze the brownies in the pan, then invert onto a cutting board, peel off the parchment paper, and slice into squares). See page 37, storing your baked goods. May be frozen.

Butterscotch Blondies with Chocolate Chips and Goji Berries ✱ SF, CF, NF ✱

Makes 16

These are a favorite dessert in our house. They are rich tasting and chewy, and the combination of lucuma with coconut sugar and coconut nectar is, I think, very reminiscent of butterscotch. I love using dried, super-healthy goji berries in these bars, but dried cherries or cranberries work just as well. In fact, feel free to stir in any additions you like, as long as you keep the same proportions. For instance, one alternative I really enjoy is pistachios and chopped dried apricots.

- 1 cup (135 g) Ricki's All-Purpose Gluten-Free Flour Mix (see page 22)
- ¾ cup (75 g) whole oat flour (to make your own, see page 35)
- 3 Tbsp (45 ml) lucuma powder
- 1 tsp (5 ml) baking powder
- ½ tsp (2.5 ml) baking soda
- ¼ tsp (1 ml) fine sea salt
- 1 tsp (5 ml) xanthan gum (use only Bob's Red Mill brand if you are concerned about a corn allergy)
- ⅓ cup (25 g) coconut sugar
- 1 Tbsp (15 ml) water
- ½ cup (120 ml) coconut nectar
- ⅛ tsp (.5 ml) pure stevia powder or ¼ tsp (1 ml) pure plain or vanilla stevia liquid, or to taste
- ⅓ cup (90 ml) sunflower or other light-tasting oil, preferably organic
- 1 Tbsp (30 ml) pure vanilla extract
- ¼ tsp (1 ml) rum, butterscotch, or brandy flavoring (optional)
- ½ cup (100 g) unsweetened carob chips or dairy-free dark chocolate chips
- ⅓ cup (80 ml) dried goji berries, cherries, cranberries, or dried fruit of your choice

Preheat the oven to 325°F (170°C). Line an 8-inch (20-cm) square pan with parchment paper, or spray well with nonstick spray.

In a medium bowl, sift together the flours, lucuma powder, baking powder, baking soda, salt, and xanthan gum.

In a large bowl, mix the coconut sugar and water until the sugar begins to dissolve. Add the coconut nectar, stevia, oil, vanilla, and flavoring, if using, until well blended. Gently stir in the chips and gojis.

Pour the dry mixture over the wet ingredients and stir to blend. You will have a thick and sticky batter. Turn the batter into the prepared pan and smooth the top.

Bake for 20 to 25 minutes, rotating the pan about halfway through baking, until a tester inserted in the center comes out just barely clean (a moist crumb or two is fine). Take care not to overbake, as these will dry out! The top may fall a little as it cools; this is fine. Allow to cool completely in pan before cutting into squares. See page 37, storing your baked goods. May be frozen.

Happy Hemp Two-Bite Brownies ✱ SF, CF ✱

Makes 9

These brownies are a perfect little treat for after school, with tea, or when you want a little pick-me-up. The combination of almonds and hemp seeds provides a good hit of protein, making these a healthy indulgence. Because of the wetness of this batter, it bakes best in small, individual quantities, making a mini-muffin pan ideal. If you don't have a mini-muffin pan, you might try making them in a regular-size muffin pan, filling them halfway.

- ¼ cup (20 g) coconut sugar
- ⅛ tsp (.5 ml) pure stevia powder or ¼ tsp (1 ml) pure plain or vanilla stevia liquid, or to taste
- 3 Tbsp (45 ml) water
- 2 tsp (10 ml) pure vanilla extract
- 1 Tbsp plus 1 tsp (20 ml total) olive or nut oil of your choice (see *Note*)
- 1 cup (160 g) natural raw skin-on almonds, preferably organic
- ¼ heaping cup (30 g) hemp seeds
- 2 heaping Tbsp (15 g) unsweetened cocoa powder, preferably non-alkalized
- ¼ tsp (1 ml) baking soda
- ¼ tsp (1 ml) baking powder
- ¼ tsp (1 ml) fine sea salt

Preheat the oven to 350°F (180°C). Line 9 mini-muffin cups with mini paper liners. If you don't have the liners, spray 9 compartments of a mini-muffin tin with nonstick spray or grease with coconut oil, then dust with cocoa. Tap out any excess cocoa by inverting the pan and tapping on the bottom of each compartment; place upright and set aside.

In a small bowl or glass measuring cup, combine the coconut sugar, stevia, water, vanilla, and oil and stir to begin dissolving the sugar. Set aside.

In the bowl of a food processor, whir together the almonds, hemp, cocoa powder, baking soda, baking powder, and salt until you have what looks like a powder (there should be no pieces of almond or hemp seed visible — this may take a few minutes). Add the wet ingredients and blend for a second or two, just until combined. Scrape the sides of the processor bowl if necessary.

Using a small ice-cream scoop or tablespoon (15 ml), divide the batter (it will be thick and sticky) evenly among the prepared muffin cups; they should be very full. Bake for 15 to 18 minutes, rotating the pan about halfway through baking, until a tester comes out clean (it's okay if it still has a few moist crumbs clinging to it). Allow to cool 10 minutes before removing from the pan. Cool completely before consuming (if you can stand it!). See page 37, storing your baked goods. May be frozen.

Note: I use macadamia oil for these brownies; however, walnut or almond oil would be great in these, too.

Best Bean Brownies ✸ CF, can be NF or SF ✸

Makes 1 dozen

There are several bean-brownie recipes on the Internet, but when I created these, I'd never come across another gluten-free version. These brownies are moist, dense, and fudgy, with the added bonus of fiber from the white beans (and yes, that really is 2 tablespoons or 30 ml of vanilla extract in the recipe!). Don't worry: You won't be able to tell the beans are in them after they're baked.

2 cups (480 ml) very well-cooked, drained white or navy beans (see Note)
½ cup (120 ml) chocolate or vanilla soy or almond milk or coconut beverage (the kind that comes in a carton)
3 Tbsp (30 ml) tahini (sesame seed paste), sunflower seed butter, or almond butter, at room temperature
⅓ cup (80 ml) sunflower or other light-tasting oil, preferably organic
2 Tbsp (30 ml) pure vanilla extract
1 tsp (5 ml) wheat-free tamari or soy sauce
1 cup (160 g) coconut sugar
⅓ cup (80 ml) coconut nectar
⅛ tsp (.5 ml) pure stevia powder or ¼ tsp (1 ml) pure plain or vanilla stevia liquid, or to taste
½ cup (80 g) teff flour
½ cup (70 g) unsweetened cocoa powder (preferably non-alkalized)
¼ cup (20 g) whole psyllium husks
½ tsp (2.5 ml) baking powder
¼ tsp (1 ml) baking soda
¼ tsp (1 ml) fine sea salt
½ cup (100 g) unsweetened carob chips or dairy-free chocolate chips

Preheat the oven to 350°F (180°C). Line a 9-inch (22.5-cm) square pan with parchment paper, or spray with nonstick spray.

In a powerful blender (a food processor is not suitable for this recipe), blend the beans and milk until you have a very smooth puree. Add the tahini, oil, vanilla, tamari, coconut sugar, coconut nectar, and stevia, and blend again, scraping down the sides as necessary, until you have a perfectly smooth, velvety puree with not even a trace of graininess or grit, up to 10 minutes. (This may take some patience — you may need to scrape down the sides up to a dozen times, depending on the style and strength of your blender.)

In a large bowl, sift together the teff flour, cocoa powder, psyllium, baking powder, baking soda, and salt. Add the wet mixture to the dry and top with the carob chips. Stir until well combined (the batter should be quite thick). Spread the batter evenly in the prepared pan and smooth the top.

Bake for 50 to 65 minutes, rotating the pan about halfway through baking, until a tester inserted in the center comes out moist but clean (it may have one or two crumbs still clinging to it). Remove from the oven and cool completely before cutting. To speed the cooling process, you can place the pan in the refrigerator until cool and then cut the brownies; note that they will crumble apart if you try to cut them while still warm. Serve chilled or at room temperature. Store, covered, for up to 4 days in the refrigerator. May be frozen.

Note: I used about ¾ cup (135 g) dried beans, soaked overnight, then drained and cooked; if using canned beans, rinse well with water and drain very well before measuring.

Sweet Potato Brownies ✱ SF, CF, NF ✱

Makes 12 to 16

One of my favorite cookbooks is *Simple Treats* by Ellen Abraham. I've been inspired by many of Abraham's recipes, but her Double Fudge Pecan Brownies are my all-time favorite. This is my spin on her brownie recipe, the first I encountered that used sweet potato.

¾ cup (120 g) packed sweet potato puree (see page 23)
¾ cup (55 g) coconut sugar
¼ cup (125 g) coconut nectar
1½ Tbsp (22.5 ml) pure vanilla extract
⅓ cup (80 ml) sunflower or other light-tasting oil, preferably organic
1 Tbsp (15 ml) whole psyllium husks
½ cup (50 g) old-fashioned rolled oats (not instant or quick-cooking)
½ cup (65 g) Ricki's All-Purpose Gluten-Free Flour Mix (see page 22)
⅔ cup (60 g) unsweetened cocoa powder, preferably non-alkalized
½ tsp (2.5 ml) pure stevia powder, or 1 tsp (5 ml) pure plain or vanilla stevia liquid, or to taste
Scant ½ tsp (2 ml) baking powder
¼ tsp (1 ml) fine sea salt
⅓ cup (65 g) unsweetened carob chips or dairy-free chocolate chips

Preheat the oven to 350°F (180°C). Line an 8½-inch (21.5-cm) square pan with parchment paper, or spray with nonstick spray.

In a medium bowl, whisk together the sweet potato puree, coconut sugar, coconut nectar, vanilla, oil, and psyllium until the sugar has begun to dissolve. Set aside.

Using a coffee grinder, grind the oats until they resemble a coarse meal. Transfer to a large bowl and sift in the flour, cocoa powder, stevia, baking powder, and salt; stir a few times to evenly distribute the ingredients.

Stir the sweet potato mixture once more, then pour over the dry ingredients and mix just until blended. Gently stir in the chips.

Spread the mixture evenly in the pan and smooth the top. Bake for 25 to 30 minutes, rotating the pan halfway through baking, until a tester inserted in the middle comes out clean (it may appear moist; this is fine). Cool completely before cutting into squares.

Dalmatian Cheesecake Brownies * CF *

Makes 16 to 20

This fantastic combination of a dark, not-too-sweet brownie topped with a layer of chocolate-dotted "cheesecake" makes a spectacular dessert for a special occasion. These confections are very rich, so a little goes a long way.

FOR THE CHEESECAKE TOPPING:

1 (12-oz or 350-g) box aseptically packaged firm or extra-firm silken tofu, such as Mori-Nu (see page 30); not the kind packed in water and displayed in refrigerated coolers

½ cup (120 ml) natural smooth cashew butter, at room temperature

½ cup (120 ml) light agave nectar

1 Tbsp (15 ml) fresh lemon juice

1 tsp (5 ml) pure vanilla extract

½ tsp (2.5 ml) pure almond extract

Pinch fine sea salt

⅔ cup (135 g) unsweetened carob chips or dairy-free chocolate chips

FOR THE BROWNIE BASE:

5 oz (140 g) pitted prunes (dried plums), coarsely chopped (if they're not soft, soak in hot water for 5 minutes and drain before using; 10 to 12 large or 18 to 23 small prunes)

½ cup (120 ml) water or rice milk

¾ cup plus 2 Tbsp (120 g total) coconut sugar

¼ cup (60 ml) coconut nectar

⅛ tsp (.5 ml) pure stevia powder or ¼ tsp (1ml) pure plain or vanilla stevia liquid, or to taste

1 Tbsp (15 ml) pure vanilla extract

2 Tbsp (30 ml) finely ground flax seeds (from about 1 Tbsp or 15 ml whole seeds)

6 Tbsp sunflower or other light-tasting oil, preferably organic

1 cup (135 g) Ricki's All-Purpose Gluten-Free Flour Mix (see page 22)

2 Tbsp (30 ml) coconut flour

¾ cup (90 g) unsweetened cocoa powder, preferably non-alkalized

¼ tsp (1 ml) baking powder

½ tsp (2.5 ml) baking soda

¾ tsp (7.5 ml) xanthan gum (use only Bob's Red Mill brand if you are concerned about a corn allergy)

¼ tsp (1 ml) fine sea salt

Preheat the oven to 350°F (180°C). Line a 9-inch (22.5-cm) square pan with parchment paper, or spray with nonstick spray.

Make the cheesecake topping: In the bowl of a food processor, process the tofu and cashew butter until smooth and no pieces of tofu are visible. Add the agave nectar, lemon juice, vanilla, almond extract, and salt and process again, stopping to scrape the sides of the bowl occasionally, until you have a perfectly smooth mixture. Turn the mixture into a medium bowl, scraping as much as you can from the processor, but don't bother to wash it (you'll use it again in a moment). Fold the chocolate chips into the cheesecake mixture. Set aside.

Make the brownie base: Combine the prunes, water, coconut sugar, coconut nectar, stevia, and vanilla in the bowl of a food processor and process until smooth. Add the flax, oil, all-purpose flour, coconut flour, cocoa powder, baking powder, baking soda, xanthan gum, and salt and process until combined. The mixture should be very thick, like a soft cookie dough; if it's truly too thick, add another tablespoon (15 ml) of water and process again. Spread or press into the bottom of the prepared pan and pat with a spatula to smooth the top.

Bake and serve: Bake for 12 minutes, then remove the partially baked brownie and pour the cheesecake topping over it, smoothing the top with a rubber spatula. Bake for an additional 30 to 40 minutes, rotating the pan about halfway through baking, until the top begins to brown around the edges and the center of the cheesecake jiggles just a bit when you shake the pan (the regular testing methods don't work for this recipe, as the center will test underdone even when the brownie is ready).

Allow to cool completely at room temperature, then cover and refrigerate. The brownie should be served cold. See page 37, storing your baked goods. May be frozen; defrost, covered, in the refrigerator overnight before serving.

Coconut Macaroons * SF, CF *

Makes 14 to 16

One of the most requested cookies when I had my bakery, Bake It Healthy, these sweet treats combine both ground almonds and coconut for an ultra-chewy base. Tahini is a terrific source of calcium. (If you're not a fan, don't worry; the flavor isn't prominent here).

- ¾ cup (135 g) natural raw skin-on almonds, preferably organic
- 2 Tbsp (15 g) finely ground flax seeds (from about 1 Tbsp or 15 ml whole seeds)
- ⅛ tsp (.5 ml) fine sea salt
- 2 cups (135 g) unsweetened shredded coconut, medium shred
- ¼ cup (60 ml) coconut nectar
- ¼ cup (60 ml) light agave nectar
- 20 to 25 drops pure plain or vanilla stevia liquid, or to taste
- ¼ cup (60 ml) tahini (sesame seed paste)
- 1 tsp (5 ml) pure vanilla extract
- ½ tsp (2.5 ml) pure coconut extract (optional)

Preheat the oven to 350°F (180°C). Line 2 cookie sheets with parchment paper, or spray with nonstick spray.

In the bowl of a food processor, whir the almonds, flax, and salt together until they resemble a coarse meal, about the texture of cornmeal, without any identifiable pieces of almond visible. Add the coconut and pulse once or twice to combine.

Next pour the coconut nectar, agave nectar, stevia, tahini, vanilla, and coconut extract, if using, over the dry ingredients. Process again until everything is incorporated and the mixture forms a sticky ball (you may need to stop and scrape down the sides of the processor bowl once or twice). Stop as soon as the mixture holds together, to avoid grinding the coconut too fine.

Using a small ice-cream scoop or tablespoon (15 ml), drop small mounds of the mixture onto the cookie sheets about 1 inch (2.5 cm) apart. Wet your palms (or use a silicone spatula) and flatten the cookies slightly.

Bake for 10 to 12 minutes, rotating the cookie sheets about halfway through baking, until the cookies are deep golden brown on top. Cool completely before removing to a rack (the cookies will firm up as they cool). See page 37, storing your baked goods. May be frozen.

Pecan Coconut Chews — Raw or Baked! ✸ GF, SF, CF ✸

Makes 20 to 22

When I first learned I could no longer eat wheat, I created these cookies, assuming "no wheat" meant "no flour of any kind." These days, I bake with alternate flours, but these cookies remain a grain-free favorite. Because the ingredients can all be eaten raw, you can also pat the mixture into a 9-inch (22.5-cm) square pan, refrigerate, and cut into squares for an equally delicious unbaked treat.

- 3½ oz (110 g) pitted prunes (dried plums)
- Boiling water, to cover prunes (see instructions)
- 3 Tbsp (45 ml) coconut sugar
- 1 tsp (5 ml) pure vanilla extract
- 2 cups (235 g) raw pecan halves or pieces
- 1 Tbsp finely grated orange zest (about 1 large orange), preferably organic
- 1 Tbsp (15 ml) finely ground flax seeds (from about 1 Tbsp or 15 ml whole seeds)
- ¼ tsp (1 ml) ground ginger
- ⅛ tsp (.5 ml) fine sea salt
- 1 cup (80 g) unsweetened shredded coconut

Preheat the oven to 350°F (180°C). Line 2 cookie sheets with parchment paper, or spray with nonstick spray.

Place the prunes in a heatproof bowl and cover with boiling water. Allow to soak 5 minutes, then drain, reserving 1 Tbsp (15 ml) of the soaking water. Return the prunes to the bowl along with the reserved soaking water, coconut sugar, and vanilla; stir to dissolve the sugar. Set aside.

In the bowl of a food processor, whir together the pecans, orange zest, flax, ginger, and salt. Add the coconut and whir just to break the coconut up a bit.

Add the prune mixture, and process until the mixture comes together in a moist "dough."

Using a small ice-cream scoop or tablespoon (15 ml), scoop the dough and roll into balls. Place on the prepared cookie sheets about 1 inch (2.5 cm) apart. Wet your palms (or use a silicone spatula) and flatten the cookies to about ¼ inch (6 mm) thick. Alternately, for unbaked bars, pat the mixture into a 9-inch (22.5-cm) square pan that's been lined with parchment paper or sprayed with nonstick spray, and refrigerate.

Bake for 12 to 15 minutes, rotating the cookie sheets about halfway through, until cookies are golden on the edges and dry on top. Allow to cool completely before removing from the cookie sheets. May be frozen.

Chapter 3: *Cakes, Cupcakes, Toppings & Frostings*

Holiday Apple Cake (Bundt Cake) * CF, SF or NF *

Makes 1 Bundt cake, serves 20 to 24

A cake this big and bursting with apples really does evoke a celebration. My mom used to bake a similar cake for the holidays in our house. With its double layer of cinnamon-soaked apples and moist cake layers, this beauty will likely become a favorite at your house, too. My favorite varieties of apple for this cake are Spartan and Northern Spy.

FOR THE FILLING:

2 medium apples, cored and thinly sliced, peeled or unpeeled
¼ cup (60 ml) coconut sugar
1 Tbsp (15 ml) ground cinnamon

FOR THE CAKE:

½ cup (40 g) coconut sugar
½ cup (120 ml) coconut nectar
1½ cups (360 ml) unsweetened plain or vanilla soy or almond milk
1 Tbsp (15 ml) pure vanilla extract
1 Tbsp (15 ml) apple cider vinegar
1 tsp (5 ml) pure lemon extract
2 tsp (10 ml) finely ground chia seeds (from about 1 tsp or 5 ml whole seeds)
⅓ cup (80 ml) sunflower or other light-tasting oil, preferably organic
1¾ cups (230 g) Ricki's All-Purpose Gluten-Free Flour Mix (see page 22)
½ cup (60 g) quinoa flour
¼ tsp (1 ml) pure stevia powder, or scant ½ tsp (2 ml) pure plain or vanilla stevia liquid
1 Tbsp (15 ml) baking powder
1 tsp (5 ml) baking soda
2 tsp (10 ml) xanthan gum (use only Bob's Red Mill brand if you are concerned about a corn allergy)
½ tsp (2.5 ml) fine sea salt

Preheat the oven to 350°F (180°C). Lightly grease a 12-cup (27-cm or 2.9-L) Bundt pan with coconut oil, or spray with nonstick spray.

Make the filling: In a medium bowl, toss the apple slices with the coconut sugar and cinnamon; set aside.

Make the cake: In another medium bowl, combine the coconut sugar, coconut nectar, milk, vanilla, vinegar, and lemon extract; stir until the sugar dissolves. Add the chia and oil and stir again. Set aside.

In a large bowl, sift the all-purpose flour, quinoa flour, stevia, baking powder, baking soda, xanthan gum, and salt. Pour the wet mixture over the dry and stir to blend.

Assemble and bake: Spoon about ⅓ of the batter into the bottom of the pan (you can just estimate) and spread to cover the bottom. Cover with a layer of about ½ the apples, taking care not to let apples touch the sides of the pan (it's not a tragedy if they do happen to touch the sides, but it will make it a bit more difficult to remove the cake from the pan without it breaking). Top with another ⅓ of the batter, gently spreading to cover the apples as completely as possible. Add the rest of the apples, again taking care not to touch the sides of the pan; finish with the last ⅓ of the batter, and gently smooth the top. All the apples should be covered with batter; if a tiny edge or point of apple sticks out from the batter on top, this is fine, but most should be under batter. Lift the pan 1 or 2 inches (2.5 or 5 cm) off the counter and then drop it down again to help the batter settle into the spaces between the apple slices; repeat once more.

Bake for 55 to 65 minutes, rotating the pan about halfway through baking, until a tester inserted halfway between the outside and inside walls of the pan comes out clean (it can be moist from the apples, but shouldn't have any batter on it). The cake should be domed on top and very well browned.

Allow the cake to cool in the pan for 20 to 30 minutes before turning out onto a rack and cooling completely. This cake is lovely plain, with ice cream, or with Coconut Whipped "Cream" (page 168). Store, covered, in the refrigerator, for up to 3 days. Serve cold or at room temperature. May be frozen.

Lemon Poppy Seed Bundt Cake * CF, SF or NF *

Makes 1 Bundt cake, serves 20 to 24

This is a "major" cake, big enough for a grand occasion. If you've got a party to feed or a buffet table to fill, a Bundt cake like this one makes an impressive offering. For smaller occasions, halve the recipe and bake the cake in an 8-inch (20-cm) square pan instead.

- 2 Tbsp (30 ml) finely grated lemon zest (about 3 very large or 4 medium lemons), preferably organic
- ¾ cup (125 g) coconut sugar
- ½ tsp (2.5 ml) pure stevia powder or 1 tsp (5 ml) pure plain or vanilla stevia liquid, or to taste
- ½ cup (120 ml) freshly squeezed lemon juice
- ¼ cup (60 ml) water
- 3 Tbsp (45 ml) finely ground flax seeds (from about 1½ Tbsp or 22.5 ml whole seeds)
- 1½ cups (360 ml) unsweetened plain or vanilla soy or almond milk
- ⅔ cup (160 ml) sunflower or other light-tasting oil, preferably organic
- 2 tsp (10 ml) pure vanilla extract
- 2 tsp (10 ml) pure lemon extract
- 1 tsp (5 ml) apple cider vinegar
- 2 Tbsp (10 ml) poppy seeds
- 3¼ cups (425 g) Ricki's All-Purpose Gluten-Free Flour Mix (see page 22)
- ½ cup (80 g) sweet rice flour
- 1 Tbsp (15 ml) xanthan gum (use only Bob's Red Mill brand if you are concerned about a corn allergy)
- 2 tsp (10 ml) baking powder
- 2 tsp (10 ml) baking soda
- ½ tsp (2.5 ml) fine sea salt

Preheat oven to 350°F (180°C). Lightly grease a 12-cup (27-cm or 2.9-L) Bundt pan with coconut oil, or spray with nonstick spray.

In a medium bowl, combine the lemon zest, coconut sugar, stevia, lemon juice, water, flax, milk, oil, vanilla, lemon extract, vinegar, and poppy seeds; stir until the sugar begins to dissolve. Set aside.

In a large bowl, sift together the all-purpose flour, sweet rice flour, xanthan gum, baking powder, baking soda, and salt. Pour the wet ingredients over the dry and use a whisk to blend just until smooth. Alternately, beat with electric beaters at low speed just until combined, but take care not to overmix. The batter will begin to foam up a bit; this is as it should be (you don't want to deflate it by overmixing).

Gently turn the batter into the pan and smooth the top. Bake for 55 to 65 minutes (or 25 to 35, if making a half recipe in an 8-inch or 20-cm square pan), rotating the pan once about halfway through baking, until a tester inserted in the center comes out clean. Allow to cool in the pan for 10 minutes before inverting onto a rack to cool completely. If desired, top with Lemon Coconut Buttercream Frosting (see Variations, page 170) or Lemon Whipped Cream (see Variations, page 169). See page 37, storing your baked goods; serve at room temperature. May be frozen.

Pear and Cranberry Cornmeal Cake * SF or NF *

Makes one 10-inch (25-cm) cake, serves 8 to 10

This cake offers the perfect marriage of a light, tender crumb and a tart, fruity filling. Use it as a great ending to a meal or as a snack to carry you through to the next one. Because most conventional corn is genetically modified, I recommend using organic cornmeal in this recipe. Feel free to substitute apples for the pears.

- ⅓ cup (55 g) coconut sugar
- ½ to 1 tsp (2.5 to 5 ml) pure stevia powder or 1 to 2 tsp (5 to 10 ml) pure plain or vanilla stevia liquid, or to taste
- ¾ cup (360 ml) unsweetened plain or vanilla almond or soy milk
- 1 tsp (5 ml) apple cider vinegar
- 1 Tbsp (15 ml) finely ground chia seeds (from about 1½ tsp or 7.5 ml whole seeds)
- 2 tsp (10 ml) pure vanilla extract
- 2 tsp (10 ml) finely grated lemon zest (about 1 large lemon), preferably organic
- ¼ cup (60 ml) coconut oil, melted (at low temperature), preferably organic
- 1½ cups (200 g) Ricki's All-Purpose Gluten-Free Flour Mix (see page 22)
- ¼ cup (35 g) brown rice flour
- 1 Tbsp (15 ml) baking powder
- ½ tsp (2.5 ml) baking soda
- ½ tsp (2.5 ml) fine sea salt
- ¾ tsp (7.5 ml) xanthan gum (use only Bob's Red Mill brand if you are concerned about a corn allergy)
- ½ cup (85 g) cornmeal, preferably organic
- 2 pears, such as Anjou or Bartlett, cored and diced, peeled or unpeeled
- 1 cup (105 g) fresh or frozen cranberries

Preheat the oven to 350°F (180°C). Line a 10-inch (25-cm) flan pan, springform pan, or pie plate with parchment paper, or spray with nonstick spray.

In a medium bowl, whisk together the coconut sugar, stevia, milk, vinegar, chia, vanilla, and lemon zest until the sugar has dissolved. Add the coconut oil and whisk to blend. Set aside.

In a large bowl, sift the all-purpose flour, rice flour, baking powder, baking soda, salt, and xanthan gum. Add the cornmeal and stir together to distribute everything evenly.

Pour the wet mixture over the dry and stir to blend well. Fold in the pears and cranberries. Turn the batter into the prepared pan and gently smooth the top.

Bake in the preheated oven for 35 to 45 minutes, rotating the pan about halfway through, until a tester inserted in the middle comes out clean. Serve warm or at room temperature. See page 37, storing your baked goods. May be frozen.

Blueberry Coffee Cake * CF, SF *

Makes one 9-inch (22.5-cm) cake, serves 9 to 12

My mom used to bake a wonderful coffee cake topped with a mixture of cinnamon and sugar. This is my revamped, gluten-free, and low-glycemic version. An easy, delicious cake that's really satisfying without being too sweet, it's perfect for a light dessert, yet also substantial enough to serve at brunch. Feel free to substitute other berries if you prefer.

FOR THE TOPPING:

½ cup (55 g) chopped walnuts or pecans

¼ cup (35 g) Ricki's All-Purpose Gluten-Free Flour Mix (see page 22)

¼ cup (30 g) old-fashioned rolled oats (not instant or quick-cooking)

2 Tbsp (30 ml) coconut sugar

2 tsp (10 ml) ground cinnamon

1 Tbsp (15 ml) sunflower or other light-tasting oil, preferably organic

FOR THE BATTER:

⅓ cup (80 ml) sunflower or other light-tasting oil, preferably organic

⅓ cup (55 g) coconut sugar

¼ tsp (1 ml) pure stevia powder or ½ tsp (2.5 ml) pure plain or vanilla stevia liquid, or to taste

1 cup (240 ml) plain or vanilla soy or almond milk

½ tsp (2.5 ml) apple cider vinegar

2 Tbsp (30 ml) finely ground flax seeds (from about 1 Tbsp or 15 ml whole seeds)

2 tsp (10 ml) finely grated lemon zest (about 1 large lemon), preferably organic

1 tsp (5 ml) pure vanilla extract

½ tsp (2.5 ml) pure lemon extract

1¼ cups (165 g) Ricki's All-Purpose Gluten-Free Flour Mix (see page 22)

⅓ cup (45 g) sorghum flour

¾ tsp (7.5 ml) xanthan gum (use only Bob's Red Mill brand if you are concerned about a corn allergy)

1 Tbsp (15 ml) baking powder

¼ tsp (1 ml) fine sea salt

2 cups (310 g) blueberries, fresh or frozen (DO NOT thaw if frozen), divided

Preheat the oven to 350°F (180°C). Line a 9-inch (22.5-cm) square baking pan with parchment paper, or spray with nonstick spray.

Make the topping: In a small bowl, blend the nuts, flour, oats, coconut sugar, and cinnamon. Drizzle with the oil and toss until crumbly. Set aside.

Make the batter: In a medium bowl, combine the oil, coconut sugar, stevia, milk, vinegar, flax, lemon zest, vanilla, and lemon extract. Set aside while you prepare the dry ingredients.

In a large bowl, sift the all-purpose flour, sorghum flour, xanthan gum, baking powder, and salt. Pour the wet ingredients over the dry and stir just to blend (it's okay if a few small dry spots remain here and there). Gently fold one cup (155 g) of the blueberries into the batter. Spread the batter in the pan.

Assemble and bake: Sprinkle the top of the batter with the topping mixture, then sprinkle the remaining blueberries over all. Press the topping lightly into the batter.

Bake for 50 to 60 minutes, rotating the pan about halfway through, until a tester inserted in the center comes out clean. Serve warm or at room temperature. See page 37, storing your baked goods. May be frozen.

Carrot Snack Cake ✷ CF, can be SF or NF ✷

Makes one 9-inch (22.5-cm) cake, serves 9 to 12

When I was a child, a major cake-mix company came out with mixes marketed as after-school snacks. On the rare occasion when my mother actually bought them, my sisters and I would fight over who got more of the moist and fruity cakes. This is my updated, healthier version. Still moist and flavorful without being too sweet, it's the perfect midafternoon snack.

- 1½ cups (155 g) finely grated carrot, loosely packed (about 2 large carrots)
- 2 tsp (10 ml) ground chia seeds or chia meal (from about 1 tsp or 5 ml whole seeds)
- ⅓ cup (55 g) coconut sugar
- ¼ tsp (1 ml) pure stevia powder or ½ tsp (2.5 ml) pure plain or vanilla stevia liquid, or to taste
- 1½ cups (360 ml) plain or vanilla soy or almond milk
- ⅓ cup (80 ml) sunflower or other light-tasting oil, preferably organic
- 1 tsp (5 ml) pure vanilla extract
- ¾ tsp (3.5 ml) apple cider vinegar
- 1 Tbsp (15 ml) freshly grated lemon zest, preferably organic, or 1 tsp (5 ml) pure lemon extract
- ½ cup (70 g) raisins, goji berries, chopped prunes (dried plums), or dates
- ⅓ cup (35 g) walnut or pecan pieces or halves (optional)
- ½ cup (40 g) unsweetened shredded coconut
- 1¼ cups (165 g) Ricki's All-Purpose Gluten-Free Flour Mix (see page 22)
- ⅓ cup (45 g) sorghum flour
- ¼ cup (20 g) whole psyllium husks
- 1 Tbsp (15 ml) ground cinnamon
- ½ tsp (2. 5 ml) ground ginger
- 2¼ tsp (11 ml) baking powder
- ¾ tsp (3.5 ml) baking soda
- ¼ tsp (1 ml) fine sea salt

Preheat the oven to 350°F (180°C). Line a 9-inch (22.5-cm) square pan with parchment paper, or spray with nonstick spray.

In a medium bowl, combine the carrots, chia, coconut sugar, stevia, milk, oil, vanilla, vinegar, lemon zest or extract, raisins, walnuts, and coconut. Set aside while you measure the dry ingredients.

In a large bowl, sift together the all-purpose flour, sorghum flour, psyllium, cinnamon, ginger, baking powder, baking soda, and salt. Stir briefly to distribute the spices.

Pour the wet ingredients over the dry and stir just to combine (it's okay if a few dry spots remain here and there). Turn the batter into the prepared pan and smooth the top.

Bake for 20 to 30 minutes, rotating the pan about halfway through baking, until a tester inserted in the center comes out clean. Cool in the pan before slicing. See page 37, storing your baked goods. May be frozen.

Cinnamon Crumb Coffee Cake ✱ CF, SF ✱

Serves 9 to 12

This quick and easy cake will impress your guests with its light, delicate crumb and cinnamon-walnut center and topping. It's perfect for impromptu visitors or just an afternoon snack.

FOR THE TOPPING/FILLING:

⅓ cup (80 ml) old-fashioned rolled oats (not instant or quick-cooking)
⅓ cup (25 g) coconut sugar
¼ cup (60 ml) coconut flour
1 Tbsp (15 ml) ground cinnamon
Pinch fine sea salt
2 Tbsp (30 ml) coconut oil, at room temperature, preferably organic
½ cup (55 g) walnut pieces or coarsely chopped walnuts

FOR THE CAKE BATTER:

½ cup (120 ml) unsweetened applesauce
1 Tbsp (15 ml) finely ground flax seeds (from about 1½ tsp or 7.5 ml whole seeds)
½ tsp (2.5 ml) apple cider vinegar
⅛ tsp (.5 ml) pure stevia powder or 20 to 30 drops pure plain or vanilla stevia liquid, or to taste
⅓ cup (80 ml) coconut sugar
1 cup (240 ml) unsweetened plain or vanilla soy, almond, or rice milk
⅓ cup (80 ml) sunflower or other light-tasting oil, preferably organic
1 tsp (5 ml) pure vanilla extract
1 tsp (5 ml) pure lemon extract
2 cups (265 g) Ricki's All-Purpose Gluten-Free Flour Mix (see page 22)
1½ Tbsp (22.5 ml) baking powder
¼ tsp (1 ml) baking soda
1¾ tsp (8.5 ml) xanthan gum (use only Bob's Red Mill brand if you are concerned about a corn allergy)
¼ tsp (1 ml) fine sea salt

Preheat the oven to 350°F (180°C). Line an 8-inch (20-cm) square pan with parchment paper, or spray with nonstick spray.

Make the topping/filling: In a medium bowl, stir the oats, coconut sugar, coconut flour, cinnamon, and salt. Stir to combine. Add the coconut oil and pinch the mixture between your thumb and fingers until it's evenly moistened and crumbly. Add the walnuts and toss to combine. Set aside.

Make the cake batter: In a small bowl, whisk together the applesauce, flax, vinegar, stevia, coconut sugar, milk, oil, vanilla, and lemon extract. Set aside while you measure the dry ingredients, or at least 2 minutes.

In a medium bowl, sift the flour, baking powder, baking soda, xanthan gum, and salt. Add the wet ingredients to the dry and whisk just until blended (do not overmix!).

Assemble and bake the cake: Spread about half the cake batter in the bottom of the pan (you can measure it, or just estimate). Sprinkle with about half the topping mixture. Scooping out heaping tablespoonsful of the remaining batter, dot the top of the topping mixture with the rest of the batter in spoonfuls, covering as much as you can. Use the back of the spoon to carefully spread the top layer of batter evenly over the surface, filling any spaces as best you can. Sprinkle with the remainder of the topping, covering the batter as evenly as possible (it's okay if there are a few empty spots here and there). Press the topping lightly into the top of the cake.

Bake for 30 to 35 minutes, rotating the pan about halfway through baking, until a tester inserted in the middle of the cake comes out clean. Cool at least 20 minutes before serving. See page 37, storing your baked goods. May be frozen.

Golden Vanilla Cake or Cupcakes * CF, NF or SF *

Makes one 2-layer, 8-inch (20-cm) cake (serves 8 to 10) or 2 dozen cupcakes

Sweetened only with agave nectar, this vanilla cake resembles a traditional "yellow" cake. It's moist and light and perfect baked in layers for a special occasion or divided into golden, domed cupcakes as individual treats. Try it layered with Chocolate Buttercream Frosting (see page 166) or topped with Lemon Coconut Buttercream Frosting (see Variations, page 170).

- 3 Tbsp (45 ml) finely ground flax seeds (from about 1½ Tbsp or 22 ml whole seeds)
- ¾ cup (180 ml) light agave nectar
- ¾ cup (180 ml) vanilla soy or almond milk
- ⅓ cup (80 ml) sunflower or other light-tasting oil, preferably organic
- 2 Tbsp (30 ml) pure vanilla extract
- 2 tsp (10 ml) apple cider vinegar
- 2 cups (265 g) Ricki's All-Purpose Gluten-Free Flour Mix (see page 22)
- 1½ tsp (7.5 ml) xanthan gum (use only Bob's Red Mill brand if you are concerned about a corn allergy)
- 1¾ tsp (8.5 ml) baking powder
- 1 tsp (5 ml) baking soda
- ¼ tsp (1 ml) fine sea salt

Preheat the oven to 350°F (180°C). Line two 8-inch (20-cm) round layer pans with parchment paper, or spray with nonstick spray, or line 24 cupcake cups with paper liners.

In a medium bowl, whisk together the flax, agave nectar, milk, oil, vanilla, and vinegar. Set aside while you measure the dry ingredients, or at least 2 minutes.

In a large bowl, sift the flour, xanthan gum, baking powder, baking soda, and salt. Pour the wet mixture over the dry and whisk again to combine; do not overmix.

Divide the batter evenly between the two pans (you can weigh it, or just estimate by setting the pans side by side on a counter as you pour and aiming for equal levels). If making cupcakes, use a large ice cream scoop or ⅓ cup (80 ml) measuring cup to fill the muffin cups ⅔ full.

Bake for 35 to 40 minutes or 20 to 25 minutes for cupcakes, rotating the pans about halfway through baking, until a tester inserted in the center of each pan comes out clean (depending on where they were situated in the oven, the two layers may not be ready at exactly the same time). Cool in the pans at least 15 minutes before removing to a cooling rack.

Frost using the frosting of your choice, or the Chocolate Buttercream Frosting (see page 166). If you will be frosting the cake, this works best if you freeze the cake for an hour or two first, then remove from the pan and frost while still frozen, as this helps prevent crumbling (the cake is quite delicate otherwise). May be frozen (depending on frosting used). Store frosted cake in a covered container in the refrigerator for up to 4 days. Serve chilled or at room temperature.

Chocolate Mystery Cupcakes * CF, SF or NF *

Makes 1 dozen regular or 2 dozen mini cupcakes

These cupcakes are the product of my early zeal, when I first started baking with healthier ingredients, to include vegetables in every item, and these offer a great way to sneak in some extra nutrition. Be sure to cool the cupcakes completely before sampling, however, as any veggie flavors disappear completely once they're cooled.

- 2 oz (70 g) fresh or frozen spinach (you may include the stems)
- 3½ oz (100 g) loosely packed grated zucchini with skin, fresh or frozen (about 1 cup)
- 1 cup (240 ml) unsweetened plain or vanilla soy or almond milk
- ½ cup (85 g) coconut sugar
- ¼ tsp (1 ml) pure stevia powder or ½ tsp (2.5 ml) pure plain or vanilla stevia liquid, or to taste
- ¼ cup (60 ml) sunflower or other light-tasting oil, preferably organic
- 1 Tbsp (15 ml) finely ground flax seeds (from about 1½ tsp or 7.5 ml whole seeds)
- 1 tsp (5 ml) apple cider vinegar
- 2 tsp (10 ml) pure vanilla extract
- 2 tsp (10 ml) instant-coffee substitute, such as Dandy Blend, or 1 tsp (5 ml) instant coffee (see page 34)
- 1 cup (135 g) Ricki's All-Purpose Gluten-Free Flour Mix (see page 22)
- ½ cup (60 g) whole oat flour (to make your own, see page 35)
- 1 tsp (5 ml) xanthan gum (use only Bob's Red Mill brand if you are concerned about a corn allergy)
- ⅓ cup (45 g) unsweetened cocoa powder, preferably non-alkalized
- 1½ tsp (7.5 ml) baking powder
- ¾ tsp (3.5 ml) baking soda
- ¼ tsp (1 ml) fine sea salt
- ½ cup (100 g) unsweetened carob chips (or dairy-free chocolate chips)

Preheat the oven to 350°F (180°C). Line 12 muffin cups with paper liners, or spray with nonstick spray (or spray 24 mini-muffin cups).

In a food processor or blender, blend the spinach and zucchini to a paste. Add the milk, coconut sugar, stevia, oil, flax, vinegar, vanilla, and coffee substitute and process again until smooth. (There may be a few small flecks of spinach visible; this is fine).

In a large bowl, sift the all-purpose flour, oat flour, xanthan gum, cocoa powder, baking powder, baking soda, and salt. Pour the wet mixture over the dry and top with the chips. Stir well to combine.

Using a large ice-cream scoop or ⅓-cup (80-ml) measuring cup, fill the muffin cups about ¾ full. Bake for 35 to 40 minutes, or 20 to 25 minutes for mini muffins, rotating the pan about halfway through baking, until a tester inserted in a center cupcake comes out clean. Allow to cool 5 minutes before removing to a cooling rack. Cool completely before sampling — the flavor changes as they cool, and any trace of veggie flavor disappears in the cold cupcakes. Frost if desired. See page 37, storing your baked goods. May be frozen.

Coconut Mini Loaves or Cupcakes ✱ CF, SF ✱

Makes 6 mini loaves or 9 cupcakes

These cakes are tender, not too sweet, and boast a pronounced coconut flavor. For fancier loaves, drizzle with your favorite glaze, or bake as cupcakes and frost with Coconut Butter Buttercream Frosting (see page 170) or Chocolate Buttercream Frosting (see page 166).

- 2 Tbsp (30 ml) coconut oil, melted (at low temperature), preferably organic
- 2 Tbsp (30 ml) natural smooth cashew or macadamia butter, at room temperature
- ⅓ cup (80 ml) light agave nectar
- ⅛ tsp (.5 ml) pure stevia powder or ¼ tsp (1 ml) pure plain or vanilla stevia liquid, or to taste
- 1 Tbsp (15 ml) pure vanilla extract
- ⅓ cup (80 ml) plain or vanilla soy, almond, or rice milk
- ½ tsp (2.5 ml) pure coconut extract
- 1 tsp (5 ml) apple cider vinegar
- 1 Tbsp (15 ml) finely ground flax seeds (from about 1½ tsp or 7.5 ml whole seeds)
- 1 cup (135 g) Ricki's All-Purpose Gluten-Free Flour Mix (see page 22)
- 1½ tsp (7.5 ml) baking powder
- ¼ tsp (1 ml) baking soda
- ½ tsp (2.5 ml) xanthan gum (use only Bob's Red Mill brand if you are concerned about a corn allergy)
- ¼ tsp (1 ml) fine sea salt
- ½ cup (40 g) unsweetened shredded coconut

Preheat the oven to 350°F (180°C). Line 6 mini loaf pans or 9 muffin cups with paper liners, or spray with nonstick spray. If using individual loaf pans, place them on a cookie sheet.

In a medium bowl, whisk together the coconut oil and cashew butter. Slowly stir in the agave nectar, stevia, vanilla, milk, coconut extract, vinegar, and flax, stir well to combine. Set aside while you measure the dry ingredients.

In a larger bowl, sift the flour, baking powder, baking soda, xanthan gum, and salt. Whisk to combine. Add the coconut and stir to blend.

Pour the wet ingredients over the dry and stir to mix well. Using a large ice-cream scoop or ⅓-cup (80-ml) measuring cup, fill the loaf pans or cupcake cups about ¾ full.

Bake for 20 to 28 minutes, rotating the pan(s) about halfway through baking, until a tester inserted in a center loaf or cupcake comes out clean (the tops will begin to crack and brown a bit). Cool in pans for 5 minutes before removing to a rack to cool completely. See page 37, storing your baked goods. May be frozen.

Chocolate Layer Cake or Cupcakes ✱ CF, SF or NF ✱

Makes one 2-layer, 8- or 9-inch cake (serves 8 to 10) or 18 cupcakes

What would a dessert cookbook be without a classic chocolate layer cake? After experimenting with various recipes for vegan chocolate cakes, I came up with my own. This cake bakes up incredibly light and moist. This was also my "go-to" birthday-cake recipe when I owned my bakery, and it received raves from virtually all of the customers for whom I baked it.

- 1 Tbsp (15 ml) instant-coffee substitute, such as Dandy Blend, or 1½ tsp (7.5 ml) instant coffee (see page 34)
- 1 Tbsp (15 ml) pure vanilla extract
- ¾ cup (125 g) coconut sugar
- ½ tsp (2.5 ml) pure stevia powder or 1 tsp (5 ml) pure plain or vanilla stevia liquid, or to taste
- 1¾ cups (420 ml) unsweetened plain, vanilla, or chocolate almond or soy milk
- 1 Tbsp (15 ml) apple cider vinegar
- ⅔ cup (160 ml) sunflower or other light-tasting oil, preferably organic
- 1½ cups (200 g) Ricki's All-Purpose Gluten-Free Flour Mix (see page 22)
- 2 Tbsp (30 ml) sweet rice flour
- ½ cup (70 g) sorghum flour
- ½ cup (80 g) unsweetened cocoa powder, preferably non-alkalized
- 1 tsp (5 ml) xanthan gum (use only Bob's Red Mill brand if you are concerned about a corn allergy)
- 1½ tsp (7.5 ml) baking powder
- ¾ tsp (3.5 ml) baking soda
- ¼ tsp (1 ml) fine sea salt

Preheat the oven to 350°F (180°C). Line two 8- or 9-inch (20-22.5-cm) round layer pans with parchment paper, or spray with nonstick spray; or line 18 muffin cups with paper liners, or spray with nonstick spray.

In a large bowl, whisk together the coffee substitute, vanilla, coconut sugar, stevia, milk, vinegar, and oil until the sugar appears dissolved.

Sift in the all-purpose flour, sweet rice flour, sorghum flour, cocoa powder, xanthan gum, baking powder, baking soda, and salt and whisk just to blend; do not overmix.

Divide the batter evenly between the 2 pans or else scoop into the muffin cups. If making cupcakes, use a large ice cream scoop or ⅓ cup (80 ml) measuring cup to fill the muffin cups ⅔ full. Bake for 35 to 40 minutes for cakes or 20 to 25 minutes for cupcakes, until a tester inserted in the middle comes out clean. Allow layers to cool completely before removing from the pan; allow cupcakes to cool at least 10 minutes.

To frost layers, it helps to freeze the cake for at least 2 hours before frosting; this will prevent the sides from crumbling into the frosting. Cupcakes may be frosted at room temperature with Coconut Butter Buttercream Frosting (see page 170) and drizzled with melted chocolate. See page 37, storing your baked goods. May be frozen.

Chocolate Buttercream Frosting * GF, SF, CF, NF *

Makes about 1 cup (240 ml), enough for 1 layer cake or 6 cupcakes

This frosting contains no butter — nor does it include dairy, nuts, soy, corn, grain products, or refined sugar. In other words, this frosting is for everyone! At room temperature, the frosting can be used as soon as it's mixed as a dark, fudgy chocolate frosting that can be piped and will hold its shape, or it can be chilled and then whipped into a lighter buttercream-style frosting. Either way, no one will believe what is — and isn't — in this frosting!

½ cup (120 ml) plus up to 2 Tbsp (150 ml) more canned or homemade unsweetened sweet potato puree (see page 23)

½ cup (40 g) coconut sugar

⅛ tsp (.5 ml) pure stevia powder or 25 to 35 drops pure plain or vanilla stevia liquid, or to taste

2 tsp (10 ml) pure vanilla extract

Pinch fine sea salt

¼ cup (25 g) raw cacao powder, unsweetened cocoa powder, carob powder, or a combination (see *Note*)

2.5 oz (65 g) good-quality unsweetened chocolate (100% cacao)

¼ cup (60 ml) natural smooth sunflower seed butter or tahini (sesame seed paste), at room temperature (see second *Note*)

2 Tbsp (30 ml) coconut oil, at room temperature, preferably organic

Place sweet potato puree, coconut sugar, stevia, vanilla, and salt in a food processor and process to blend. Add the cacao powder and process until combined. Set aside, but leave the sweet-potato mixture in the processor.

In a small, heavy-bottomed pot, heat the chocolate, sunflower seed butter, and coconut oil over low heat. Stir constantly until the chocolate melts; remove from the heat. Turn the mixture into the food processor and blend everything until smooth and creamy, scraping down the sides as necessary.

Note: If the coconut oil begins to separate (the mixture will appear oily and a bit curdled) OR if you find that the mixture is too thick, add 1 tablespoon (15 ml) more of the sweet potato puree at a time and blend again; it should come together in a silky, spreadable frosting.

May be used immediately as a fudgy frosting, or else refrigerate until firm, then beat with electric beaters until fluffy and lighter in color for a buttercream frosting (it will resemble milk chocolate rather than dark chocolate when beaten). In either case, avoid the urge to eat most of it straight from the spoon. Store, covered, in the refrigerator, up to 5 days.

May be frozen; defrost overnight in the refrigerator, then bring to room temperature and stir well (for fudgy frosting) or beat with electric beaters (for buttercream) before using.

Note: If you can tolerate additional sugar to get a more chocolatey frosting, use cocoa powder and add more coconut sugar or even a couple of tablespoons (30 ml) agave nectar. For a lower-glycemic frosting, use cacao or carob powder, or a combination, along with stevia. Because raw cacao powder has a milder flavor than cocoa powder, it can be combined with stevia without producing a bitter aftertaste that sometimes occurs with stevia and cocoa powder. Combining the cocoa with part carob powder (use between 25% and 50% carob) has the same effect, enabling you to use stevia without a bitter aftertaste.

You can also use natural smooth cashew butter in place of the sunflower seed butter or tahini, if you can tolerate nuts.

Pastry Cream or Custard * SF, CF, can be NF *

Makes enough for one 9- to 10-inch (22.5- to 25-cm) pie or tart, or filling for 10 to 12 cupcakes

Years ago at a cooking class, I tasted pastry cream for the first time. Immediately smitten, I continued to use the classic egg-and-cream-based, sugary filling as a staple in fruit tarts for many years. When my diet changed, I thought I'd given up this rich, creamy filling — until now. It takes some time and work, but the results are worth it for a sugar-free, egg-free, and butter-free pastry cream this good! This also makes a wonderful custard all on its own or layered in a parfait with fresh berries. If you have it, I suggest including the almond extract, which adds a touch of richness to the cream without a really prominent almond flavor.

¼ cup (50 g) dry millet
½ cup (120 ml) water or plain or vanilla rice milk, plus more if needed
1 can (14 oz or 400 ml) full-fat canned coconut milk, preferably organic
Pinch fine sea salt
⅓ cup (80 ml) light agave nectar
1 Tbsp (15 ml) pure vanilla extract
¼ tsp (1 ml) pure almond extract (optional)

Place the millet and water or rice milk in a medium pot and bring to boil; lower heat to simmer, cover, and cook until the liquid is completely absorbed, about 15 to 20 minutes.

Add the coconut milk, salt, and agave nectar, and return to boil over medium heat. Lower heat to simmer once more and continue to cook, stirring frequently to avoid scorching (I find a silicone spatula works beautifully for this, as you can scrape clean the bottom of the pot), until the liquid is almost absorbed, the grains of millet have begun to break open and disintegrate into the liquid, and the mixture has a texture of thick wallpaper paste (or very thick oatmeal), for 30 to 40 minutes. If necessary, add a bit more water or rice milk, about ¼ cup (60 ml) at a time, to ensure that the mixture has cooked long enough (don't worry about overcooking at this point —the longer it cooks, the better!).

Remove from the heat; stir in the vanilla and almond extract, if using, and allow to cool for a couple of minutes.

Working in ½-cup (120-ml) batches, blend the mixture in a powerful blender (a hand blender or food processor is not suitable for this recipe), scraping down the sides of the blender repeatedly, until the texture is perfectly smooth and velvety. (Using my conventional blender, I had to stop and scrape the sides about 10 to 15 times to achieve this result.) Turn each pureed batch into a clean bowl, and continue until all the mixture has been blended and poured into the bowl. Use immediately or refrigerate for later use.

Spread the smooth pastry cream over pie crust, or use as a custard in a parfait, tarts, or as a filling for a layer cake. Chill for 4 hours or overnight before serving.

If not using immediately, store, covered, in the refrigerator, for up to 3 days. Not suitable for freezing.

Coconut Whipped Cream ✷ GF, can be SF, CF and NF ✷

(see photograph of Strawberry Whipped Cream on page 86)

Makes about 1½ cups (360 ml)

Coconut whipped cream has become a staple in vegan kitchens in recent years. The usual recipe, I've found, produces a cream that's a bit heavier than what I remember dairy whipped cream to be. With this version, I've lightened it up somewhat to re-create more of the traditional texture. And the bonus: There's no need for beaters! This cream also mounds and pipes beautifully if refrigerated first for at least 12 hours before using. Each of the flavor variations is just as delectable; choose according to your recipe.

BASIC WHIPPED CREAM:

1 can (14 oz or 400 ml) full-fat canned coconut milk, preferably organic

2 to 3 Tbsp (30 to 45 ml) rice milk or other nondairy milk, or 3 to 4 Tbsp (45 to 60 ml) reserved coconut water from can

1 tsp (5 ml) pure vanilla extract

Pinch fine sea salt

Scant ⅛ tsp (.5 ml) pure stevia powder or ¼ tsp (1 ml) pure plain or vanilla stevia liquid, or to taste

½ tsp (2.5 ml) xanthan gum (use only Bob's Red Mill brand if you are concerned about a corn allergy)

Note: At least 24 hours before you make the whipped cream, refrigerate the can of coconut milk.

Make the whipped cream: Remove the coconut milk from the fridge, turn the can upside down, and open it from the bottom. You will see a clear, slightly viscous liquid on top (this is the coconut water that has separated out). Gently pour the coconut water into a bowl or glass and reserve if you wish to use it in the whipped cream (or use for some other recipe — it's very nice in smoothies).

Using a spoon, scoop out the thick white cream left in the can and place it in the bowl of a food processor or blender. If you notice any more coconut water pooled under the cream, add it to the rest of the coconut water.

Add 2 tablespoons (30 ml) of the rice milk or 3 tablespoons (45 ml) of the reserved coconut water to the cream in the processor. Next, add the vanilla, salt, and stevia and blend until smooth. Sprinkle with the xanthan gum and process again until well combined. You should have a light and fluffy cream that can be spooned on top of desserts or spread over trifles, pies, etc. If the cream seems too thick, add the additional tablespoon (15 ml) of rice milk or coconut water and process again.

Coconut Whipped Cream *continued* ✷ GF, can be SF, CF and NF ✷

Chill the whipped cream: If you wish to pipe the cream, you will need to cover the bowl with plastic wrap and refrigerate it for an additional 24 hours at this point. After 24 hours, gently spoon the cream into a piping bag and use as desired. Prepared cream will keep, covered, in the refrigerator, for up to 3 more days.

Variations:

Lemon Whipped Cream: Add the finely grated zest of 1 lemon, preferably organic, with the coconut milk, rice milk, vanilla, salt, and stevia; replace 1 Tbsp (15 ml) of the rice milk or coconut water with fresh lemon juice; continue as above.

Chocolate Whipped Cream: Add 1 Tbsp (15 ml) unsweetened cocoa powder to the mixture in the processor with the coconut milk, rice milk, vanilla, salt, and stevia; increase liquid stevia by 10 drops, or to taste (you can also use 2 Tbsp or 30 ml coconut sugar instead of more stevia). Continue as above.

Strawberry Whipped Cream: Use ½ cup (150 g) quartered fresh strawberries in place of the liquid in the recipe. Add the finely grated zest of 1 lime, preferably organic, to the mixture in the processor as well, and process as above.

Coconut-Butter Buttercream Frosting ✱ GF, SF, CF ✱

(see photograph on page 164)

Makes about 1 cup (240 ml)

With the same light, fluffy texture as traditional buttercream, this recipe makes perfect use of the naturally firm texture of coconut butter. When combined with the liquid ingredients, the final result is a smooth, light frosting that holds its shape at room temperature, without an overpowering coconut flavor.

½ cup (120 ml) coconut butter, melted, preferably organic
2 Tbsp (30 ml) natural smooth macadamia or cashew butter, at room temperature
2 Tbsp (30 ml) unsweetened applesauce
2 Tbsp (30 ml) light agave nectar
10 to 15 drops pure plain or vanilla stevia liquid, or to taste (optional)
1 tsp (5 ml) pure vanilla extract
Pinch fine sea salt
¼ cup (60 ml) unsweetened coconut beverage (the kind that comes in a carton), plus up to 2 Tbsp (30 ml) more, as needed

Place all ingredients in a small food processor or blender, and blend until perfectly smooth and creamy. You may need to add a touch more coconut beverage to attain spreading consistency. This frosting will firm up considerably when refrigerated, so if you think you've added too much liquid, try refrigerating for an hour first to see what happens. If you make the frosting in advance and find it too firm to spread when you remove it from the fridge, simply place back in the processor and blend until spreadable. It will keep, covered, in the refrigerator, up to a week. May be frozen. Defrost, overnight, in the refrigerator, and then stir or process again before using.

Variations:
Lemon Coconut Buttercream Frosting: Add finely grated zest of 1 medium lemon, preferably organic, and ½ teaspoon pure lemon extract.

Caramel Buttercream Frosting: Replace the applesauce with ¼ cup (60 ml) homemade unsweetened sweet potato puree (see page 23) and add 1 tablespoon (15 ml) lucuma powder.

Chapter 4: *Cheesecakes, Pies, Tarts & Puddings*

Butter Tarts ✱ SF, can be CF, NF ✱

Makes 8

For those who don't know, butter tarts are a Canadian confection much like mini pecan pies, except with raisins instead of pecans and with a slightly runnier, gooier filling. I include raisins as an option here just for authenticity, even though I don't normally eat them because of their high sugar content; you can easily replace them with walnut pieces (or pecans!) if you prefer. My recipe testers adored these sweet treats. Note that in this recipe, chia is necessary in the filling; do not substitute with ground flax or another egg substitute.

FOR THE CRUST:

- 1⅔ cups (215 g) Ricki's All-Purpose Gluten-Free Flour Mix (see page 22)
- 1½ tsp (7.5 ml) xanthan gum (use only Bob's Red Mill brand if you are concerned about a corn allergy)
- ¼ tsp (1 ml) fine sea salt
- ½ cup (120 ml) coconut oil, melted (at low temperature), preferably organic
- 3 Tbsp (45 ml) coconut nectar
- 1 Tbsp (15 ml) water, if necessary

FOR THE FILLING:

- ½ cup (120 ml) coconut nectar
- ¼ cup (60 ml) light agave nectar
- ¼ tsp (1 ml) pure stevia powder or ½ tsp (2.5 ml) pure plain or vanilla stevia liquid, or to taste
- 2 Tbsp (30 ml) arrowroot or tapioca starch
- 2 Tbsp (30 ml) coconut oil, melted (at low temperature), preferably organic
- 1 tsp (5 ml) pure vanilla extract
- 1 tsp (5 ml) brandy or rum extract (or use another 1 tsp or 5 ml vanilla)
- 2 Tbsp (30 ml) finely ground chia seeds (from about 1 Tbsp or 15 ml whole seeds)
- ¼ tsp (1 ml) baking powder
- ¼ cup (35 g) raisins or pecan pieces

Preheat the oven to 325°F (165°C). Lightly grease 8 individual tart pans, or line 8 muffin cups with paper liners. If you're using solid tart pans (without removable bottoms), it's worth lining these with parchment paper rounds and then greasing the rounds of parchment, as the bottoms may stick to the pan otherwise.

Make the crust: In a medium bowl, sift the flour, xanthan gum, and salt. Set aside.

In a small bowl, pour the ½ cup (120 ml) melted coconut oil and then whisk in the coconut nectar until combined.

Pour the coconut oil–coconut nectar mixture over the flour mixture and toss with a fork until it comes together. Knead with your hands just until the wet ingredients are well incorporated. You should have a very soft dough that just holds its shape. (If the dough is too dry, sprinkle with the 1 tablespoon (15 ml) of water and knead again; if it turns out that it's too soft, sprinkle more flour, about 1 tablespoon (15 ml) at a time, until you reach a just barely firm texture (this dough should be quite soft!). Divide dough into 8 equal portions among the tart pans.

Dust your hands with flour. Beginning with the sides of the tart pans or muffin cups, press the dough evenly to cover each pan; dust your hands with flour periodically to prevent the dough from sticking. Place the tart pans or muffin tin on a cookie sheet and bake for 10 to 15 minutes, until the crust is just starting to puff up.

(continued on page 176)

Butter Tarts *continued* ✷ SF, can be CF, NF ✷

While the crusts bake, make the filling: In a medium bowl, whisk together the coconut nectar, agave nectar, stevia, and arrowroot until the mixture is smooth. Whisk in the melted 2 tablespoons (30 ml) coconut oil, vanilla, brandy or rum extract, and chia; continue whisking until there are no little lumps of chia left in the mixture. Add the baking powder last and mix quickly just to blend.

Fill the shells: After 15 minutes, when the shells are just beginning to puff up, remove them from the oven and sprinkle about ½ tablespoon (7.5 ml) of the raisins or pecan pieces in the bottom of each shell. Divide the filling equally among the tart pans so the pans are about ¾ full, or the filling is almost even with the top of the crusts. (You may have a bit of filling left over — it makes a nice topping over ice cream or pancakes.)

Bake another 25 to 30 minutes, rotating the cookie sheet about halfway through baking to ensure even baking. The tarts are ready when the crust is lightly browned, and the filling appears slightly foamy on top and bubbles a little onto the sides of the crust in the pans. It will begin to brown on top but will still appear quite liquid when you jiggle the pans; this is as it should be. Remove the tarts carefully from the oven and allow to cool to room temperature, then refrigerate until firm.

These can be eaten cold or at room temperature; for the latter, chill first and then return to room temperature. Store, covered, in the refrigerator, for up to 5 days. May be frozen.

Berries and Cream Tart * SF, CF, can be NF *

Serves 9 to 12

This tart makes a spectacular summer dessert. It takes a bit of planning to prepare the cream in advance, but once you've got the parts mixed up, it's a snap to assemble. And your guests will be very impressed!

FOR THE FILLING:

1 recipe Pastry Cream or Custard (see page 167)

1 recipe pie crust from Chocolate Pecan Pie (see page 180) or Chai Cheesecake (see page 184)

About 2 cups (310 to 325 g) fresh mixed berries, such as strawberries, raspberries, and blueberries

FOR THE GLAZE (OPTIONAL):

¼ cup (60 ml) light agave nectar

2 tsp (10 ml) tapioca starch

½ cup (120 ml) water

Make the pastry cream: Prepare the pastry cream according to the recipe, and allow it to cool to room temperature.

Meanwhile, make the pie crust: Line a 9-inch (22.5-cm) pie plate or springform pan with parchment paper or spray with nonstick spray. Mix the dough for the pie crust according to the recipe, and pat it evenly over the bottom and up the sides of the pie plate, or on the bottom of the springform pan. Bake according to recipe and allow to cool.

Assemble the tart: Sort and wash the berries, and then spread them on paper towels to absorb excess moisture. If using strawberries, slice them. Set aside.

Spread the pastry cream evenly over the cooled pie crust. Place the berries in a decorative pattern over the pastry cream, leaving as little space between berries as possible. Refrigerate while you make the glaze, if using, or for 4 hours (up to overnight) if serving without the glaze.

Make the glaze (optional): In a small bowl, whisk together the light agave nectar and tapioca starch until smooth. Pour the water into a small, heavy pot, and slowly whisk in the agave mixture. Bring to boil over medium heat and boil for 30 seconds, stirring constantly. Allow to cool for at least 10 minutes before brushing on the tart.

Once the glaze has cooled, brush it gently over the surface of the berries, allowing it to drip between the berries over the top of the tart. Store, covered, in the refrigerator, for up to 5 days. Not suitable for freezing.

Rustic Glazed Peach and Mascarpone Tart * CF, SF *

Serves 8

This tart looks fancy enough for company, but the ease of preparation means you can whip it up for you and the family any day. It's a perfect dish for a summer brunch as well — and a great way to use leftover steel-cut oats from yesterday's breakfast. The "mascarpone" will turn out a light eggshell color because of the coconut sugar; if you prefer a whiter cheese, use more stevia, as directed in the ingredients section. Adding lucuma lends a subtly rich, caramel flavor to the cheese, but it will still be luscious without it.

FOR THE MASCARPONE:

1 can (14 oz or 400 ml) full-fat canned coconut milk, preferably organic

¾ cup (120 g) natural raw cashews

1½ Tbsp (22.5 ml) fresh lemon juice

1 Tbsp (15 ml) lucuma powder (optional)

1 to 1⅛ tsp (5 to 5.5 ml) pure stevia powder or ¾ tsp (7.5 ml) pure plain or vanilla stevia liquid, or to taste

¼ cup (20 g) coconut sugar, or ⅛ tsp (.5 ml) more pure stevia powder, or ¼ tsp (1 ml) more pure plain or vanilla stevia liquid

Pinch fine sea salt

FOR THE OATCAKE CRUST:

⅔ cup (160 ml) precooked, chilled steel-cut oats (regular rolled oats are not suitable here)

2 Tbsp (30 ml) coconut sugar

¼ tsp (1 ml) pure stevia powder or ½ tsp (2.5 ml) pure plain or vanilla stevia liquid, or to taste

⅔ cup (160 ml) unsweetened plain or vanilla soy or almond milk

1 tsp (5 ml) apple cider vinegar

3 Tbsp (45 ml) sunflower or other light-tasting oil, preferably organic, or coconut oil, melted (at low temperature), preferably organic

1 tsp (5 ml) pure vanilla extract

1½ cups (195 g) Ricki's All-Purpose Gluten-Free Flour Mix (see page 22)

1 tsp (5 ml) xanthan gum (use only Bob's Red Mill brand if you are concerned about a corn allergy)

2½ tsp (12. 5 ml) baking powder

½ tsp (2.5 ml) baking soda

¾ tsp (3.5 ml) fine sea salt

2 tsp (10 ml) ground cinnamon

FOR THE PEACH TOPPING:

2 medium fresh peaches, peeled or unpeeled, pitted and sliced into ¼-inch (.5-cm) thick slices (28 to 36 slices), or 8 to 9 oz (225 to 250 g) frozen, sliced peaches

¼ cup (20 g) coconut sugar

Make the mascarpone: Place all ingredients in a high-powered blender (such as a Vitamix) and blend until perfectly smooth, scraping down the sides if necessary. Set aside.

Make the crust: Preheat the oven to 375°F (190°C). Line the bottom of an 8½-inch (21.5-cm) springform pan with parchment paper, or spray with nonstick spray. (You can use a 9-inch (22-cm) pan for this tart, but note that it won't need to bake as long and the "cheese" layer will be thinner and less luxurious as a result.)

In a medium bowl, whisk together the cooked oats, 2 tablespoons (30 ml) coconut sugar, stevia, milk, vinegar, oil, and vanilla to begin dissolving the coconut sugar. Set aside.

In a large bowl, sift the flour, xanthan gum, baking powder, baking soda, salt, and cinnamon. Stir once or twice to distribute the ingredients evenly.

Pour the wet mixture over the dry and stir to combine; do not overmix. The batter will be very thick and almost like cookie dough. Spread the mixture in the bottom of the prepared pan. Pour the mascarpone over the batter and smooth the top.

Bake for 40 to 45 minutes, until the edges are beginning to brown and the top appears firm. Remove from the oven and turn on the broiler. (If your oven has no broiler, increase temperature to 500°F (260°C).) Top with the peach slices, then sprinkle with the ¼ cup (20 g) coconut sugar. Broil for an additional 5 minutes, until the peaches begin to brown and the sugar begins to caramelize. Remove from the oven and cool completely, then refrigerate for at least 6 hours (or overnight) before serving. Serve chilled. See page 37, storing your baked goods. May be frozen; defrost, covered, overnight in the refrigerator before serving.

Chocolate Pecan Pie * SF, CF *

Serves 8 to 12

A cross between a regular pecan pie and chocolate ganache, this dense, rich, and uber-chocolatey pie filling works perfectly nestled in a flaky crust. While it may be unconventional, this pie will make a show-stopping holiday treat, especially topped with some Coconut Whipped Cream (see page 168).

FOR THE CRUST:

1 Tbsp (15 ml) coconut sugar

6 Tbsp (90 ml) cold water, plus up to 2 tablespoons (30 ml) more if needed

¼ cup (60 ml) coconut oil, melted (at low temperature), preferably organic

2 Tbsp (30 ml) sunflower or other light-tasting oil, preferably organic

1½ cups (195 g) Ricki's All-Purpose Gluten-Free Flour Mix (see page 22)

¼ tsp (1 ml) baking soda

½ tsp (2.5 ml) fine sea salt

¼ cup (20 g) whole psyllium husks

1 Tbsp (15 ml) ground chia seeds (from about 1½ tsp or 7.5 ml whole seeds; white works best in this crust recipe)

FOR THE FILLING:

⅔ cup (50 g) coconut sugar

⅓ cup (80 ml) coconut nectar

2 Tbsp (30 ml) natural smooth cashew butter, at room temperature (see *Note*)

5.25 oz (150 g) unsweetened chocolate, chopped (the size of chocolate chips)

⅛ tsp (.5 ml) fine sea salt

⅛ tsp (.5 ml) pure stevia powder or ¼ (1 ml) pure plain or vanilla stevia liquid, or to taste

1 Tbsp (15 ml) arrowroot powder

1 tsp (5 ml) pure vanilla extract

1½ cups (120 g) pecan pieces, raw or lightly toasted

½ cup (40 g) pecan halves, raw or lightly toasted (about 30), for decoration (optional)

Preheat the oven to 375°F (190°C). Line an 8½- or 9-inch (21.5- or 22-cm) pie plate with parchment paper, or spray with nonstick spray.

Make the crust: In a small bowl, mix the coconut sugar and water until the sugar begins to dissolve. Add the oils and whisk until well blended. Set aside.

In a medium bowl, sift the flour with the baking soda and the salt. Add the psylliom and chia and stir to blend. Pour the oil mixture over the dry ingredients and toss with a fork until it comes together. Use your hands to mix into a firm, but still pliable, dough. (If you absolutely need more water, add about a teaspoon (5 ml) at a time — you don't want the dough to be too soft.

Starting with the sides of the pie plate, press bits of dough along the edges and then the bottom, until evenly distributed (you may need to press fairly hard). Flute the edges if you wish, or press with the tines of a fork. Dock the crust by pricking the bottom 10 to 12 times with a fork.

Bake for 20 to 30 minutes, rotating the pie plate about halfway through baking, until edges are browned and the rest of the crust is golden.

Make the filling: About 15 minutes before the crust is finished baking, begin making the filling. In a medium, heavy-bottomed pot, combine the coconut sugar, coconut nectar, cashew butter, chocolate, salt, and stevia. Cook and stir over medium heat until everything is melted and the mixture is smooth. Sprinkle with the arrowroot powder and whisk to combine.

(continued on page 182)

Chocolate Pecan Pie *continued* ✸ SF, CF ✸

Continue to cook the mixture, for another minute, stirring constantly and scraping the bottom of the pot to prevent scorching. The filling should become thicker and slightly glossy, with a texture similar to corn syrup or molasses. Turn off the heat and add the vanilla, then stir in the pecan pieces to coat.

Fill, chill, and serve: Remove the baked pie crust from the oven and pour the hot filling into it, smoothing the top if necessary.

If you'd like to decorate the pie with the pecan halves, now is the time to do so, while the filling is still hot. Place the halves in a decorative pattern over the filling and press slightly so they adhere to the surface. Allow the pie to cool completely at room temperature; then refrigerate until ready to serve. Remove from refrigerator about 20 minutes before serving. See page 37, storing your baked goods. May be frozen.

Note: You can substitute macadamia butter or tahini (sesame seed paste) for the cashew butter in the filling.

Chocolate Satin Tart ✱ CF, SF ✱

Makes one 8- or 9-inch (20- or 22-cm) tart (serves 6 to 8)

Filled with a smooth, velvety chocolate ganache, this tart is a wonderfully rich indulgence. Top with some fresh raspberries and Coconut Whipped Cream (see page 168) for a beautiful dessert presentation.

FOR THE TART SHELL:

1 recipe Chocolate Shortbread Cookie dough (see page 103)

FOR THE GANACHE FILLING:

6 oz (170 g) unsweetened chocolate, chopped

1 cup (240 ml) full-fat canned coconut milk

2 Tbsp (30 ml) natural smooth macadamia or cashew butter, at room temperature

6 Tbsp (90 ml) coconut nectar

⅛ tsp (.5 ml) pure stevia powder, or ¼ tsp (1 ml) plain or vanilla pure stevia liquid or to taste

½ tsp (2.5 ml) pure vanilla extract

Pinch fine sea salt

Fresh raspberries and/or Coconut Whipped Cream (see page 168), for serving (optional)

Make the tart shell: Preheat the oven to 350°F (180°C). Lightly grease an 8- or 9-inch (20- or 22-cm) tart pan or pie plate.

Prepare the Chocolate Shortbread Cookie dough (see page 103) according to the recipe instructions, but do not form into a roll or refrigerate before using.

Pat the dough evenly on the bottom and up the sides of the tart pan. Dock the bottom of the tart by pricking 6 to 10 times across the bottom dough with the tines of a fork. Place the pan on a cookie sheet.

Bake the tart shell for 15 to 25 minutes, rotating the cookie sheet about halfway through, until the shell is dry on top, puffed a bit, and browned on the edges. Allow to cool completely before filling.

Once the shell is cool, make the ganache: In a small, heavy-bottomed pot, combine the chocolate, coconut milk, and macadamia butter. Cook over very low heat, scraping the bottom of the pan occasionally to prevent scorching, until the mixture is smooth and all of the chocolate is melted. Remove from heat and stir in the coconut nectar, stevia, vanilla, and salt.

Assemble the tart: Pour the ganache into the cooled tart shell. Allow the filling to cool completely at room temperature, then refrigerate until the ganache is firm. Garnish with fresh raspberries and/or Coconut Whipped Cream, if desired. Store, covered, in the refrigerator, until ready to serve. May be served cold or at room temperature. See page 37, storing your baked goods. May be frozen.

Note: You can make this recipe as individual tarts as well, by dividing the dough among 6 to 8 small tart pans, 3 inches (7.5 cm) in diameter. Bake the tart shells for 12 to 16 minutes, then fill as above.

Chai Cheesecake * CF *

Makes one 8-inch (20-cm) cheesecake (serves 6 to 8)

Even though I love the spices in chai tea, I'm not a fan of the beverage. In trying to come up with another way to enjoy this spice mix, I created this recipe. The fragrant cinnamon, cardamom, and ginger are highlighted in the dense, rich, though not-too-sweet base. This is great served with a big dollop of Coconut Whipped Cream (see page 168). Please note, if you use whipped cream, the recipe will not be corn-free.

FOR THE CRUST:

3 Tbsp (45 ml) coconut sugar
2 Tbsp (30 ml) water
¼ cup (60 ml) sunflower or other light-tasting oil, preferably organic
½ cup (65 g) Ricki's All-Purpose Gluten-Free Flour Mix (see page 22)
¼ cup (25 g) ground flax seeds or flax meal (from about 2 Tbsp or 30 ml whole seeds)
½ cup (50 g) old-fashioned rolled oats (not instant or quick-cooking)
½ cup (55 g) raw or lightly toasted walnut pieces or halves
¼ tsp (1 ml) fine sea salt

FOR THE FILLING:

1 pkg (about 1 lb or 425 to 450 g) firm Chinese-style tofu (the kind packed in water and displayed in refrigerated coolers, not the individual, aseptically packaged boxes)
½ cup (120 ml) natural smooth cashew or macadamia butter, at room temperature
⅓ cup (80 ml) full-fat canned coconut milk
½ cup (120 ml) coconut nectar
½ cup (85 g) coconut sugar
2 Tbsp (30 ml) freshly squeezed lemon juice
2 Tbsp (30 ml) potato starch
1 Tbsp (15 ml) carob or lucuma powder
1 Tbsp (15 ml) ground cinnamon
1 tsp (5 ml) ground ginger
¼ to ½ tsp (1 to 2.5 ml) ground cardamom, to taste
⅛ tsp (.5 ml) cloves
⅛ tsp (.5 ml) fine sea salt

Make the crust: Preheat the oven to 350°F (180°C). Line the bottom of a 8-inch (20-cm) springform pan or a pie plate with parchment paper or spray with nonstick spray. Set aside.

In a small bowl, combine the 3 Tbsp (45 ml) coconut sugar and water; stir until the sugar dissolves. Add the oil and set aside.

In the bowl of a food processor, combine the flour, flax, oats, walnut pieces, and salt and process until you have a fine meal about the texture of cornmeal (there should be no detectable pieces of walnut, though you may still see small bits of oats).

Drizzle the wet mixture in a ring over the dry and process again until it comes together in a moist dough. If it appears more like a thick batter, add another tablespoon (15 ml) flour and mix again. Turn the mixture into the pan, scraping the processor as clean as you can. Press the dough evenly onto the bottom of the pan. Bake for 10 to 12 minutes in the preheated oven, just until it begins to puff a bit and the top appears dry. Remove from the oven and reduce heat to 325°F (170°C).

Make the filling: In the same processor bowl (no need to wash it), process the tofu and cashew butter until smooth. Add the remaining ingredients and process again, scraping down the sides if necessary, until completely combined and silky smooth.

Pour the cheesecake into the partially baked crust and smooth the top. (For a smooth top, do this: wearing oven mitts, grab the pan on either side, at the 3:00 and 9:00 positions. Then, holding the sides, quickly rotate it first to the left a quarter turn, then to the right. Do this several times, and the top should eventually smooth out.).

Chai Cheesecake *continued* ✱ CF ✱

Bake the cheesecake at 325°F (170°C) another 45 to 55 minutes, rotating the pan about halfway through baking, until the cheesecake appears dry and firm on top and just barely jiggles in the center when you shake the pan.

Allow to cool to room temperature before refrigerating, at least 6 hours (or overnight) before serving. See page 37, storing your baked goods. May be frozen; defrost, covered, in the refrigerator overnight.

My Mother's Cheesecake * CF *

Serves 9 to 12

My dad grew up on a farm, and his grandmother made old-fashioned cheesecake for special occasions. My mom reproduced the recipe as a treat for my dad, and now I've created a new version that's vegan and free of gluten or sugar. We called this "Farmer's Cheesecake" at home, but I think the credit should go to my mom.

FOR THE FILLING:

1 (12-oz or 375-g) box aseptically packaged firm silken tofu, such as Mori-Nu (not the kind packed in water and displayed in refrigerated coolers)
½ cup (120 ml) natural smooth cashew butter, at room temperature
½ cup (120 ml) light agave nectar
2 tsp (10 ml) finely grated lemon zest (about 1 large lemon), preferably organic
2 tsp (10 ml) fresh lemon juice
½ tsp (2.5 ml) pure lemon extract
1 tsp (5 ml) pure vanilla extract
Pinch fine sea salt

FOR THE CRUST:

⅓ cup (80 ml) sunflower or other light-tasting oil, preferably organic
¼ cup (60 ml) light agave nectar
2 Tbsp (30 ml) plain or vanilla soy or almond milk
1¼ tsp (6.5 ml) pure vanilla extract
1 heaping Tbsp (20 ml) arrowroot powder or tapioca starch
1 scant cup (125 g) Ricki's All-Purpose Gluten-Free Flour Mix (see page 22)
¾ cup (110 g) sorghum flour
Heaping ¼ tsp (1.5 ml) baking powder
Heaping ¼ tsp (1.5 ml) baking soda
1½ tsp (7.5 ml) xanthan gum (use only Bob's Red Mill brand if you are concerned about a corn allergy)
Heaping ¼ tsp (1.5 ml) fine sea salt

Preheat the oven to 350°F (180°C). Line an 8-inch (20-cm) square pan with parchment paper, or spray with nonstick spray.

Make the filling: Blend the tofu and cashew butter in a food processor until well combined, scraping down the sides if necessary. Add the agave nectar, lemon zest, lemon juice, lemon extract, vanilla, and salt and process until perfectly smooth and velvety (there should be no bits of tofu visible). Set aside.

Make the crust: In a medium bowl, whisk together the oil, agave nectar, milk, and vanilla to emulsify. Sift the arrowroot, all-purpose flour, sorghum flour, baking powder, baking soda, xanthan gum, and salt over the mixture in the bowl and stir with a wooden spoon to combine to a soft dough (it will be slightly sticky, but firm enough to hold a shape). Remove about ⅓ of the dough and set aside (you can just estimate — you'll need about ½ cup or 120 ml) for the lattice top.

Assemble and bake the cake: Press the remaining dough evenly into the bottom of the prepared pan with wet fingers or a silicone spatula (the spatula works well to avoid sticking).

Pour the filling evenly over the crust in the pan. To smooth the top, grab the pan on opposite sides with your hands and, keeping the bottom of the pan flat against the surface it's on, quickly rotate it once to the left and then to the right.

(continued on page 188)

My Mother's Cheesecake *continued* ✱ CF ✱

Divide the reserved dough in half, then divide each half into 3 equal parts (you'll have 6 balls of dough). Pinching about ½ of each ball at a time, roll it between your palms to create a thin rope about ⅜ of an inch (just under 1 cm) thick.

Starting at one corner and working diagonally across to the opposite corner of the pan, place the ropes of dough in a straight line from one corner to the other (the dough doesn't necessarily have to be rolled in a single rope that spans the whole distance across the pan — you can line up shorter pieces end-to-end). Next, place ropes of dough on either side parallel to the first rope, so you end up with three diagonal lines across the pan. Continue until you have 5 lines in one direction across the pan (shorter lines toward the edges).

Repeat with ropes of dough in the opposite direction, crossing over the first ropes. You should end up with a diagonal crisscross pattern over the surface of the cheesecake. (If you prefer, you can simply crumble the remaining dough evenly over the top of the cheesecake instead.)

Bake for 30 to 40 minutes, rotating the pan about halfway through baking, until the filling appears firm and the edges of the dough are beginning to brown. Cool completely, then refrigerate until cold (at least 4 hours) before slicing. See page 37, storing your baked goods. May be frozen; defrost, covered, in the refrigerator overnight.

Quick Blueberry-Pineapple Crisp * CF, SF, and NF *

Serves 4 to 6

This crisp is the quintessential summer dessert. It is exactly the kind of easy, light fare one enjoys while sitting outside on a warm day and sipping an iced tea. Surprisingly, it also works well in winter, making use of frozen fruit. Enjoy it anytime!

FOR THE FILLING:

1½ cups (235 g) fresh or frozen blueberries
1 heaping cup (180 g) diced fresh or frozen pineapple
2 tsp (10 ml) finely grated lemon zest (about 1 medium lemon), preferably organic
1 Tbsp (15 ml) fresh lemon juice
1 Tbsp (15 ml) Ricki's All-Purpose Gluten-Free Flour Mix (see page 22)
¼ cup (60 ml) water (reduce to 2 Tbsp or 30 ml if using frozen fruit), mixed with 10 to 20 drops pure plain or vanilla stevia liquid, or to taste

FOR THE CRUMBLE TOPPING:

2 Tbsp (30 ml) coconut sugar
¼ cup (60 ml) water or unsweetened plain or vanilla soy or almond milk
1 Tbsp (15 ml) pure vanilla extract
⅛ tsp (.5 ml) pure stevia powder or ¼ to ½ tsp (1 to 2.5 ml) pure plain or vanilla stevia liquid, or to taste
1 cup (100 g) old-fashioned rolled oats (not instant or quick-cooking)
½ cup (65 g) Ricki's All-Purpose Gluten-Free Flour Mix (see page 22)
2 tsp (10 ml) ground cinnamon
½ tsp (2.5 ml) ground ginger
Pinch fine sea salt
⅓ cup (80 ml) coconut oil, melted (at low temperature), preferably organic

Coconut Whipped Cream (see page 168), for serving (optional)

Preheat the oven to 350°F (180°C). Line a 4-cup (1-L) casserole dish or 8-inch (20-cm) square pan with parchment paper, or spray with nonstick spray.

Make the filling: In a medium bowl, toss together the blueberries, pineapple, lemon zest, lemon juice, flour, and water mixed with stevia. Pour into the prepared casserole dish.

Make the crumble topping: In a small bowl or glass measuring cup, mix together the coconut sugar, water or milk, vanilla, and stevia; stir to begin dissolving the sugar. Set aside.

In a medium bowl, whisk together the oats, flour, cinnamon, ginger, and salt until everything is well distributed. Add the coconut oil in spoonfuls scattered over the top, and then pinch with your fingers until the mixture comes together in a crumbly dough (your fingers will get full of oil at first, but it will eventually come together). Drizzle with the wet mixture, then toss with a fork until well mixed. It should be moist but still crumbly.

Assemble and bake: Top the fruit mixture with the crumble topping, pressing the top down very gently (it should look bumpy, not flat). Place the casserole dish on a cookie sheet to catch any spills, and bake for 50 to 60 minutes, rotating the dish about halfway through baking, until the top is browned and the fruit is soft when pierced. Allow to cool for 10 to 20 minutes before serving. If desired, top each serving with a dollop of Coconut Whipped Cream (see page 168). This is also good at room temperature. Store, covered, in the refrigerator, up to 4 days. May be frozen.

Grain-Free Autumn Fruit Crumble * CF, GF, SF *

Serves 6 to 8

This is another one of those "desserts that can be breakfast." With the abundance of fall fruit and absence of grains, this dish offers a great lower-glycemic way to start your day. Add a bit more protein, and you're all set! For best results, select crisp, sweet apples, such as Gala, Honeycrisp, or Pink Lady, and firm pears, such as D'Anjou or Bosc.

FOR THE TOPPING:

⅓ cup (45 g) coconut sugar
½ cup (65 g) natural raw walnut pieces
½ cup (80 g) natural raw skin-on almonds, preferable organic
⅓ cup (50 g) coconut flour
¼ cup (40 g) potato starch
1 Tbsp (30 ml) ground cinnamon
Generous pinch fine sea salt
3 Tbsp (45 ml) coconut oil, at room temperature, preferably organic
30 drops pure plain or vanilla stevia liquid, or to taste
1 tsp (5 ml) pure vanilla extract
3 Tbsp (45 ml) water

FOR THE FILLING:

2 medium pears, washed, cored, and diced, peeled or unpeeled
2 medium sweet apples, washed, cored, and diced, peeled or unpeeled
1 cup (115 g) fresh or frozen cranberries
1 tsp (5 ml) ground cinnamon
¼ tsp (1 ml) ground ginger
2 Tbsp (30 ml) coconut sugar
Juice of ½ lemon
¼ tsp (1 ml) pure stevia powder or ½ tsp (2.5 ml) pure plain or vanilla stevia liquid, or to taste

Coconut Whipped Cream (see page 168), for serving

Preheat the oven to 350°F (180°C). Grease a 9-inch (22.5-cm) square pan or a 6-cup (1.4-L) casserole or soufflé dish with nonstick spray or coconut oil.

Make the topping: Place the coconut sugar, walnuts, almonds, coconut flour, potato starch, cinnamon, and salt in the bowl of a food processor and process until the mixture resembles a fine meal with no pieces of nuts visible.

In a small, heavy-bottomed pot, melt the coconut oil. Whisk in the stevia, vanilla, and water. Pour the coconut-oil mixture in a ring around the dry ingredients in the processor and pulse until it all comes together. It should look like moist clumps. Set aside.

Make the filling: In a large bowl, toss the pear, apple, and cranberries together with the cinnamon and ginger. In a small bowl, mix together the coconut sugar, lemon juice, and stevia, and stir until the sugar begins to dissolve. Drizzle over the fruit and then toss again to coat evenly.

Assemble and bake the crumble: Turn the fruit mixture into the prepared casserole dish and sprinkle with the topping. Press down gently on the topping.

Bake for 40 to 60 minutes (depending on the depth of your pan, you will need more or less time for the fruit to cook), rotating the dish about halfway through baking, until the crumble topping is deeply browned and the fruit is soft. Serve immediately or at room temperature with a little Coconut Whipped Cream (see page 168). See page 37, storing your baked goods. May be frozen.

Spiced Pumpkin Millet Pudding * CF, NF, can be SF, *

Serves 6

This pudding is rich and creamy enough to serve as a dessert, but nutritious enough for breakfast as a cooked cereal. I love this cold from the refrigerator, but it's also delicious warm. If you use Coconut Whipped Cream, please note the recipe will not be corn-free.

- ½ cup (100 g) dry millet
- ½ cup (120 ml) plain or vanilla rice, soy, or almond milk
- ½ cup (120 ml) water
- 1 can (14 oz or 400 ml) full-fat canned coconut milk, preferably organic
- ½ cup (120 ml) canned or homemade unsweetened pumpkin puree (see page 23)
- ¼ cup (60 ml) light agave nectar
- ½ tsp (2.5 ml) ground ginger
- 1 tsp (5 ml) ground cinnamon
- ¼ tsp (1 ml) nutmeg

- 1 batch Coconut Whipped Cream (see page 168), for serving (optional)
- Cinnamon for sprinkling (optional)

Preheat the oven to 350°F (180°C). Grease a 6-cup (1.4-L) casserole or soufflé dish with nonstick spray or coconut oil.

Place the millet, milk, and water in a saucepan and bring to boil over medium-high heat. Turn off heat. Add the coconut milk, pumpkin puree, agave nectar, ginger, cinnamon, and nutmeg and stir to combine. Pour the mixture into the prepared casserole dish and cover.

Bake the covered casserole for about an hour, removing the dish every 20 minutes or so to stir the contents, then replace the cover and return to the oven. After an hour, the millet should be well cooked, with the grains beginning to break apart; the pudding will still be fairly loose, but a bit more gelatinous than when it began to bake (it will continue to thicken as it cools). Remove the casserole from the oven and allow to sit, uncovered, at least 20 minutes before serving. Stir again before serving.

May be served warm, at room temperature, or cold. If desired, top with Coconut Whipped Cream (see page 168) and sprinkle with cinnamon. Store, covered, in the refrigerator for up to 4 days. May be frozen. Defrost, covered, in the refrigerator and then gently heat to serve.

Variation:
Rice Pudding: Use dried brown basmati rice in place of the millet; add ⅓ cup (40 g) raisins to the pudding before baking.

Bread Pudding with Warm Caramel Sauce * Can be CF, SF *

Makes one 8-inch (20-cm) cheesecake (serves 6 to 8)

One of my favorite "comfort food" desserts is bread pudding. When I lived alone during my undergraduate years, I was known to eat it regularly for breakfast, too. This revamped recipe tastes incredibly rich and decadent, making it perfect for a special dessert — but with its whole-food ingredients, feel free to go ahead and try it for breakfast, too, if you wish. Please note that most packaged breads use xantham gum, and not all xantham gum is corn-free. See page 23 for more information.

FOR THE PUDDING:

5 to 6 slices of your favorite mildly flavored gluten-free bread (use 6 if thinly sliced — see *Note*)

¼ cup (25 g) old-fashioned rolled oats (not instant or quick-cooking)

¼ cup (60 ml) natural smooth cashew butter, at room temperature, or ½ cup (80 g) natural raw cashews

3 cups (720 ml) unsweetened plain or vanilla soy, almond, rice, flax, or other nondairy milk

1½ Tbsp (22.5 ml) whole psyllium husks

1 tsp (5 ml) ground cinnamon

2 Tbsp (30 ml) coconut sugar

20 to 30 drops pure plain or vanilla stevia liquid, or to taste

Pinch fine sea salt

1 medium juicy apple, such as MacIntosh or Spartan, cored, peeled, and cut into chunks

FOR THE CARAMEL SAUCE:

2 Tbsp (30 ml) lucuma powder

2 tsp (10 ml) carob powder

¼ cup (60 ml) coconut nectar

15-25 drops pure plain or vanilla stevia liquid, or to taste

2 Tbsp (30 ml) coconut oil, at room temperature, preferably organic

pinch fine sea salt

1 tsp (5 ml) pure vanilla extract

1 tsp (5 ml) brandy or rum extract (optional) (or 1 Tbsp/15 ml brandy or rum)

½ cup (120 ml) unsweetened plain or vanilla soy or almond milk or coconut beverage (the kind that comes in a carton)

Make the pudding: Preheat the oven to 350°F (180°C). Spray an 8-cup (2-L) casserole dish with nonstick spray, or grease with coconut oil.

Dice the bread into large cubes and place them in a large bowl.

In a blender, whir the oats until powdered. Add remaining ingredients and blend again until smooth. Pour this mixture over the bread in the bowl and stir gently to coat all pieces. Allow to sit and absorb the liquid for 10 to 15 minutes, until the bread is well moistened throughout. Transfer the mixture to the casserole dish.

Bake for 35 to 45 minutes, until the top is slightly puffed and beginning to brown. Remove from heat and cool slightly before serving. May also be served at room temperature or cold. Top each serving with a spoonful or two of warm caramel sauce (see instructions below). Makes 6 to 8 servings. See page 37, storing your baked goods. Unsauced pudding can be frozen.

While the pudding bakes, make the sauce: In a small pot, whisk all ingredients over medium-low heat until bubbling. Lower heat slightly and continue to cook, allowing the mixture to bubble without boiling over, for another 5 minutes, stirring constantly. Remove from heat and use with bread pudding. Makes about ¾ cup (180 ml), enough for 6 servings. Keep, covered, in the refrigerator, for up to 5 days. (Also good over ice cream or pancakes!)

Note: While you can use any gluten-free bread in this recipe, you'll achieve best results with a lighter style of bread rather than a really dense loaf (such as a sourdough). I've even made this pudding using gluten-free hamburger buns, with great success.

Chapter 5: *Raw & No-Bake Treats*

Grain-Free Raw Cookie Dough Bites ✷ GF, CF, can be SF ✷

Makes 4 to 5 balls

These are a great snack when you're craving something sweet and indulgent tasting — yet they won't spike your blood sugar or crush your resolve to stay grain-free and low glycemic.

1 heaping Tbsp (20 ml) "Salted Caramel" Walnut Butter (see page 91) or natural smooth cashew, macadamia, or almond butter, at room temperature
1 Tbsp (15 ml) unsweetened plain or vanilla almond, soy, or rice milk, or coconut beverage (the kind that comes in a carton)
1 tsp (5 ml) agave nectar or coconut nectar
1 tsp (5 ml) pure vanilla extract
10 to 20 drops pure plain or vanilla stevia liquid, or to taste
¼ cup (30 g) almond flour or meal
1 Tbsp (15 ml) coconut flour
Pinch fine sea salt
½ tsp (2.5 ml) ground cinnamon (optional)
1 Tbsp (15 ml) unsweetened carob chips or cacao nibs

In a small bowl, whisk together the nut butter, milk, agave nectar, vanilla, and stevia until smooth and creamy. Add the almond flour, coconut flour, salt, and cinnamon and, using a wooden spoon, mix well to form a soft "dough." Stir in the chips.

Scoop the mixture using a melon baller or teaspoon, then roll into balls. Refrigerate until firm, or eat as is. Will keep, covered, in the refrigerator, for up to 1 week. Serve chilled; not suitable for freezing.

Marbled Halvah ✱ GF, SF, CF ✱

Makes 20 to 30 small squares

This is the kind of dessert that looks great on a candy tray alongside chocolates or truffles. At the same time, it contains so many healthy ingredients and is so packed with nutrition that you can feel just fine eating a few pieces as an afternoon snack. It's also a great way to consume more calcium, as sesame seeds are very high in this important mineral.

FOR THE HALVAH BASE:

½ cup (80 g) natural raw cashews, lightly toasted

¾ cup (180 ml) tahini (sesame seed paste)

¼ cup (35 g) sesame seeds, lightly toasted

1 tsp (5 ml) pure vanilla extract

Pinch fine sea salt

3 Tbsp (45 ml) coconut nectar or yacon syrup

10 to 20 drops pure plain or vanilla stevia liquid, or to taste

FOR THE CHOCOLATE SWIRL:

1 oz (30 g) unsweetened chocolate, preferably organic

1 Tbsp (15 ml) agave nectar

10 to 20 drops pure plain or vanilla stevia liquid, or to taste

Make the halvah base: In the bowl of a food processor, whir the cashews until they resemble a coarse cornmeal. There should be no pieces left bigger than a sesame seed.

Add the remaining ingredients and blend until the mixture comes together in a ball. It should have the consistency of a thick dough (resist the temptation to add liquid to make it blend more easily; you want it to be fairly dry, but just moist enough to hold together). Break up the ball with your fingers or a spatula and crumble it evenly around the processor bowl. Set aside.

Make the chocolate swirl: Pour enough water into a small pot to fill it about 1 inch (2.5 cm) deep. Bring to a boil, then reduce the heat to the lowest possible setting. Place a large heatproof bowl over the pot (it should be large enough that the bottom doesn't touch the water in the pot), and add the chocolate to the bowl. Stir constantly until the chocolate melts, a couple of minutes. Remove the bowl from the pot, and then stir in the agave nectar and stevia. The mixture should remain smooth and pourable.

Finish the halvah: Drizzle the chocolate mixture in a ring directly over the halvah in the processor bowl. Don't worry if it's not even or if it doesn't cover the entire halvah mixture. Replace the processor cover and pulse once or twice ONLY to barely incorporate the chocolate in rivulets through the mixture (any more than this and you will end up with chocolate halvah). You want the chocolate to be distributed between the bits of halvah, but not blended into it. (If you do happen to blend too much, chocolate halvah is lovely, too.)

Lay out a large piece of plastic wrap on your counter and turn the mixture onto it. Folding the plastic over the halvah mixture, press the mixture into place to form a compact rectangle. Cover with plastic and refrigerate until firm. Once firm, cut into small squares for serving. Store, covered, in the refrigerator, for up to 1 week. Serve chilled; not suitable for freezing.

Raw Fig & Cherry Bars * GF, SF, CF *

Makes 1 dozen

I originally developed these bars for a cooking class on bone health. Almost every ingredient here is high in calcium, resulting in a bar that delivers about 12 percent of this mineral's daily requirement for women. They're also high in protein and work as a great energy bar. I often carry these in the car with me for a mid-afternoon pick-me-up.

2 cups (290 g) natural raw skin-on almonds, preferably organic

¼ cup (25 g) finely ground flax seeds or meal (from about 2 Tbsp or 30 ml whole seeds)

1 Tbsp (15 ml) finely grated lemon zest (about 2 medium lemons), preferably organic

6¾ to 7 oz (190 to 200 g) destemmed and quartered dried figs

2 Tbsp (30 ml) to ¼ cup (60 ml) agave nectar

2 Tbsp (30 ml) raw tahini (sesame seed paste, not toasted), or regular tahini (sesame seed paste) for bars that are not completely raw

1 cup (125 g) dried tart cherries or dried cranberries

Lightly grease a 9-inch (22.5-cm) square pan with coconut oil, or line with plastic wrap.

In the bowl of a food processor, combine the almonds and flax and process until you have a fine meal (there should be no pieces of almonds bigger than sesame seeds). Do not overprocess, however, or you'll end up with nut butter!

Add the lemon zest and figs and process again until well blended and there are no large pieces of fig visible. Add 2 tablespoons (30 ml) of the agave, the tahini, and the cherries and pulse or process briefly to chop the cherries and create a moist, dough-like consistency. The mixture is ready if it sticks together and feels slightly moist when pinched between your thumb and fingers. Taste the dough to see if it's sweet enough. If necessary, to adjust sweetness and/or consistency, add up to 2 tablespoons (30 ml) more agave nectar to moisten, and pulse again until desired consistency is achieved.

Turn the mixture into the prepared pan and press down very firmly with your fist or the back of a metal spatula (it helps to cover with plastic wrap first). The mixture should be extremely compact and solid — press hard!

Refrigerate until very firm, about an hour, or at least 20 minutes. Cut into 12 bars and store in an airtight container in the refrigerator, or wrap each bar individually in plastic wrap for a grab-and-go snack. The bars will keep, refrigerated, for up to 2 weeks. Serve chilled. May be frozen; defrost, covered, in the refrigerator overnight.

Raw Chocolate Fudge-Topped Brownies ✷ GF, CF, SF ✷

Makes about 25

This is a double-fudgy treat that's reminiscent of Nutella in its chocolate-hazelnut glory. The raw cacao here imparts a distinct chocolate flavor that melds well with the sweeteners used. These are cut into small, bite-sized morsels, but that's all you'll need with these ultra-rich chocolatey treats!

FOR THE BROWNIES:

1½ cups (170 g) raw walnut halves or pieces (see *Note*)

1½ cups (225 g) raw hazelnuts (see *Note*)

⅓ cup (25 g) coconut sugar

Pinch fine sea salt

¾ cup (80 g) raw cacao powder

⅓ cup (80 ml) agave nectar or coconut nectar

2 tsp (10 ml) raw vanilla powder or pure vanilla extract

¼ tsp (1 ml) pure stevia powder or ½ tsp (2.5 ml) pure plain or vanilla stevia liquid, or to taste

FOR THE FUDGE TOPPING:

1 cup coconut butter (not solid coconut oil)

1 cup (140 g) raw hazelnuts (see *Note*)

1 heaping ¼ cup (30 g) raw cacao powder

¼ cup (60 ml) coconut sugar

1 tsp (5 ml) raw vanilla powder or pure vanilla extract

Pinch fine sea salt

20 to 30 drops pure plain or vanilla stevia liquid, or to taste

Make the brownies: Line an 8.5-inch (21.5-cm) square pan with parchment paper and set aside (for thicker brownies, recipe can be made in a loaf pan instead).

In a food processor, whir the walnuts, hazelnuts, coconut sugar, and salt until the mixture resembles coarse crumbs. Add the cacao powder, agave nectar, vanilla powder, and stevia and process until it begins to come together in a ball. Stop and scrape the sides if necessary while processing. Take care not to overprocess, or you'll end up with nut butter! The mixture should be moist enough to stick together when pinched, but not wet.

Turn the brownie "dough" into the pan and press down firmly with your hands or a stiff spatula so that the mixture is dense and there are no air bubbles. Place in the refrigerator while you prepare the fudge topping.

Make the fudge topping: Place the coconut butter, hazelnuts, cacao powder, coconut sugar, vanilla powder (if using vanilla extract, add it later), and salt in a high-speed blender. Using the tamper to push the mixture toward the blades, blend until the mixture liquefies, about 5 minutes, stopping to scrape down the sides as necessary. Add the vanilla extract, if using, and the stevia and blend again.

Pour the mixture over the brownie dough in the pan. Return to the refrigerator until the fudge sets up, about 1 hour. Using the parchment paper as a sling, pull out the brownie and place it on a cutting board. Cut into 1½-inch (4-cm) squares and store, covered, in the refrigerator until ready to serve. Will keep, covered, in the refrigerator, for up to 5 days. May be frozen; defrost, covered, in the refrigerator overnight.

Note: For brownies that are not completely raw, you can use lightly toasted nuts. Do not toast the coconut for the frosting, however, or it won't work!

"Milk Chocolate" Mint Truffles ✸ GF, SF, CF ✸

Makes 12 to 16 truffles

Although these truffles scream "holidays," they are great anytime as a "just because" treat. The filling is smooth, creamy, and melt-in-your-mouth — everything you'd want a truffle to be.

FOR THE FILLING:

½ cup plus 2 tsp (130 ml total) coconut butter, melted, preferably organic

¼ cup plus 2 tsp (70 ml total) natural smooth cashew or macadamia butter, at room temperature

⅓ cup (55 g) coconut sugar, ground to a fine powder in a coffee grinder

Pinch fine sea salt

1.5 oz. (40 g) unsweetened chocolate

1 tsp (5 ml) pure vanilla extract

½ tsp (2.5 ml) pure peppermint extract

¼ tsp (1 ml) pure stevia powder or ½ tsp (2.5 ml) pure plain or vanilla stevia liquid, or to taste

FOR THE CHOCOLATE COATING:

4 oz (115 g) unsweetened chocolate

1 Tbsp (15 ml) coconut oil, at room temperature, preferably organic

2 Tbsp (30 ml) carob powder, sifted

20 to 30 drops pure plain or vanilla stevia liquid, or to taste

Make the filling: Line a small square plastic container (about 2-cup or 500-ml capacity), single-serving loaf pan, or other small square container with plastic wrap. Alternately, for round truffles, you could use miniature silicone muffin cups. Set aside.

In a small, heavy-bottomed pot, combine the coconut butter, cashew butter, coconut sugar, salt, and chocolate. Heat over the lowest heat possible, stirring constantly, until the chocolate is melted and very smooth. Add the vanilla, peppermint extract, and stevia and stir well. (For a glassy-smooth filling, at this point you can pour this mixture into a blender and blend for 30 seconds to smooth out any last remnants of graininess from the coconut sugar. But this is totally not necessary — they're still delicious without this extra step.)

Pour the mixture into the prepared container and refrigerate until solid, 40 to 60 minutes. Once solid, invert onto a small cutting board lined with plastic and allow to sit for 5 minutes to soften slightly (this will happen fairly quickly, but if you cut it right away, it will splinter and crack). Using a very sharp knife, cut into 12 to 16 squares. Alternately, pour the mixture into the silicone cups and refrigerate as above. Pop out of the cups and place on a small cutting board.

Place the cutting board with the squares or rounds on it in the freezer until completely solid, about an hour.

About ten minutes before you will coat the truffles, make the chocolate coating: Bring about 1 inch (2.5 cm) of water to a boil in a small pot; turn down to lowest heat. Set a heatproof bowl over the pot (the bowl should be big enough that the bottom isn't touching the water in the pot). Add the chocolate and coconut oil to the bowl. Allow to sit about 30 seconds, then stir until the chocolate melts. Remove the bowl from the pot and whisk in the carob powder and stevia. Mix well to eliminate any lumps.

Coat the truffles: Place the bowl of chocolate on the counter. Get yourself a large dinner fork.

Bring the board with the cut-out squares or rounds of filling to the counter. Working quickly, grab each piece and dip the bottom in the chocolate; let it drip off a bit, then place it chocolate-side-down back onto the board. When they're all done, return the board to the freezer so the chocolate can firm up a bit (about 5 minutes).

One at a time, place each square or round chocolate-side-down on the fork. Hold the truffle over the bowl and, using a spoon or spatula, spoon more chocolate over the top and sides of each square, allowing the excess to drip through the tines of the fork and back into the bowl. Tap the fork on the side of the bowl to remove any furthur excess. At this point, it's really important to ensure that the entire filling is coated, with no uncovered spots peeking through the chocolate! Using the tip of a knife or another fork, slide the truffle off the fork back onto the cutting board. Repeat with each square or round.

Once all the truffles are coated, pop them in the fridge for another 10 to 15 minutes to firm up completely (no need to go back in the freezer at this point).

After the truffles are firm, you can drizzle any leftover chocolate coating over them to create pretty patterns, or dip a dried cranberry or goji berry in a bit of the leftover chocolate to "glue" it to the top of a truffle as decoration.

Store the truffles in a covered container in the refrigerator for up to one week. Remove them from the fridge at least 10 minutes before serving to allow the filling inside to soften up for a smoother, more ganache-like consistency. If you've covered the entire filling with chocolate, the truffles should be fine at room temperature, as the coating is solid and will prevent any of the filling from oozing out.

Raw Gingersnap Cookie Bon Bons ✷ CF, can be SF ✷

Makes about 20

These indulgent-tasting bites are so pretty that you'll want to serve them at parties and holiday events (just don't tell your guests how healthy they are). For a quicker, "everyday" variation, omit the coating and enjoy the base rolled into balls as high-energy snacks.

FOR THE COOKIE "DOUGH":

⅔ cup (110 g) natural raw almonds

⅔ cup (110 g) natural raw cashews, lightly toasted

⅔ cup (65 g) old-fashioned rolled oats (not instant or quick-cooking)

2 tsp (10 ml) ground cinnamon

¼ tsp (1 ml) ground cloves

4 tsp (20 ml) ground chia seeds (from about 2 tsp or 10 ml whole seeds)

Pinch fine sea salt

1 Tbsp (15 ml) finely grated fresh ginger

2 Tbsp (30 ml) yacon syrup

¼ to ⅜ tsp (1 to 1.5 ml) pure stevia powder or ½ or ¾ tsp (2.5 to 3.5 ml) drops pure plain or vanilla stevia liquid, or to taste

2 Tbsp (30 ml) almond or soy milk, if needed

FOR THE "WHITE CHOCOLATE" COATING

1 cup (240 ml) coconut butter, melted

2 Tbsp (30 ml) coconut oil, melted (at low temperature), preferably organic

1 Tbsp (15 ml) coconut sugar

15 to 25 drops pure plain or vanilla stevia liquid, or to taste

½ tsp (2.5 ml) pure vanilla extract

Extra ground cinnamon, if desired, for sprinkling

Set out a cookie sheet lined with plastic wrap or parchment paper, or line an 8-inch (20-cm) loaf pan with plastic.

Make the dough: Place the almonds, cashews, oats, cinnamon, cloves, chia, and salt in the bowl of a food processor and process until the mixture resembles a very fine meal (there should be no pieces of nut bigger than a sesame seed). Add the remaining ingredients and process until the mixture begins to come together in a ball. It should look fairly dry but stick together when pinched between your thumb and fingers. Add milk only if absolutely necessary to make the dough stick together; it should not be wet.

Using a small scoop or a teaspoon, scoop the dough and form into balls. Place on a plate in the freezer to firm up, 10 to 20 minutes. Alternately, press the dough in the bottom of the loaf pan and refrigerate. Once firm, invert onto a cutting board and cut into 20 small squares. Return the squares to the refrigerator until ready to coat.

Make the coating: Place all coating ingredients in the container of a high-powered blender or food processor and blend until perfectly smooth and liquid, about 5 minutes, scraping down the sides as necessary. Pour the mixture into a small, deep bowl.

Coat the bon bons: Line a large, flat plate with plastic wrap and set aside. Dip each ball or square in the coconut coating until it is completely covered. Scoop out carefully with a fork, and tap the fork handle on the edge of the bowl so that excess coating drips back into the bowl. Place on the plate and return to the freezer until coating is solid (about 5 minutes); then repeat the coating process once more for each ball or square. Sprinkle gently with cinnamon, if desired. Once the coating is hard, the bon bons may be kept in the refrigerator. Store, covered, in the refrigerator, for up to 1 week.

Raw Frosted Lemon-Poppy Seed Squares * SF, CF *

Makes about 1 dozen

A while back, I hosted a friend's birthday party at our house. I made these squares so that I'd have something to eat while everyone else feasted on the conventional (white flour and white sugar) cake. When I brought out my plate of lemon bars, someone asked to taste them — and within minutes the plate was empty! These treats are tasty and impressive enough to serve to anyone, restricted diet or not.

FOR THE BASE:

2 heaping Tbsp (35 ml) ground chia seeds (from about 1 Tbsp or 15 ml whole seeds)

1 cup (165 g) natural raw skin-on almonds, preferably organic

¾ cup (115 g) natural raw cashews

Pinch fine sea salt

2 tsp (10 ml) grated lemon zest (about 1 large lemon), preferably organic, divided in half

Juice of 1 lemon, preferably organic, divided in half

2 Tbsp (30 ml) agave nectar or yacon syrup

15 to 20 drops pure plain or vanilla stevia liquid, or to taste

1 tsp (5 ml) pure vanilla extract

Up to 1 tablespoon (15 ml) water, if needed

2 Tbsp (30 ml) poppy seeds

FOR THE FROSTING:

Heaping ¼ cup (70 ml) ground chia seeds (from about 2 Tbsp or 30 ml whole seeds)

⅓ cup (80 ml) coconut oil, at room temperature, preferably organic

1 Tbsp (15 ml) raw smooth cashew or macadamia butter, at room temperature

Reserved lemon zest (from making base, above)

Reserved lemon juice (from making base, above)

15 to 20 drops pure plain or vanilla stevia liquid, or to taste

FOR THE GARNISH (OPTIONAL)

Extra grated lemon zest (from an additional lemon)

Extra poppy seeds

Make the base: Line a regular loaf pan with plastic wrap. Set aside.

Combine the chia, almonds, cashews, and salt in the bowl of a food processor and process until the mixture looks like a fairly fine meal (no pieces of almond should be visible).

In a small bowl, mix together half of the lemon zest, half of the lemon juice (about 2 tablespoons or 30 ml), the agave nectar, stevia, and vanilla until everything is well combined. Pour the lemon-juice mixture over the dry ingredients in the processor and blend until it comes together in what looks like a sticky dough (if it's too dry, add up to 1 tablespoon or 15 ml water). Sprinkle with the poppy seeds and pulse just until they are incorporated.

Turn the base into the prepared loaf pan and, using wet hands or a silicone spatula, press it down firmly and evenly. Place the pan in the fridge while you prepare the frosting.

Make the frosting: In the bowl of a food processor or using a hand blender, blend the chia, coconut oil, nut butter, reserved lemon zest, reserved lemon juice (you should have about 2 tablespoons or 30 ml), and stevia until perfectly smooth. The mixture may liquefy as the coconut oil melts; this is fine.

Frost and unmold: Pour the frosting over the base in the pan and swirl the top. If desired, sprinkle with additional lemon zest and poppy seeds to garnish (see photo, page 208). Refrigerate until firm, at least 2 hours. (Tip: If the frosting is too liquid to hold a shape when you first pour it over the base, refrigerate about 15 minutes until it firms up a bit, and then add any swirls that you like.) Once the top is firm, fold the plastic wrap over it to cover.

To unmold, peel back the plastic on top and invert onto a cutting board; turn right-side-up and cut into 12 or more pieces (they should be relatively small). Serve immediately; store leftovers, covered, in the refrigerator, for up to 5 days. May be frozen. Defrost in refrigerator.

Raw Superfood Cupcakes with Coconut-Butter Buttercream Frosting * GF, SF, CF *

Makes 18 mini cupcakes or balls, or 6 regular cupcakes

These elegant little bites are a great postprandial treat. For a more pronounced "caramel" flavor, opt for pecans instead of almonds in the base. Feel free to top with your choice of Coconut Butter Buttercream Frosting (see page 170; my favorite variation is caramel). And while I enjoyed pressing the "dough" into mini silicone cupcake molds to make cupcakes, you could just as easily omit the frosting and roll these into balls for a great portable snack.

FOR THE CUPCAKES:

2 Tbsp (30 ml) coconut sugar
1 tsp (5 ml) pure vanilla extract
2 Tbsp (30 ml) coconut nectar or agave nectar
⅛ tsp (.5 ml) pure stevia powder or ¼ to ½ tsp (1 to 2.5 ml) pure plain or vanilla stevia liquid, or to taste
2 Tbsp (30 ml) water
½ cup (80 g) natural raw cashews
½ cup (50 g) natural raw pecans or natural raw almonds (80 g)
½ cup (70 g) raw hemp seeds
⅓ cup (45 g) lucuma powder
⅛ tsp (.5 ml) fine sea salt

Coconut Butter Buttercream Frosting (see page 170)

If making cupcakes, have on hand 2 miniature silicone muffin molds (with 12 mini muffin cups in each) or 1 regular silicone muffin mold (with 6 muffin cups). Alternately, if making balls, line a rimmed baking sheet with plastic wrap and set aside.

Make the cupcakes: In a small bowl, stir together the coconut sugar, vanilla, coconut nectar, stevia, and water to partially dissolve the sugar. Set aside.

In the bowl of a mini food processor (or small food processor), whir together the cashews, pecans, hemp seeds, lucuma, and salt until the mixture resembles a powder. Rub a little of it between your thumb and fingers; if you can still see whole hemp seeds, process a bit more, but take care not to create nut butter (it should remain dry).

Stir the wet mixture one more time and pour it in a ring over the dry mixture in the processor bowl. Blend until it comes together in a sticky dough. It will likely stick to your fingers and the processor bowl, but should be thick enough to hold its shape. Resist the urge to add more dry ingredients; the raw ground nuts and seeds will absorb any excess liquid while the cupcakes chill, and they will firm up considerably after a few hours.

Using a small ice-cream scoop or tablespoon (15 ml) for mini cupcakes, scoop the mixture and pack it into the molds flush with the top, spreading the dough flat across the top. For regular-sized cupcakes, use a large ice-cream scoop or ⅓-cup (80-ml) measuring cup. Alternately, roll into balls and set on the prepared baking sheet. Refrigerate at least 2 hours, and up to overnight.

To frost the cupcakes: Pop the cupcakes out of the molds and place them on a plate or tray. Either pipe or spread your choice of Coconut Butter Buttercream Frosting (see page 170) over each cupcake. Refrigerate until ready to serve. Store, covered, in the refrigerator for up to 1 week. Serve chilled. Defrost, covered, in refrigerator overnight.

Decadent Chocolate Paté ✱ GF, SF, CF, NF ✱

Serves 4 to 6

With heart-healthy flavonoids from the dark chocolate and monounsaturated fats from the avocado, this is a cholesterol-free indulgence that's actually good for you!

½ cup (115 g) packed avocado puree from a barely ripe avocado (1 medium avocado)
1 tsp (5 ml) pure vanilla extract
⅛ tsp (.5 ml) pure stevia powder or ¼ tsp (1 ml) pure plain or vanilla stevia liquid, or to taste
Pinch fine sea salt
6 oz (170 g) unsweetened chocolate, chopped (or use 6 oz or 170 g dairyfree chocolate chips, if you can tolerate sugar)
⅓ cup (80 ml) freshly squeezed orange juice (from approximately 1 medium orange)
½ cup (85 g) coconut sugar

Fresh berries and/or Coconut Whipped Cream (see page 168), for serving

Line a miniature loaf pan with plastic wrap and set aside.

In the bowl of a food processor, whir the avocado puree, vanilla, stevia, and salt. Set aside while you melt the chocolate.

In a heavy-bottomed pot set over the lowest heat possible, combine the chocolate, orange juice, and coconut sugar. Stir constantly until the chocolate is melted and smooth, about 5 minutes. Immediately scrape the chocolate mixture into the food processor with the avocado mixture, and blend again until perfectly smooth and glossy. Turn the mixture into the loaf pan and smooth the top.

Refrigerate, uncovered, until the top is firm and dry; then cover the top with more plastic wrap and refrigerate until the entire loaf is firm, for 4 to 6 hours or overnight.

To unmold, remove the plastic from the top of the loaf. Invert over a serving dish and remove the loaf pan, then carefully peel away the rest of the plastic. Serve in thin slices with fresh berries and/or Coconut Whipped Cream (see page 168). May be frozen; defrost, wrapped in plastic, in the refrigerator overnight.

Caramel Ice Cream (no ice-cream maker required!)

✷ GF, CF, can be SF ✷

Serves 6 to 9

Don't be deterred by this unusual combination of ingredients. You will be amazed at how much this ice cream tastes like caramel! I love it with bits of cookie or brownie mixed in; try it made with Chocolate–Almond Butter Fudgies (see page 109) or Sweet Potato Brownies (see page 140). This recipe can be made in either a food processor or an ice-cream maker.

- 1 cup (155 g) natural raw cashews
- 1 cup (240 ml) canned or homemade unsweetened sweet potato puree (see page 23)
- 1 cup (240 ml) full-fat canned coconut milk, preferably organic
- ⅔ to 1 cup (160 to 240 ml) unsweetened plain or vanilla soy, almond, or rice milk
- ⅓ cup (55 g) coconut sugar
- 2 tsp (10 ml) pure vanilla extract
- 1 Tbsp (15 ml) lucuma or carob powder
- ⅛ tsp (.5 ml) pure stevia powder or ¼ tsp (1 ml) pure plain or vanilla stevia liquid, or to taste
- ½ tsp (2.5 ml) brandy or rum flavoring (or 1 Tbsp or 15 ml brandy or rum) (optional)
- ⅛ tsp (.5 ml) fine sea salt

Optional add-ins: cacao nibs, unsweetened carob chips, nondairy chocolate chips, or crumbled cookies or brownies, about 1 Tbsp (15 ml) per serving

Make the ice cream: If you have an ice-cream maker, set it up according to the manufacturer's directions. Alternately, place 9 silicone liners in a muffin pan and set aside, or line an 8-inch (20-cm) square pan with waxed paper and set aside.

Place the cashews, sweet potato puree, coconut milk, ⅔ cup (160 ml) of the milk, coconut sugar, vanilla, lucuma powder, stevia, brandy flavoring, if using, and salt in a high-powered blender and blend until smooth and creamy; it should have the texture of a light pudding. (Alternately, blend in smaller batches in a regular blender, and transfer each batch to a large bowl before proceeding.) If the ice cream is too thick, add up to ⅓ cup (80 ml) more milk as needed. You may need to scrape down the sides a few times during blending. Divide evenly among the muffin liners or pour into the pan.

If using an ice-cream maker: Pour the mixture into it at this point and follow manufacturer's directions. Serve. If using add-ins, add them during the final 5 minutes of churning.

If using a food processor: If using the muffin liners, freeze until firm, 5 to 6 hours, then peel off the silicone cups and place the disks in a sealed Ziploc bag or container in the freezer. If using the pan, freeze just until firm, 2 to 3 hours. Invert on a cutting board, peel off the waxed paper, and cut the square into 6 large or 9 small equal-sized pieces, depending on the number of people you would like to serve and/or how small or large you would like the serving size to be. Place the pieces in a sealed plastic bag or container in the freezer.

When ready to make the ice cream, remove 1 muffin-sized disk or square per person. Cut each disk or square into 3 to 4 smaller pieces and place in the bowl of a food processor. Process until the pieces start to come together in a ball (at first they will resemble crumbs), then press down with a rubber spatula and process briefly once more until smooth. Serve. Will keep, frozen, for up to 3 months.

Incorporate the add-ins, if using: Prepare the ice cream as directed. Once it's ready, sprinkle the add-ins over the ice cream in the processor, then pulse once or twice only to incorporate.

Chai Ice Cream (no ice-cream maker required!) * GF, SF, CF *

Serves 6 to 8

Although I'm not fond of chai tea, I adore this combination of spices in other desserts — like this ice cream. Of course, you could use any tea flavor you prefer, as long as it's robust and flavorful. Some people find the natural sweetness of the pears sufficient in this recipe; if that's you, feel free to omit the stevia. This recipe can be made in either a food processor or an ice-cream maker.

1 cup (240 ml) plain or vanilla rice milk
2 chai tea bags, herbal or regular black chai
2 medium ripe pears (any kind), cored, peeled or unpeeled
½ cup (80 g) natural raw cashews
1 cup (240 ml) full-fat canned coconut milk
¼ cup (60 ml) agave nectar or coconut nectar
Pinch fine sea salt
10 to 15 drops pure plain or vanilla stevia liquid, or to taste (optional)

If you have an ice-cream maker, set it up according to the manufacturer's directions. Otherwise, set 8 silicone muffin cups in a muffin pan, or set out 3 silicone ice-cube trays.

Pour the rice milk into a small pot and add the tea bags. Bring to a boil over medium heat, and lower heat to simmer; cover and allow to cook for 5 minutes. Turn off heat. Press the tea bags with the back of a spoon to bring out as much flavor as possible, then remove the tea bags from the liquid.

Pour the milky tea into a blender and add the remaining ingredients. Blend until perfectly smooth.

If using an ice-cream maker: Pour the mixture into your ice-cream maker and follow the manufacturer's directions for ice cream. Serve.

If using a food processor: Divide the mixture evenly among the silicone muffin cups or silicone ice-cube trays and freeze until firm; pop out of the cups or trays and into Ziploc bags. Store in the freezer until ready to use.

When you're ready to make the ice cream, remove 1 muffin-sized disk or 4 ice cubes per serving. Chop the muffin disk into 4 pieces (use whole ice cubes). Place in the food processor and process until it resembles bread crumbs. Press down with a rubber spatula, then continue to process just until the mixture begins to come together in a ball. Will keep, frozen, for up to 3 months.

Mint Carob Chip Ice Cream (no ice-cream maker required!)

✷ GF, CF, can be SF or NF ✷

Serves 8 to 10

I was never a huge fan of ice cream — until I started making my own. This recipe is incredibly easy to make and, once frozen, will provide you with an almost-instant dessert that is hard to resist! The mint extract in this recipe is optional, but it really does bring out the fresh mint-leaf flavor, so I highly recommend adding it.

- 1 large ripe pear, cored, peeled or unpeeled
- About ⅓ cup (80 ml) avocado puree (from 1 small to medium just-ripe avocado)
- 2¼ to 2¾ oz (65 to 80 g) fresh mint leaves (45 to 70 leaves, depending on the size of leaves and your taste)
- 2 Tbsp (30 ml) agave nectar or yacon syrup
- ⅛ tsp (.5 ml) pure stevia powder or 20 to 30 drops pure plain or vanilla stevia liquid, or to taste
- 1 tsp (5 ml) pure vanilla extract
- 1 can (14 oz or 400 ml) full-fat canned coconut milk, preferably organic
- ½ cup (120 ml) unsweetened plain or vanilla soy or almond milk
- ½ tsp (2.5 ml) pure mint extract (optional)
- Pinch fine sea salt
- ½ cup (65 g) unsweetened carob or chocolate chips, total, or 1 Tbsp (15 ml) per serving

Line an 8-inch (20-cm) square pan with two pieces of waxed paper, overlapping the paper in either direction to cover all sides of the pan; or place 10 silicone muffin cups in a muffin tin; or set out 3 silicone ice-cube trays.

If using a blender: Place all ingredients except the carob chips in a high-powered blender (such as a Vitamix) and blend until perfectly smooth.

If using an ice-cream maker: Prepare according to the manufacturer's directions, reserving the chips until the final 5 minutes of churning.

Pour the mixture into the pan, muffin cups, or ice-cube trays and freeze until solid (you will not have enough mixture to fill all 3 ice-cube trays completely; this is as it should be). (The mixture will take about 3 hours to freeze in the muffin cups or ice-cube trays, but will take longer, about 4 hours, in the pan.) Pop the mixture out of the muffin cups or ice-cube trays and place in a Ziploc bag; store in the freezer until ready to use. If using the square pan, remove from the pan by flipping out onto a cutting board as soon as the mixture is frozen solid, and peel off the waxed paper. Cut into 8 to 10 equal squares and place in a Ziploc bag; put in the freezer until ready to use.

Remove the desired servings from the freezer bag (1 muffin cup per serving, or 4 ice cubes, or 1 square from the square pan) and place in the bowl of a food processor. Process until the mixture resembles the texture of bread crumbs, then scrape down the sides and continue to process just until it begins to form a ball. Using a rubber spatula, spread out the mixture in the processor bowl to cover the bottom; sprinkle with the carob chips (enough for the number of servings selected). Replace the processor cover and pulse 5 to 10 times, just enough to break up most of the chips and distribute them through the mixture.

Cocoa Nibbles * GF, SF, CF *

Makes 20 to 25 nibbles

Incredibly easy to throw together, these delicious and satisfying bites provide good amounts of calcium, magnesium, and iron. And they're so much fresher and less expensive than store-bought raw bars!

½ cup (80 g) natural raw almonds, preferably organic

1¼ cups (150 g) unsweetened prunes (dried plums), chopped (they should be soft)

6 Tbsp (60 g) coconut sugar

6 Tbsp (55 g) cocoa powder, preferably non-alkalized

Pinch fine sea salt

1 tsp (5 ml) pure vanilla extract

Optional add-ins (choose 1 or 2): 6 fresh mint leaves, chopped; ¼ to ½ tsp (1 to 2.5 ml) chili flakes; 1 Tbsp (15 ml) raw cacao nibs; 1 Tbsp (15 ml) unsweetened carob chips; 1 Tbsp (15 ml) goji berries; 2 tsp (10 ml) freshly grated lemon or orange zest, preferably organic; ½ tsp (2.5 ml) ground cinnamon; 1 to 2 tsp (5 to 10 ml) instant-coffee substitute, such as Dandy Blend, or instant coffee (see page 34)

In the bowl of a food processor, process the almonds, prunes, coconut sugar, cocoa powder and salt until you have what looks like a fine meal (there should be no large pieces of almond visible). Sprinkle with the vanilla and any optional add-ins, if using, and continue to process another 2 to 3 minutes, until the mixture is well blended; stop occasionally to scrape the sides of the processor and push the mixture toward the blade).

The "dough" is ready when, if you pinch some and press it between your thumb and fingers, it sticks together readily and appears a bit shiny. (Sometimes, if the prunes are too dry, this doesn't happen easily. In that case, sprinkle up to 2 tsp or 5 ml of water over the dough and proceed as above). The mixture should not be as soft as cookie dough, but more like clay in texture.

Place a clean piece of plastic wrap on the counter and turn the mixture onto it. Using your hands, form a log about 8 inches (20 cm) long. Try to compress the dough as much as possible, so you have a very dense log. Wrap with the plastic and roll the log one or two times, compressing it more with your hands, to squeeze out any air pockets. (Alternately, pat the mixture into an 8-inch or 20-cm loaf pan; press down as hard as you can to remove any air pockets, then cover with plastic.)

Refrigerate until firm, for at least 4 hours and up to overnight. Cut into small rounds or squares. Store, covered, in the refrigerator, for up to 10 days.

Acknowledgments

The process of recipe development and creation, like many artistic endeavors, is often a solitary experience. Testing those recipes and compiling them into the book you now hold, on the other hand, is definitely a group effort. This book would never have come together as it has without the input of many talented people, and I truly wish I could thank each one individually — but then there might be no room left for the actual recipes! Here, then, is a partial list of those who've contributed to *Naturally Sweet & Gluten-Free*. And to those of you not listed here, please know that your input is no less appreciated.

To readers of my blog, *Diet, Dessert and Dogs*, as well as the thousands of customers who own Sweet Freedom, I am deeply grateful for your continued support, encouragement, and feedback. This book really exists primarily because of all of you. Thank you for reading, for commenting, and for continuing to visit my blog. And thank you for inundating me with requests for a new book with gluten-free recipes!

Anyone who has been blogging for some time knows that the friendships forged through our online connection are just as powerful and meaningful as the ones with people who may live next door. So, to the following friends and colleagues, I thank you for your suggestions, consistent support, and encouragement, from the inception to the final edits of this book: Adrienne Urban, Alexa Croft, Alisa Fleming, Alison Shefler, Allyson Kramer, Alta Mantsch, Amie Valpone, Amy Green, Andrea Nakayama, Angie Azouz, Beverly Verstege, Carla Flamer, Carol Kicinski, Cara Lyons, Cheryl Harris, Christy Morgan, Deborah Salsberg, Dreena Burton, Ela Borenstein, Eric Marsden, Gena Hamshaw, Hallie Klecker, Hannah Kaminsky, Hannah Terry-Whyte, Heather Nauta, Jacqueline Betterton, Jaime Karpovich, Jan Ravens, Jeff Moore, JL Fields, Johanna Monk, Judith Carson, Kim Maes, Lisa Cantkier, Lisa Pitman, Maggie Savage, Martha Greenfield, Michelle Spring, Nava Atlas, Robin Flamer, Rosemary FitzGerald, Shari Heller, Sharon Sheldon, Shirley Braden, Susan Baker, and Tess Masters.

To the incredible group of dedicated testers who baked, frosted, mixed, chilled, tasted, and provided feedback on everything from serving size to ideas for garnishing cupcakes, thank you for your consistent efforts, your conscientiousness, and your insightful feedback. I'm sure every cookbook author believes s/he has the best testers, but I really did have the best testers! You have all helped to shape this book and make it better. Huge, heartfelt thanks go out to Michelle Anderson, Jeanne Barnum, Courtney Blair, Shereé Britt, Gwen Card, Sarah Draper, C. Favreau, Katja Haudenhuyse, Abby Heckendorn, Valerie Kramer, Cara Lyons, Geanna Marek, Laurel McBrine, Jenni Mischel, Irene Prasad, Alethea Raban, Kimberly Richer, Michele Silvester, Tessa Simpson, Linda Stiles, Sheree Welshimer, and Blaine Wilkes.

To my publisher, Robin Haywood, thank you for taking a chance on this newbie author, and for nurturing and caring about this project as much as you do (and even while on holiday!).

To Charlotte Cromwell, Holly Jennings, and Renee Rooks Cooley, thank you for your keen eyes, attention to detail, and useful suggestions for both the text and visual aspects of the book.

To Celine Saki, the incredibly talented photographer for *Naturally Sweet & Gluten-Free*, thank you for your patience, your diplomacy, and your amazing work ethic. It was a privilege and pleasure to work with you on these photos.

To my agent, Marilyn Allen, thank you for your always-sage advice, and for being the calm, reasonable counterpart any time my type A tendencies bubble to the surface.

To Cameron, thank you. I love you.

And finally, to Elsie and Chaser, thank you for enthusiastically disposing of the leftovers.

Resource Guide

If you live in an urban area in North America or the United Kingdom, you are likely to have an easy time finding the baking ingredients to make the recipes in *Naturally Sweet & Gluten-Free.* Large health-food grocers such as Whole Foods have stores in both places, and they carry extensive inventories. But if you live outside a big city, be assured that you will find what you need on the Internet. If you want to avoid shipping charges from one continent to another, check out a site such as glutenfreepassport.com for Web sites in your country where you can order locally. These are some of my favorite brands.

Agave nectar:

- Madhava (madhavasweeteners.com)
- Xagave (xagave.com)

All-purpose gluten-free flours (and most individual GF flours):

- Bob's Red Mill (bobsredmill.com)
- King Arthur (kingarthurflour.com)
- Arrowhead Mills (arrowheadmills.com)

Blanched almond flour:

- Honeyville (honeyvillegrain.com) a fine texture
- JK Gourmet (jkgourmet.com) a fine texture
- Bob's Red Mill (bobsredmill.com) a coarser texture

Coconut beverage:

- So Delicious Dairy Free (sodeliciousdairyfree.com)
- Coconut Dream (tastethedream.com)

Coconut butter (not oil):

- Artisana (artisanafoods.com)
- Nutiva (nutiva.com) **Note:** Nutiva calls their product "coconut manna," but it is the same as coconut butter.

Coconut, coconut flour, and coconut oil:

- Tropical Traditions (tropicaltraditions.com) shredded coconut, coconut oil, coconut flour
- Omega Nutrition (omeganutrition.com) coconut oil, coconut flour

Coconut sugar and coconut nectar:

- Cocovie (cocovienaturals.com) sugar and nectar; Canada only
- Wholesome Sweeteners (wholesomesweeteners.com) sugar
- Coconut Secret (coconutsecret.com) sugar and nectar

Coconut milk (canned):

- Thai Kitchen (thaikitchen.com)
- Native Forest (edwardandsons.com) BPA-free cans

Stevia:

- NuNaturals (nunaturals.com) pure liquid and powdered stevia
- NOW Foods (nowfoods.com)

General Online Retailers/Stores

U.S.:

- **Amazon (amazon.com).** A surprisingly extensive list of products at reasonable prices. They carry most gluten-free flours, sweeteners, coconut products, cocoa, spices, vanilla, xanthan gum, and more.
- **Navitas Naturals** (navitasnaturals.com) Superfood seeds (chia, flax, hemp) as well as cacao nibs, lucuma, goji berries, and yacon syrup.
- **Nuts.com.** Source of almond flour and other natural foods such as dried fruits, nuts, seeds, etc.
- **iHerb.com.** Broad selection of all types of natural ingredients and superfoods, including flours, nuts/seeds, dried fruits, sweeteners, and cacao.

Canada:

- **Canadian Alternative Foods** (gluten-free-grocery.com). This online store offers a range of prepared products as well as a section on "baking ingredients" where you'll find Bob's Red Mill all-purpose flours and certified gluten-free oats.
- **Upaya Naturals** (upayanaturals.com). A great source for superfoods like goji berries or lucuma powder; all raw ingredients and natural sweeteners. Free delivery with minimum purchase.
- **Well.ca.** Huge selection of items, including many that are naturally gluten-free, such as coconut flour, nuts, seeds, bean flour, and others.
- **Grain Process Enterprises.** A wholesaler with a retail store open to the public in the Toronto area. Will deliver to businesses. Great source for flours, nuts/seeds, sweeteners, unsweetened carob chips, and dried fruits.

United Kingdom

- **Norwich:** Rainbow Wholefoods — check for city centre shop AND warehouse wholesaling!
- **Penzance Cornwall:** Archie Brown's
- **Surrey:** Ocado local, online delivery http://www.allergyessex.co.uk http://www.allergyuk.org/general-avoidance/shopping-and-cooking-for-a-restricted-diet

Index

Page numbers in *italic* indicate photos.